THE INMOST LEAF

OTHER BOOKS BY ALFRED KAZIN

A Walker in the City

On Native Grounds

ALFRED KAZIN

THE INMOST LEAF

A Selection of Essays

HARCOURT, BRACE AND COMPANY
NEW YORK

first edition

Essays 3, 7, 8, 10, 13, 15, 18, 19, 21, 22, 24, and 25 appeared originally in slightly different form in *The New Yorker*. The remaining essays appeared originally in the following magazines: *The Atlantic Monthly, Commentary, The Harvard Advocate, The Kenyon Review, The New York Herald Tribune Weekly Book Review, The New Republic, The New York Times Book Review, Partisan Review,* and *The Quarterly Review of Literature.*

The author wishes to thank The Viking Press for permission to reprint the Introduction from *The Portable Blake,* copyright, 1946, by The Viking Press, Inc.

The quotation on pages 268-270 from *Intruder in the Dust* by William Faulkner, copyright, 1948, by Random House Inc., is used with the permission of the publisher.

LIBRARY OF CONGRESS CATALOG CARD NUMBER: 55-10810

PRINTED IN THE UNITED STATES OF AMERICA

FOR MY DEAR ANN

Contents

I am like one of those seeds taken out of the Egyptian Pyramids, which, after being three thousand years a seed and nothing but a seed, being planted in English soil, it developed itself, grew to greenness, and then fell to mould. So I. Until I was twenty-five, I had no development at all. From my twenty-fifth year I date my life. Three weeks have scarcely passed, at any time between then and now, that I have not unfolded within myself. But I feel that I am now come to the inmost leaf of the bulb, and that shortly the flower must fall to the mould.

Melville to Hawthorne: June, 1851

One

THE DEATH OF JAMES JOYCE

January, 1941

> *My intention was to write a chapter of the moral history of my country, and I chose Dublin for the scene because that city seemed to me the center of paralysis.*
> —Joyce to Grant Richards, 1906.

He was an outlaw to the very end. Of most innovators in modern literature, rebels, expatriates, heroes of the *avant-garde,* it can be said that if they began by shocking conventional society they eventually found their place in it by forcing society to accept them at their own evaluation—or by yielding to it. Yeats became a Senator, Valéry an academician, Shaw a kind of permanent Majesty's Opposition, as indispensable to English life as Queen Mary. Stefan George was taken over by the Nazis, Ezra Pound gave himself to Fascism, Eliot became a pillar of the Church, the Greenwich Village rebels of 1910 are members of the Academy, Pulitzer and Nobel Prize winners, best sellers, subjects of dissertations. Joyce never yielded, and society—even official literary society—never absorbed him. To the end his personality and his daemon furnished one of the "comic" legends of our time. Joyce, the funny man! The salacious Bohemian! "But does he have to write like that? What does it all mean?" Any columnist in need of an idea could ridicule him, any professor could patronize him, any critic could explain him away, any snooper defame him. And he was always fair game.

He never apologized for his "queerness," he never explained his work, he never gave interviews, he never made a public speech in his life. He had no politics, save to remain an Irishman; he won no prizes, belonged to no institute, never announced his opinion of Hitler, the Five-Year Plan or the New Deal. He was fifty-eight years old when he died early this month in Zurich, and for thirty-eight of those years he devoted himself unremittingly to the composition of four books of fiction, two slender sheaves of poetry and a three-act play. For more than thirty of those years he lived below the level of a third-rate clerk, and but for his language lessons and the generous help of Harriet Weaver and other friends would have starved.

II

His passing removes one of the few lights of greatness our contemporary world has known. Whatever one is to say of his development and his personality, he was one of the most moving exemplifications of pure genius in the whole history of English letters. His abilities were phenomenal, too phenomenal if you like; but at a time when the written word has become so abundant and so cheap, when the world is bursting with merely good writing, efficient and clever and sober writing, Joyce's will to greatness was its own distinction. It is easy to say that he brought writing into a blind alley; perhaps he did. But if he killed the novel it is only for those who may follow him literally and on his own ground, and no one ever will. For the rest, his work gave a new dimension to literature.

I am not sure that he was as satisfying a novelist as Thomas Mann or as great a spirit as Lawrence; but Lawrence and Mann, like Dickens and Fielding before them, imposed their gifts upon a conception of the novel which, compared with the progress of poetry, had been relatively uniform. Joyce riddled that conception and hence transformed the novel for others. He threw off the fear of science which had haunted the literary imagination for a hundred years and so adroitly incorporated science into the novel that he proved it to be as illimitable a type of inquiry into human life as any science has furnished. He dissolved mechanism in literature as effectively as Einstein destroyed it in physics. Of so great an innovator in the novel as Zola one can say that he forced writers after him to work with new tools; of Joyce, that he taught them to see experience itself with new eyes. That had been done long before in painting; it had not been attempted in literature since Blake and Wordsworth.

But this was but one phase of his influence on the novel, and as obvious a one as his elimination of quotation marks around dialogue. How much Joyce contributed to the art of the novel is incalculable. He proved, like Henry James (and his influence was greater in this respect than James's, for it is almost as difficult to follow James as it is not to wish to), that the novel demanded as much seriousness as poetry, as precise an attention and as scrupulous a sense of form. From those first twilit sketches in *Dubliners* to the subterranean sleep-tossed world of *Finnegans Wake* he showed that the material of fiction could rest upon as tense a distribution and as delicate a balance of its parts as any poem.

Joyce's passion for form, in fact, is the secret of his progress as a novelist. He sought to bring the largest possible quantity of human life under the discipline of the observing mind, and the mark of his success is that he gave an epic form to what remains invisible to most novelists. That passion was deceptive in its energy, but it was as austere and unremitting as Flaubert's.

Hence, though his own poetry was juvenilia and sentimental, he restored poetry to the novel not by lacquering it with "poetic" phrases, like Pater or Wilde or some Irish novelists one could name, but by imagining the very context of his novel in poetic terms. What John LaFarge said of Henry Adams's feeling for history applies even more vividly to Joyce's feeling for the novel: it amounted to poetry.

III

There were many paradoxes in Joyce (his habits were as bourgeois as Lenin's), but none so perplexing as the fact that though he was light years ahead of everyone else in technical audacity and sheer exuberant originality, he remained a colossal sentimentalist. In a sense his was the last great Romantic effort in literature to parade one's personal soul in epic form. He was absorbed entirely in himself, wrote all his books frankly as personal history, was mellifluous with self-love even when he was unintelligible, and fundamentally more conventional in most spheres of thought than any other modern writer of his stature. His monkishness was hardly an affectation; he seems to have noticed contemporary developments in politics and the arts chiefly for the purpose of mimicry, like the note on Auden in *Finnegans Wake*. Had the Vichy government not forced him back to Zurich, where he died, one could very easily picture him writing away with his legendary crayons and brushes to the tread of Nazi boots outside his door in Paris. When he lived in Zurich during the World War, for example, his chief feeling about the war seems to have been that it was all a blasted nuisance—but it did not keep him from plowing away sixteen hours a day at *Ulysses*. His prime subject to the end was the James Joyce who first left Ireland at twenty determined to justify his genius ("silence, exile, and cunning") to his family and friends. He returned to Ireland only when his mother died, and when he left it forever in 1904 he invested his exile with a gargantuan historic mission comparable only to Dante's. Even the history of each book, its composition, publication, reception, became an epic, and when he wrote "Dublin, 1904—Trieste, 1914" on the last page of *A Portrait of the Artist* (originally entitled *Stephen Hero*) the conventional notation had its drama. He had promised his scornful college friends in 1904 to produce his justification in ten years, and he did.

The depth of Joyce's pride has already become a legend. He seems seriously to have thought of Parnell and himself as the two great figures in modern Irish history. When, some years ago, Yeats, in behalf of the Irish Academy, asked him to return to Ireland, Joyce refused, and remarked bitterly to his friends that an Irish mob had flung quicklime into the eyes of Parnell when he stepped off at Castlecomer. This pride had its comic side; the narrowness of application is vivid enough in Joyce's work. But no one who knows anything of his life can fail to see that the inexpressible difficulties under which he labored for so many years emphasized his belief in his mission. He so fused his feeling for Ireland, his contempt for complacent mediocrity, the sense of his own powers, that his need to justify himself to Ireland became inextricable from his desire to justify Ireland to the world. Only a profound nationalist can take his exile so dramatically as did Joyce, and the virulence with which the Irish attacked him gave his characteristically Irish martyrdom an appropriate place beside Wolfe Tone and Parnell. That there was a comic-opera element of calculated romanticism and melodramatic heroism in all this needs hardly to be said. Joyce not only lived this dramatic legend, he wrote it up in his early twenties so that no one should ever miss it. "Try to be one of us," pleads Davin in *A Portrait of the Artist*. "In your heart you are an Irishman but your pride is too powerful." Ashplant in hand, Dedalus-Joyce-Hamlet answers proudly, "No honorable and sincere man has given up to you his life and his youth and his affections from the days of Tone to those of Parnell but you sold him to the enemy or failed him in need or reviled him and left him for another. And you invite me to be one of you. I'd see you damned first. . . . Do you know what Ireland is? Ireland is the old sow that eats her farrow." . . . The same book has a very eloquent remembrance of the young Joyce's love for *The Count of Monte Cristo.*

Yet, if that were all, Joyce's legend would be merely pathetic. In reality, he invested it with an almost classic sense of tragedy. "I will not serve that in which I no longer believe. . . . I will try to express myself in some mode of life or art as freely as I can and as wholly as I can, using for my defence the only arms I allow myself to use—silence, exile, and cunning. . . . I will tell you also what I do not fear. I do not fear to be alone or to be spurned for another or to leave whatever I have to leave. And I am not afraid to make a mistake, even a great mistake, a lifelong mistake and perhaps as long as eternity too." . . . He was a very young man when he wrote that in Trieste, and the quavery eloquence meant more than he may have realized. But that he followed it through with a staggering devotion contributes to whatever little heroism of the mind our time can show. Joyce means many things to different people; for me his importance has always been primarily a moral one. He was, perhaps, the last man in Europe who wrote as if art were worth a human life. He entered literature at a time when science and the brutalization of common life had made the writer's function ambiguous; he stopped writing at a time when literature itself had vanished from Europe and the most elementary intellectual discrimination and activity had become dangerous on a fascist continent. Yet, from first to last he asserted the writer's claim to sovereignty as stubbornly as he illustrated the value of the writer's need to exist. Hence, the greatness of his service: he at once mirrored the disintegration of our world and proved himself superior to it. By living for his art he may yet have given others a belief in art worth living for.

Two

WILLIAM AND HENRY JAMES: "OUR PASSION IS OUR TASK"

. . . the method of narration by interminable elaboration of suggestive reference (I don't know what to call it, but you know what I mean) goes agin the grain of all my own impulses in writing; and yet in spite of it all, there is a brilliancy and cleanness of effect, and in this book especially a high-toned social atmosphere that are unique and extraordinary. . . . But why won't you, just to please Brother, sit down and write a new book, with no twilight or mustiness in the plot, with great vigor and decisiveness in the action, no fencing in the dialogue, no psychological commentaries, and absolute straightness in the style? . . .

I mean . . . to try to produce some uncanny form of thing, in fiction, that will gratify you, as Brother—but let me say, dear William, that I shall greatly be humiliated, if you *do* like it, and thereby lump it, in your affection, with things of the current age, that I have heard you express admiration for and that I would sooner descend to a dishonoured grave than have written. . . . I'm always sorry when I hear of your reading anything of mine, and always hope you won't—you seem to me so constitutionally unable to "enjoy" it. . . . how far apart and to what different ends we have had to work out (very naturally and properly!) our respective intellectual lives.

Thus William James to Henry James on the publication of *The*

Golden Bowl in 1905, and the latter's unusually sharp reply to the older brother whom he adored—and could barely read. There is always an obtrusive irony in honoring the Jameses together: they could never fully honor or, after a certain point, really understand each other. This was something that both recognized and that William almost enjoyed. They were always seeking to gratify each other, "as Brother," for the Jameses loved each other as passionately as they debated their differences, and delighted in each other's careers. Never as in the James family, indeed, was so little envy or indifference brought to so many conflicting intellectual ambitions, and never was so much fraternity brought to so little mutual understanding. How deeply the elder James delighted in his genius sons, though he could only, from his vast intimacy with God, look down on both science and art as frivolously incomplete! How ready William always was to read each of Henry's essays and novels as it came along, so quick with eager brotherly praise, so ready to define Henry's subtlest triumphs and to miss them! How much Henry stood in awe of William, showered him with adulation, professed himself a "pragmatist," and resented it when William forgot to send even a technical monograph!

Yet though their devotion to each other was profound, their essential antipathy of spirit went deeper still. But antipathy is not the word: there was only a kind of loving non-recognition. Similar as they were in their studies of human consciousness, in raising to an ideal end the operative supremacy and moral serenity of an individual "center of revelation," they could only smile to each other across the grooves in which each had his temperament. Henry at least knew his failure to recognize the design unfolded in William's empiricism, where William so genially slid over the symbolic design stamped on Henry's every effort, praised him for his "high-toned social atmosphere," patronized him, and missed that need to *use* the novel as a medium of inquiry that cut Henry's career off from the Anglo-American fiction of his generation. Henry was always an isolated figure in the philosophic James household, where William was its reigning active heir, the versatile young naturalist who spoke in his father's hearty voice even when he revolted against his father's foggy theology, the naturalist in a scientific era whose interests drew him everywhere. William could at least follow Henry's works and comment on them (he commented on everything)—praise the early style or deplore the later, admire a character and confer a judgment. When William's first book, the great *Psychology,* appeared in 1890, Henry could only fidget in embarrassment and complain that he was too absorbed properly to appreciate "your mighty and magnificent book, which requires a stretch of leisure and an absence of 'crisis' in one's own egotistical little existence." Or, later, say of *A Pluralistic Universe* that he had read it "with enchantment, with pride, and almost with comprehension. It may sustain and inspire you a little to know that I'm *with* you, all along the line. . . . Thank the powers—that is, thank *yours*—for a relevant and assimilable and referable philosophy . . . Your present volume seems to me exquisitely and adorably cumulative. . . ."

There it was always: William's thought was "adorable," but Henry was too absorbed. Henry had always been absorbed, where William's mind opened outwards to all the world from his father's notations on Swedenborg to psychical research, from Kant to William Jennings Bryan; Henry was absorbed in making novels. William tried to be an artist and a chemist, went to Brazil with Agassiz to collect fishes, took an M.D. between periods of almost suicidal depression, debated endlessly with his opponents and loved them all, learned psychology by teaching it, wrote letters to all the cranks about their manias, gravitated into philosophy, fought against imperialism; Henry went on making novels. He made novels as he had made his first critical essays, his famous "impressions" and the enduring myth of England he absorbed from his childhood reading Punch: by storing and molding what he had, and by never taking in anything he would not use. They had tried to make a lawyer out of him, they tried to teach him some elementary facts of science; Henry went on collecting impressions—impressions of Italy and of the pictures he found in Italy (Emerson loved these), impressions of Newport, Paris, Geneva and Saratoga; impressions of the mourned cousin, Mary Temple, whose face was the face of Milly Theale, Maggie Verver and Isabel Archer. The only culture he had was literature and pictures, and the only literature he sought was the nineteenth-century novel—he did not care even for poetry; but he had a mission and his mind and life composed a single order of desire: he made novels.

To the other Jameses Henry was always the marvelous unknown child who sat quietly alone, dreaming pictures and studying novels, and always bewilderingly content with his own mind. He seemed so little to adhere to anything except his own tropisms of taste; he had no "message," no positive belief or apparent need of one. William, on the other hand, was racked until he could find an ontology as plastic as life and true of every last thing in it; and he ran excitedly through all the disciplines, rejecting, disputing, extracting, until he could square the "irreducible facts" with the highest fact of his own nature. To Henry he might have said what their father had said to Emerson: "Oh, you man without a handle! shall one never be able to help himself out of you, according to his needs, and be dependent only upon your fitful tippings-up?" William always needed a handle; and he could use one only by reacting against something. What he principally reacted against was his father. Henry drew from the elder James by enclosing himself in the independence the father preached; he did not react against his father's theology, he was indifferent to it.

William, however, was too much like his father in combativeness and vivacious curiosity to reproduce anything but his temperament. Nothing could have seemed more lethal to him than his father's glacial metaphysics, poetic as many of its elements were. The elder James had escaped the dreariness of Calvinism—its belief in a kind of haphazard criminality of human nature—by nailing the human mind and will to the dreariness of a perpetual mysticism. The world was now joy, where Calvin's had been the fear of fate; but the only release allowed man was submission; the only hope a projected union with God. Utopian socialist though he fancied himself, he saw the natural world only as a medium of communication with supernatural truth. Thought was reduced to the labored ecstasy of extracting mystic "secrets"; man lived in an automatic effort at revelation.

Nothing was more alien to William than any belief which bound man to something not in his particular nature and experience. In his biological theory of mind the mind was not a mere faculty, as the soul was not a region; it was an effect and transmission of consciousness, and purposive; the endlessly probing antennae of the whole human organism, and the exercise of it. All of a man's life was engaged in his thought or spoke or hid in it; the mind did not "receive" ideas, it shaped them in seeking adaptability; it sought ends. Yet what was so significant in William's psychology, often condemned as "literary," was that it buttressed in moral philosophy a theory of knowledge. Though he was almost the first American to establish psychological studies in the laboratory, he was always impatient with laboratory psychology and a mere corpus of facts. What he was getting at, as in his pragmatism, was not only a more elastic sense of reality, a more honest and imaginative perception that all life and thought begin in discrete individuals and are shaped by their differences, but a need to show that what was not a real experience to an individual had no existence that one could name and take account of.

To the merely bookish, who would rather intone their knowledge than be shaped by it; to the merely devout, who would rather worship their God than be transformed by Him; to the formal logicians and contented monists, for whom the world's disorder and depths are so easily sacrificed, William James has always seemed loose or even vulgar because he preached that an idea has meaning only as it is expressed in action and experience. That he was so misunderstood is partly James's own fault, since he *would* speak of "the cash-value" of an idea in his characteristic attempt to reach the minds even of those for whom cash-value was the only value. But it is largely the fault of ourselves and our personal culture, since the rarest thing in it is still moral imagination. For what James was leading to in his pragmatism—once it had served as a theory of knowledge—was moral in the classic sense of conduct, moral in the enduring sense of the order and use of a human life. Tell me, he seemed always to be saying to those who were so content with ideas rather than with thinking, with metaphysics rather than with morality, what is it you *know,* what is it that is changed in you or by you, when you have achieved your certainty or knowledge? What is it you live by, appreciably, when you have proved that something is true? James knew well enough, and could formulate the ends and satisfactions of his opponents better than many of them could; but that was only incidental to his essential aim. Knowledge is for men that they may live—and men may live for ideal ends. So is the monist happy in his all-enveloping unity, the rationalist in his ideal symmetry, the mystic in his visions. And all of these exist, said James; all of these must be taken into our account of the human experience and the demands of our nature. But do not confuse, he went on, your individual need of certainty with the illusion that some supra-human order is ascertained by it; do not confuse your use of reason—and delight in it—with the illusion that what cannot be named or verified by rationalism does not exist.

To say this is not to forget how treacherous James's ideal of the provisional can be, and that he is particularly dissatisfying when he merely brings us to the borders of moral philosophy. He triumphed by disproving all the cults and systems which ignored the shaping power of man's individuality, by threshing his way through pre-scientific myths and post-scientific arrogance. But like so many American naturalistic thinkers, he took a certain necessary definition of the good life for granted (or confused it with the Elysian fields of the Harvard Department of Philosophy?); whereas it is the unrelenting consciousness of it that is most lacking. Yet what is most important here is that the great particular for him, as for all the Jameses, was the human self, and that out of it they made all their universals (though it is always a question what Henry's universals were). For the elder James the center of existence was the self that seeks to know God and to be sublimated in Him; William's theory of knowledge began with the knowing mind that *initiates* the ideas to which the test of experience is to be applied; Henry found his technical—and moral—triumph in the central Jamesian intelligence which sifts the experience of all the other characters and organizes them. This, had William not so clearly pined for Stevenson when he read Henry's novels, he might have recognized as Henry's "handle." For in an age when all the materials through which William was running so eagerly demanded large positive answers, wholesale reconstructions and a world view, Henry had quietly and stubbornly reproduced his father's mystical integrity in the integrity of the observing self. The novel for him was to be *histoire morale,* a branch of history that sought the close textures and hidden lights of painting; but the highest morality was not so much in the story as it was in the exercise of the creative principle behind it.

That devotion to a creative principle was the great epic of Henry's integrity, as everything he ever sought or wrote was a commentary on it. In most writers their works exemplify their ambition; Henry's were about his ambition, as they were, in one sense, only his ambition written large. Just as William's vision always came back to a loose sea of empiricism in which man could hold on only to himself, so Henry's was to define and to fill out the moral history of composition. His theory of art was not preparatory to a manipulation of experience; it *was* his experience. His interest was fixed on writing about the symbolic devotion of writing, as so many of his stories were of writers (but only of depressed or unsuccessful writers: there was no "dramatic process" in the surface of success). And the central Jamesian intelligence, in all his disguises as "the foreground observer," "the center of revelation," the artist planning his effects, the critic "remounting the stream of composition," was always sifting and commenting in turn. "The private history of any sincere work," he wrote once, "looms large with its own completeness"; it was his symbol of man's completeness. He studied his novels endlessly as he wrote them, corrected them endlessly when they were published, wrote a preface to each in which he summarized the history of its composition, defined his every intent and use of means, speculated on the general principles they illustrated, and at the end, as he hinted to Grace Norton, might have written a preface to the prefaces, commenting on *them* in turn. Secretions within secretions, knowingness within knowingness: out of so self-driven an integrity, as out of the intense interior life of his characters, there could be grasped the central fact of the effort, the search, the aura of devotion, that gave meaning to the artist's life and form to his work. And always the thread remained firmly in the artist's hand, pulling it back to himself—the story of Henry James was the story of Henry James writing his novels.

Life for both always returned to the central self. Significantly, it was always the richness of their personal nature that distinguished all the Jameses, and the overflow of life in them that gave them their vascular styles. Ralph Barton Perry says of the elder James that he felt his visions so intensely, and had so many together, that he had to get them all out at once. The elder James was always running over, laughing at himself for it, and never stopped running over. Like William, he had so many possible thoughts about so many things; and he had the James exuberance (the seed *was* Irish) that always ran so high in them despite the unending family history of illness. Superficially, of course, no two styles would seem to be so different as William's and Henry's: the one so careful to be spontaneous, the other so spontaneously labored; the one so informal in its wisdom, flinging witticisms, philosophical jargon, homeliness and hearty German abstractions about with a seeming carelessness, protesting doubt at every point, yet probing with angelic friendliness in all the blocks of the human mind; the other so *made* a style, solemnly and deliciously musical, reverberating with all the tones of all the books Henry had ever read, forever sliding into cozy French idioms, shyly offering the commonest spoken expressions in quotation marks—Henry always sought to be friendly. Yet both were great spoken styles, intimate and with an immense range of tone: the only difference being that William talked to friendly Harvard seniors and Henry later dictated to his secretary. What no one has ever said enough about Henry's style, of course, is that it was the family style become molten: like all the Jameses, he wrote instinctively out of his amplitude. He gushed in his letters and he gushed in his novels, but there was always the James motor power behind him, their terrible need to seize and define everything within their range. And more, there was that "blague and benignity" in his style that Ezra Pound caught: the tricky interior changes of pace, the slow mandarin whisperings, the adjectives that opened all vistas for him like great bronze doors, the extraordinary *soundings* he could make with words, and covering them all, always his deceiving gentleness, the ceremonial diffidence, and his sudden barbs and winks.

To think of their styles is to be aware of the great innocence that was in all the Jameses, an innocence of personal spirit if not of moral perception. Financially secure, encouraged by their father to be different and uncontrolled, even to be without a profession, both ranged at will in what was still the household age of modern thought—a period when the security of their society encouraged those first studies in the naturalism of the psyche, and a voracious interior life. The only revolution either could envision was in new ways of knowing; and it is significant that William led the way to "the stream of consciousness." They all had the natural outpouring that came with innocence, the innocence that trusted in all the data of their inquiry, took the social forms for granted, and based life upon the integrity of the observing self. "In self-trust are all the virtues comprehended." It was the Emersonian faith of their culture, in all its genteelism and instinctive trust in individuality. Just as the elder James's theology committed man, as it were, to be a recording angel, to seek the necessary revelation and inscribe it, so they were all recording angels, much as William said of Henry that under all his "rich sea-weeds" and "rigid barnacles and things" he cared only for making novels. Life was here and now, in all that system of relations between minds in which experience immediately consists; man *studied* it. The highest aim, somehow, was to be an author. But there is no very great sense of tragedy in any of them (compare them with the Adamses), no sense of that world process which is something more than William's metaphysical novelty and pluralism; the great depths of life are not in them.

In a time like our own, when men are so lost in themselves

because they are so lost from each other, the Jamesian integrity can seem small comfort to us. We can take no social form for granted; we cannot possess or be possessed by those explorations in human consciousness which only parallel—or at best reveal—our quest for security. To say this is not to make a judgment on the Jameses, but to define our predicament. Our enforced sense of evil has nothing so creative in it as their innocence; and their legacy is still most precious for its symbolic integrity, its trust in mind, its superiority to our "failure of nerve." Even Henry James's greatest contributions to human pleasure and self-comprehension, or his insistence on the integrity of a work of art, are less important now than the emblem his pride raises before us. Even William's full devotion to realism, his imaginative projection of complexity, are less important to us now than the respect he breeds in us for all the forms of reality and our necessary understanding of them. And it is this which is now most visible in them and most important to us: the simplicity of their respect for life and the intensity of their elucidation of it. They both worked in that period of modern history when the trust of man in his power to know was at its highest, when the revolution of modern political democracy, science and materialism carried along even those who were skeptical of the idea of progress. And if we feel at times that they are even greater than their thought, more far-ranging than the forms that contain them, it is because they burned with that indestructible zeal we need so badly to recover—the zeal that cannot blind men to illusion, but must always rise above it, the zeal that cries that life does have a meaning: we seek to know.

In one of those exquisite stories, "The Middle Years," in which Henry James was always writing out the lesson of his own loneliness and neglect in the story of the celebrated writer neglected and misunderstood by those nearest him, the writer cries on his deathbed: "It *is* glory—to have been tested, to have had our little quality, and cast our little spell." "You're a great success!" his young attendant assures him. And Dencombe replies, wearily, but with mounting exaltation: "We work in the dark—we do what we can—we give what we have. Our doubt is our passion, and our passion is our task."

Three

PROUST IN HIS LETTERS

Letters of Marcel Proust, edited and translated by Mina Curtiss, is a selection made, "primarily, to provide readers of *Remembrance of Things Past* with clues to the development of the personality and the creative process out of which the novel grew." It hadn't occurred to me that there could be a better reason than this for going to the letters; Mrs. Curtiss's editorial tone is unnecessarily humble, particularly since she has met some difficult problems with the required sympathy and taste rather than with a merely laborious and showy display of scholarship. Of course this book is not, whatever the publishers say, a "definitive" edition of the letters; there is none even in France. Proust never dated them, said he never wanted them to be published; his brother Robert had great trouble buying some back from collectors for the six volumes of the *General Correspondence* published in France, and many were reserved for volumes of reminiscence by his friends, some of whom had no other way of sharing in his fame. Parts of some letters have always been withheld from publication, and Mrs. Curtiss has been forced to omit the passages from her book, but it does contain three letters that have never been published before. The trail of Proust's correspondence leads into so many thorny patches of French literary politics, personal vanity, old and mysteriously disturbed friendships that Mrs. Curtiss deserves praise for the deftness with which she managed to get what she needed. But her notes on Proust's correspondents—no doubt a matter of diplomacy, since some are still living—do not always indicate enough of their relationship to him to explain his tone.

For the translations, Mrs. Curtiss has avoided "the king's English or the native American tongue," adopting, as a "convention," "a kind of English that it seemed to me Proust might have written, had he been bilingual." When I read this statement, before turning to her versions, I was not sure what it meant, and now I have read them, I am still unsure, for though the idea sounds good and the translations are faithful and sensitive, the gulf between Proust and the English language is not that easily bridged. Had Proust ever turned to English, he might very possibly have written in the style Mrs. Curtiss has given him; a writer's first language usually haunts his second, and *his* sense of his own language was too traditional and ornamented by personal compulsions ever to yield to the counterforce of another language. But Proust was not bilingual and could not have been. Although he was a virtuoso of style, his skill was peculiarly of a kind given to building up new formal patterns in his own language; he was absorbed in forcing the medium of the classic French moralists to the farthest limits of his own consciousness. In this, he was very unlike his great rival in the twentieth-century novel, James Joyce, who was a master of European languages and who logically (with an Irishman's irreverence for a language not quite his own) split English apart to show the universal roots of language and myth. Proust worked at his style just the other way, by invocations of classic splendor, by enormous agglutinations of detail, instead of by questioning the language itself; he wrote as if there were no medium in the world but French, and never had been. To imagine Proust as "bilingual" is to deprive ourselves of a key to his mind—his conception of style as a fatality for the individual and a characterization of nations. In translating him, there is a definite need to throw a shadow from his language onto our own, to show all the revolutions of his mind's wheel, as it were, turning so incongruously on the alien ground of English, to keep always before the reader's mind the particular slopings and formations of a writer for whom "style"—with all his unresting demands on it—was, as he says here, "like color with certain painters, a quality of vision, a revelation of a private universe which each one of us sees and which is not seen by others."

And this Mrs. Curtiss has done for the letters, not by turning Proust into an unnaturally effeminate dandy with an odd predilection for upper-class British slang, as C. K. Scott-Moncrieff did in his version of *A la Recherche du Temps Perdu,* a tour de force which is brilliant but always slightly off key, but by reminding us in every bland circumlocution and overmannered stroke of politeness that he was thinking in French. "I discovered long ago," he writes to Count Robert de Montesquiou, whom he flattered sickeningly and unceasingly in order not to lose touch (so it is said) with a principal model for the Baron de Charlus, "that you stood far above the type of exquisite decadent with whose features (never as perfect as yours, but common enough in these times), you are depicted. . . . And I think that never before has this supreme refinement been combined with such energy, and this creative force, typical of the past, with this almost seventeenth-century intellectuality, so little has there been of it since." This is hardly the English of a bilingual man, but it is Proust, just as Scott-Moncrieff, beginning the passage on the death of the writer Bergotte with "He was dead. Permanently dead?," is a thickening of both Proust and English.

Still, it must be admitted that Scott-Moncrieff had greater problems, for the letters are really a handbook to the novel; they do not have the independent interest of D. H. Lawrence's letters or the journals of André Gide. In fact, unless one goes to the letters with a very keen sense of how great the novel is, how much, in Proust's mind, it was the grand justification of a life that up to the time he began the book had been largely "wasted"—on just the social career that these elaborately deferential letters to all and sundry had to feed—it is easy to misjudge the man who wrote them. They are full of his intellectual radiance, often winning—almost too winning—with the gifted neurotic's special need and knowledge of how to please, but they purr so evenly that they often become in the reader's mind indistinguishable expressions of the same social manner. Throughout the first period of his life, Proust appeared simply a fashionable young man-about-town and, if not aggressively a snob, certainly a good deal of a climber; he was the gifted amateur of whom great things may be expected, the dilettante trying to edge his way into literary circles. He did social notes for *Le Gaulois,* articles and parodies for *Figaro;* he was soon to publish (with a necessary preface by Anatole France) a collection of stories, essays, and poems lightly entitled *Pleasures and Days*. Even after *Swann's Way* had been published, in 1913, at his own expense, he was so little known—or known only for minor achievements—that he was afraid of being confused with the popular novelist Marcel Prévost; one of his closest friends, the Countess de Noailles, found after his death that she had actually filed his letters under Prévost's name. He had the fashionable interest of young French gentlemen of the time in things English, and though he hardly knew the language, he somehow managed, by intuition, by saturation in the material, and with the help of friends, to produce two translations of Ruskin. Yet Ruskin was not the most obvious choice for a young French dilettante, nor was his affection for Emerson, Thoreau, or George Eliot. And for all his extravagant deference to Robert de Montesquiou,

Proust could defend his dignity if needed, as when that gentleman, who no doubt went along with the savage anti-Semitism of French "society" during the Dreyfus affair, evoked from him the quiet rejoinder that for "reasons of the highest rectitude" (he was brought up a Catholic, but his mother was Jewish) he would prefer not to discuss these things, not to be put in a position where he might be misinterpreted as agreeing with his friend. But even here his tone was that of a man anxious to avoid a social rupture at all costs: "Because since our ideas do differ, or rather since I have no choice of opinion on this subject as I might under other circumstances have had, you could involuntarily have hurt me in a discussion."

Yet actually Proust was a passionate Dreyfusard. He might flatter "society," but, as he was later to write about his novel, "In spite of my desire to be extremely fair and impersonal, it happens, things being what they are, that in *Temps Perdu* the class that is slandered, that is always wrong, talks only nonsense, the vulgar and hateful class, is *'le monde.'*" For he was slowly finding his way to his vocation, outside the society that had always been so important to him, superior even to friendships (and these were peculiarly necessary to him, for he was often anxious and usually ill), which, as he was to confess in a summary passage of the novel apropos of his beloved Robert de Saint-Loup, diminished loneliness but could not involve a man's essential self. It was his mother who had seemed to embody the only disinterested love in the world. She had spoiled him, had indulged him in all his illnesses from childhood on, and had sat patiently and humbly outside his door for hours, waiting for his call. His idea of misery, he had once noted in a children's questionnaire, was "to be separated from Mamma." When she died, in 1905, he could be grateful that she died first, for he knew what anguish his death would have caused her.

But the separation from *"le monde"* was final, and if he retired to his cork-lined room, it was certainly not to find safety or tranquillity but to fit the skin of language over the whole world he had once known. Two years before his mother's death, he had written that "Literary work makes perpetual demands on the emotions that are linked with suffering. It is like the pain one feels when one moves an injured part of the body that should be held still. What I need, on the contrary, is frivolity and distraction." But now, as he wrote to Antoine Bibesco, "From the moment I emerged from that long torpor and for the first time turned my eyes inward towards my thoughts, I have felt the complete void of my life, while hundreds of characters for a novel, thousands of ideas beg me to give them body, like those shades in the *Odyssey* who ask Ulysses to let them drink a drop of blood to bring them back to life. . . . I have awakened the sleeping bee and I feel far more keenly his cruel sting than his impotent wings. I had fettered my intelligence to my peace of mind. In undoing its chains I thought only of freeing a slave. Instead, I have given myself a master whom I lack the physical strength to satisfy and who will kill me if I don't resist him." Cutting himself off from his friends and doctors—even from his brother, a distinguished physician—writing in bed, in a room whose windows were tightly shut and where a fire blazed on the hearth winter and summer, covered with sweaters and a barman's white jacket, he was not afraid to meet those "perpetual demands on the emotions that are linked with suffering." On the contrary, he gave himself to them with the ecstasy of an anchorite in the desert before his God; always "dying," yet not quite ready to die so long as the book waited, he allowed himself to be consumed for a work that people on the outside might still—so little were his intention and his originality understood—discount in advance as just another collection of articles.

The letters from the cork-lined room bring us near the Proust of the novel—not the "I" who tells the story, since he is a personification of human consciousness, but the heroic invalid who detached himself from his narrator to write the book—the Proust who was interested *not* in doing a self-portrait but in "general laws." And it is only in this period, as we watch him forced to communicate with the outside world largely by letters, yet—through all his pain and desperate fatigue, his appeals to friends to understand how very ill he is, his instinctive demands for sympathy—slowly building his novel up through the years, that we grasp how much its grand style had been formed by his long uneasiness in *"le monde,"* out of the effusiveness that had always hidden his deepest feelings. He would have liked to be "concise" in the manner of certain admired friends, but he knew that for him there was only one way of writing. "I must perforce weave these long silken threads as I spin them, and if I shortened my sentences, the results would be fragments, not whole sentences. So I continue like a silkworm, and live in the same temperature." His indirectness had been one way of withholding himself from a society to which he had been forced to pay tribute, in which he had always felt his position to be slightly false. Now, as he converted his social manner into an instrument of vision, still formal, still polite, he was dazzled by his own abundance. The sentences rose up like cathedrals, infinitely and secretly joined by a continuous rapture at how much could be seized by his consciousness.

Four

MAXIM GORKY AND THE MASTER FRIENDS

In the course of his long revolutionary career, marked by so much painful self-education, literary success, and a stubborn dedication to basic human values stronger than his formal political beliefs, Maxim Gorky wrote several reminiscences of Russian writers that are peculiarly valuable. The finest of these are the notes on Tolstoy, which are surely among the most beautiful things ever written by one human being on the character of another. There is a memoir of Chekhov that is almost as fine, less notable only because the subject is less complex, and acrid memories of two friends from the "decadent" generation—the novelist Leonid Andreyev and the poet Alexander Blok. Gorky on Tolstoy, on Chekhov, and then on the melancholy and eccentric Andreyev and Blok, is like moving from the high blaze of summer in the Crimea, where Gorky knew Tolstoy in the latter's last years, to the dull winter of the Russian mind that followed the aborted revolution of 1905. Putting together Gorky's portraits of four master friends, we have his basic conception of Russia, of the writer in Russia, and of his quarrel with himself.

The portrait of Tolstoy is a masterpiece, set down in scattered notes that Gorky himself evidently did not mind losing at one time, so much had he revealed of himself in grappling with the fascinating mystery that was Tolstoy. Great in its insight into the "old magician," whom Gorky adored and feared, it reveals more than he realized the liberating effect of Tolstoy's genius. Gorky was a man who gave himself passionately and gratefully to anything which called out his longing for a spiritual hero. He was able to gain from Tolstoy, despite all their differences, an absolute concentration of moral judgment by which to oppose him. That is the curious secret background of their meetings, one not to be guessed from the outward scene. The older writer was exactly forty years older, and at the very top of his influence and massive self-reliance, all the more striking because of the withered and contracted appearance he presented; crushingly direct in all his observations, "beautiful," but with something secretive in him that Gorky disliked, and for all his pleasure in his own genius, curiously baffled by it and following on a road all his own the estrangement he felt from friends and Russian society. The younger writer was awkward and tensely contradictory, full of Western ideas that were like shrill pipings against Tolstoy's Slavic abundance and deep passivity; enthusiastic about culture, science and revolution, and somehow calling up in Tolstoy a curious dislike.

Gorky had been a tramp, an itinerant laborer, and was now a passionate realist. Tolstoy was transcribing his genius from art into moralism, yet remained the patrician and baron despite his peasant blouse, and able to call up an insight into men and books that threatened Gorky's flimsy self-confidence. Their meeting was a conflict between the emperor of all the literary Russias, the social aristocrat who wanted to identify himself with the suffering of the masses, but in his religiosity seemed more aloof than ever, and the young self-made author who had taken the name of "Gorky" (bitter) to describe his experience in the lower depths. They clashed at many points. Gorky disliked Tolstoy's moralism and his social passivity, both of which seemed to him a regression to Slavic "backwardness" and the inertia and superstitions of the Russian village. He probably disliked even more Tolstoy's ability to expose the weakness of his culture. They irritated each other deeply, and Tolstoy provoked in Gorky, by his ruthless manner of instruction, an unexpected competitiveness. Deeper than this went the struggle between the lordly father and Homeric author, who knew his greatness too well, and the gauche son, whose approach to literature was still political and journalistic. Tolstoy exerted so much force on everyone around him that it was impossible not to resent him. "His surroundings become like a desert where everything is scorched by the sun and the sun itself is smoldering away, threatening a black and eternal night." Where Tolstoy was not, there was only dullness and mediocrity; but his presence eclipsed everything else.

To cope with Tolstoy, Gorky saw, was like struggling with Russia's immense distances and her deep suspicion of the West; he was a gigantic figure, but backward in his thinking and repellent in his approach to contemporary problems. It was Tolstoy's religion that he could not bear, for he could not believe that Tolstoy was truly religious. He saw too much of his immense pride; he could not believe that Tolstoy needed enough of another even to ask it of God. The meek Christ had in Tolstoy's mouth a false ring. "God," he quotes Tolstoy as writing in a diary note, "is the name of my desire." When Gorky asked him what it meant, he hesitated: "An unfinished thought. . . . I must have wanted to say: God is my desire to know him. . . . No, that that." Tolstoy's pride was too great to admit hunger for God; but since it rested on an omnivorous curiosity, he needed God to round out his picture of the world. He was an unbreakable rationalist in all things, an inhuman systematizer. God would be the final identifying principle. If Tolstoy was alone, it was because he had passed to the head of the human march and beyond it. Hence Gorky saw Tolstoy as playing rival to God. Tolstoy and God reminded him of two bears in the same den. Tolstoy's interest in himself, Gorky, he felt to be "ethnological." "In his eyes I belong to a species not familiar to him—only that."

Tolstoy's religion Gorky found hard to accept for another reason; the intended mortification of the flesh, even in the old man, was a cold idea: the "riot of the flesh" was too evident, and always violent. Tolstoy liked to shock, or rather he liked the effect that his customary frankness would have on young puritans. Other men were not only lesser beings, but inferior animals. Once Tolstoy astonished everyone by turning to Chekhov and asking him blithely: "You whored a great deal when you were young?" Chekhov was confused. Tolstoy, looking at the sea, confessed: "I was an indefatigable ——." Gorky goes on to say that "he said this penitently, using at the end of the sentence a salty peasant word. And I noticed for the first time how simply he used these words, as though he knew no more fitting ones to use. Coming from his shaggy lips, they sound simple and natural and lose their soldierly coarseness and filth."

Tolstoy mocked Gorky's inexperience as a man and author. He was a fearfully shrewd critic of another writer's work, and so strong in himself that he could speak of *War and Peace* as another *Iliad,* and convey some sense of the heights on which he worked by saying: "I myself, when I write, suddenly feel pity for some character, and then I give him some good quality or take a good quality away from someone else, so that in comparison with the others he may not appear too black." He took particular pleasure in showing up the evasions and genteel slurrings in Gorky's early work. Gorky felt himself surrounded by a hydra of strength: the old nobleman and libertine had him on one side, the astonishing purity and rough honesty of Tolstoy's writing challenged him on the other. Tolstoy always gave the appearance of being as uncomplicated a craftsman as a cobbler transferring nails from his mouth to the shoe; he knew that he had a skill that went beyond all transparent strategy, and had a way of making his friends feel that other writers were corrupt, since they could not be equally simple. Nothing could have been more difficult for another than Tolstoy's simplicity; it was really a happy freedom from the endless self-corrections and qualifications in which so much of Western keenness consists. To be as "simple" as Tolstoy, one would have needed to be as self-rooted in at least one department of human activity as Tolstoy was in all. Even his suffering had in it the quality of a man transferring all his strength to the search for his own meaning. Only such a deep and secret abundance could have permitted such analytical doubts as he permitted himself. La Rochefoucauld said that the weak cannot be sincere. Tolstoy was so strong that he bent the experience of life into a grotesque new shape to locate its ultimate meaning. But his real quest was the meaning of his formidable sincerity.

That there was such a quest, especially in Tolstoy's old age, was never lost on anyone near him. What is best in Gorky's portrait is that he makes us feel this continually in Tolstoy, and always in terms of his own respect for him—a respect that transcended resentment and went out in love and awe to the great writer seeking the meaning of his human strangeness. We have an appealing record of this in Gorky's description of Tolstoy sitting alone at the edge of the sea, as if he had gone away into himself—as before his death he did flee from everyone, to die alone in the little railroad station at Astapovo:

> I once saw him as, perhaps, no one has ever seen him. . . . Behind Yussopov's estate, on the shore among the stones I saw his smallish, angular figure in a gray, crumpled, ragged suit and crumpled hat. He was sitting with his head on his hands, the wind

blowing the silvery hairs of his beard through his fingers: he was looking into the distance out to sea, and the little greenish waves rolled up obediently to his feet and fondled them as if they were telling something about themselves to the old magician. It was a day of sun and cloud, and the shadows of the clouds glided over the stones, and with the stones the old man grew now bright and now dark. . . . He, too, seemed to me like an old stone come to life, who knows all the beginnings and the ends of things, who considers when and what will be the end of the stone, of the grasses of the earth, of the waters of the sea, and of the whole universe from the pebble to the sun. And the sea is part of his soul, and everything around him comes from him, out of him. In the musing motionlessness of the old man I felt something fateful, magical, something which went down into the darkness beneath him. . . . I can not express in words what I felt rather than thought at that particular moment; in my soul there was joy and fear, and then everything blended in one happy thought: "I am not an orphan on the earth, so long as this man lives on it."

Yet even after this, one feels in Gorky's notes the positive estrangement from Tolstoy. There was that in the older man which the younger could not recognize and which he feared; there was that which he feared because he could recognize it. Gorky was afraid of the whole moralistic and Gandhiesque side of Tolstoy's teaching because it rested on an indiscriminate religious affirmation to which he was susceptible. He liked to stress the beauty of positivism and secularism because he was afraid of losing his own hard-won faith in the revolution, and thus his principle of survival for himself and the Russian people. Tolstoy aroused in him those intense longings to burst the narrow bounds of revolutionary materialism which he knew could be exploited by the reactionary forces in Russian thought and earn him disfavor with the left. We know from the history of the Russian revolutionary movement that Gorky's religious promptings, in the confused period after 1905 when so many intellectuals sought to admit an idealistic principle into their thought, provoked contempt in Lenin. At the same time Gorky had a special need to believe in "westernization," which he saw as the only counter to Russian despair and apathy. "Culture," with its special resonance to a Russian intellectual outraged by the deprivations of his people, became his great belief. He insisted on it all the more because literature had raised him from the living death of the old Russia. Hence the sharpness with which he drew himself away from Tolstoy, as if to say: He can afford a metaphysics; I cannot. But hence, too, the shrewdness with which he exposed in Tolstoy the defects of the "would-be saint." By this move he was trying to destroy simultaneously that which was genuine in him but false in Tolstoy.

When we turn to the descriptions of Chekhov, Andreyev and Blok we can see how avidly Gorky seized on those elements—particularly in Chekhov—which were overtly against the regime. He made a fellow-insurgent out of Chekhov, which the latter certainly was in his own way. But that way was so much subtler than Gorky's own, and so full of questionings and promptings on human nature in itself, that it is amusing to see how determinedly Gorky brought Chekhov's art down to his own level. His Chekhov is the tubercular doctor, rotting away in his small village, and dying of Russian life in the nineteenth century, *tout simple*. It is a very moving portrait, it is unquestionably a very true and keen portrait. But Gorky's Chekhov is too rationalist by far, too limited and thus too easily assimilable into the familiar canons of Russian criticism—a criticism always inseparable from the need to make of the writer a political demiurge.

Perhaps Gorky abbreviated Chekhov's personality so as to admit nothing which could cause him uneasiness. Tolstoy was too massively complex to bear elimination of a single trait; it was indeed just that preponderance of astonishing single traits that made him interesting. But to Chekhov Gorky could give himself with a special joy. He admired in him all that was missing or inadequate in himself—the calmness, the humor, the gift of *chiaroscuro;* and so many virtues for which one hungered, and hungers still, in Russia—respect for the dignity of the individual, the freedom to declare the value of a person or a work, despite all political "necessity," liberalism as a way of life. It is obvious that Gorky could not bear to think of Chekhov as having a single fault. He does not attempt real criticism of Chekhov's work; in that he is one with his Western admirers. It was enough for Gorky that in this little man, whom Tolstoy also loved more than anyone else, there had been revealed so much ease in speaking the truth, and so deep a fund of personal nobility. Chekhov was the beautiful friend, the Spinoza in the Russian drama—Tolstoy, on the other hand, was the oracle speaking out of the dangerous Russian God-hunger; Andreyev and Blok were the gloomy contemporaries of Gorky's own literary world, too much like him in their inner restlessness to be admired. *Their* God was a thing of streaks and patches; Tolstoy's was inaccessible; Chekhov represented the possible living beauty in man. "In front of that dreary, gray crowd of helpless people there passed a great, wise, and observant man; he looked at all these dreary inhabitants of his country, and, with a sad smile, with a tone of gentle but deep reproach, with anguish in his face and in his heart, in a beautiful and sincere voice, he said to them: 'You live badly, my friends. It is shameful to live like that.' " Out of how much deep self-hatred in the old Russian life does Gorky bring this ideal friend to us, as if to make us believe, through so astonishing a presence: "Wait and see! Life will yet be better!"

Five

AN INTRODUCTION TO WILLIAM BLAKE

The real man, the imagination.

In 1827 there died, undoubtedly unknown to each other, two plebeian Europeans of supreme originality: Ludwig van Beethoven and William Blake. Had they known of each other, they could still not have known how much of the future they contained and how alike they were in the quality of their personal force, their defiance of the age, and the fierce demands each had made on the human imagination.

It is part of the story of Blake's isolation from the European culture of his time that he could have known of Beethoven, who enjoyed a reputation in the London of the early 1800's. The Ninth Symphony was in fact commissioned by the London Philharmonic, who made Beethoven's last days a little easier. The artistic society of the day was appreciative of Beethoven. It ignored the laborious little engraver, shut off by his work and reputed madness, who was known mainly to a few painters, and held by most of them to be a charming crank.

It is hard to imagine Blake going to concerts or reading accounts of Beethoven's music. He never traveled. Except for one three-year stay at a cottage in Sussex, he hardly went out of London. Like his father and brothers, he lived the life of a small tradesman—at one time he kept a printshop. He was always very poor, and generally worked in such seclusion that at one period, near the end of his life, he did not leave his house for two years, except to go out for porter. Blake had instinctive musical gifts; in his youth and old age he spontaneously, when in company, sang melodies to his own lyrics. Musicians who heard them set them down; I wish I knew where. Even on his deathbed, where he worked to the last, he composed songs. But he had no formal musical knowledge and apparently no interest in musical thought. Self-educated in every field except engraving, to which he had been apprenticed at fourteen, his only interest in most ideas outside his own was to refute them. He always lived and worked very much alone, with a wife whom he trained to be the mirror of his mind. The world let him alone. He was entirely preoccupied with his designs, his poems, and the burden—which he felt more than any writer whom I know—of the finiteness of man before the whole creation.

Beethoven's isolation was different. He was separated from society by his deafness, his pride, his awkward relations with women, relatives, patrons, inadequate musicians. He was isolated, as all original minds are, by the need to develop absolutely in his own way. The isolation was made tragic, against his will, by his deafness and social pride. At the same time he was one of the famous virtuosos of Europe, the heir of Mozart and the pupil of Haydn, and the occasional grumpy favorite of the musical princes of Vienna. His isolation was an involuntary personal tragedy, as it was by necessity a social fact. He did not resign himself to it, and only with the greatest courage learned to submit to it. If he was solitary, it was in a great tradition. As he was influenced by his predecessors, so he became the fountainhead of the principal musical thought that came after him.

Blake's isolation was—I sometimes think it still is—absolute. It was the isolation of a mind that sought to make the best of heaven and earth, in the image of neither. It was isolation of a totally different kind of human vision; of an unappeasable longing for the absolute integration of man, in his total nature, with the universe. It was the isolation of a temperament run on fixed ideas; and incidentally, of a craftsman who could not earn a living. There are analogies to Blake's position in a world which has so many displaced persons as our own; but they are inadequate. Blake's isolation may be likened to that of the revolutionary who sits in his grubby room writing manifestoes against a society that pays him no attention, with footnotes against other revolutionaries who think him mad. It was that of the author who prints his own books. It was that of the sweetly smiling crank who sits forever in publishers' offices, with a vast portfolio under his arm, explaining with undiminishable confidence that only through his vision will the world be saved. It was that of the engraver who stopped getting assignments because he turned each one into an act of independent creation. Blake was a lyric poet interested chiefly in ideas, and a painter who did not believe in nature. He was a commercial artist who was a genius in poetry, painting, and religion. He was a libertarian obsessed with God; a mystic who reversed the mystical pattern, for he sought man as the end of his search. He was a Christian who hated the churches; a revolutionary who abhorred the materialism of the radicals. He was a drudge, sometimes living on a dollar a week, who called himself "a mental prince"; and was one.

There are other points of difference between Blake and Beethoven, important to recognize before we can appreciate their likeness. With Beethoven we are in the stream of modern secular culture. Beethoven, the enduring republican and anti-Bonapartist, the social dramatist of *Fidelio,* the jealous admirer of Goethe, the celebrant of Schiller's call to the joyous brotherhood of man, is a central figure in *our* history, as Blake never has been. We remember Beethoven the moralist, the Beethoven who felt so gratefully at home in the world of Kant that he copied out a sentence, probably at second-hand, and kept it on his work-table—"The starry heavens above us and the moral law within us. Kant!!!" To Blake the "moral law" was a murderous fiction and the stars were in the heavens because man's imagination saw them there. Beethoven speaks to our modern humanity in tones we have learned to prize as our own and our greatest, as Blake has not yet; he is uneasily religious and spiritually frustrated, in a familiar agnostic way, where Blake is the "immoralist" and "mystic" by turns. Beethoven could not hear the world, but he always believed in it. His struggles to sustain himself in it, on the highest level of his creative self-respect, were vehement because he could never escape the tyranny of the actual. He was against material despotisms, and knew them to be real. Blake was also against them; but he came to see every hindrance to man's imaginative self-liberation as a fiction bred by the division in man himself. He was against society *in toto:* its prisons, churches, money, morals, fashionable opinions; he did not think that the faults of society stemmed from the faulty organization of society. To him the only restrictions over man are always in his own mind—the "mind-forg'd manacles."

With Blake, it would seem, we are off the main track of modern secular thought and aspiration. The textbooks label him "mystic," and that shuts him off from us. Actually he is not off the main track, but simply ahead of it; a peculiarly disturbed and disturbing prophet of the condition of modern man rather than a master-builder. From any conventional point of view he is too different in kind to be related easily to familiar conceptions of the nature of the individual and society. Blake combines, for example, the formal devotional qualities of the English dissenters with the intellectual daring of Nietzsche, the Marquis de Sade, and Freud. No Christian saint ever came to be more adoring of Jesus, and no naturalistic investigator was a more candid opponent of traditional Christian ethics. He was one of the subtlest and most far-reaching figures in the intellectual liberation of Europe that took place at the end of the eighteenth century. But he had no interest in history, and easily relapsed into primitive nationalism. To the end of his life his chief symbol for man, "the eternal man," was Albion; the origin of "natural religion" he located among the Druids; he hated Newton and despised Voltaire, but painted the apotheosis of Nelson and Pitt. Like so many self-educated men, he was fanatically learned; but he read like a Fundamentalist—to be inspired or to refute. He painted by "intellectual vision"—that is, he painted ideas; his imagination was so original that it carried him to the borders of modern surrealism. Yet he would have been maddened by the intellectual traits of surrealism: the calculated insincerities, the defiant disorder, the autonomous decorative fancy, the intellectual mockery and irreverence. That part of surrealism which is not art is usually insincerity, and to Blake any portion of insincerity was a living death. As he hated church dogma, so he hated scepticism, doubt, experimentalism. He did not believe in sin, only in "intellectual error"; he loathed every dualistic conception of good and evil; the belief that any human being could be punished, here or elsewhere, for "following his energies." But he thought that unbelief—that is, the admission of uncertainty on the part of any person—was wicked. He understood that man's vital energies cannot be suppressed or displaced without causing distortion; he saw into the personal motivations of human conflict and the many concealments of it which are called culture. He celebrated in *Songs of Innocence,* with extraordinary inward understanding, the imaginative separateness of the child. He hated scientific investigation.

He could say in his old age, when provoked, that he believed the world was flat. He was undoubtedly sincere, but he did not really care what shape it was; he would not have believed any evidence whatsoever that there were many planets and universes. He did not believe in God; under all his artistic labors and intellectual heresies he seems to have thought of nothing else. He is one of the most prophetic and gifted rebels in the history of Western man—a man peculiarly of our time, with the divisions of our time. Some of his ideas were automatically superstitious, and a large part of his writing is rant. There are features of his thought that carry us beyond the subtlest understanding we have of the relations between man and woman, the recesses of the psyche, the meaning of human error, tyranny, and happiness. There are chapters in his private mythology that carry us into a nightmare world of loneliness and fanaticism, like a scream repeated interminably on a record in which a needle is stuck.

Yet Blake is very much like Beethoven in his artistic independence and universality. Like Beethoven, he is a pioneer Romantic of that heroic first generation which thought that the flames of the French Revolution would burn down all fetters. Like Beethoven, he asserts the creative freedom of the imagination within his work and makes a new world of thought out of it. There sounds all through Blake's poetry, from the boyish and smiling defiance of neo-classic formalism in *Poetical Sketches,*

> The languid strings do scarcely move!
> The sound is forc'd, the notes are few!

to the vision of man the divine in *Jerusalem* that lyric despair mingled with quickness to exaltation, that sense of a primal intelligence fighting the mind's limitations, that brings Beethoven's last quartets so close to absolute meditation and the Ninth Symphony to a succession of triumphal marches. What is nearest and first in both men is so strong a sense of their own identity that they are always reaching beyond man's conception of his powers. In both there is a positive assertion against suffering, an impatience with forms and means. As Beethoven said of the violinist who complained of the difficulty of one of the Rasumofsky quartets—"Does he really suppose I think of his puling little fiddle when the spirit speaks to me and I compose something?"—so to Blake the forms he uses in his last Prophetic Books, even to their very narrative coherence, are nothing before the absoluteness of his vision. In both life becomes synonymous with the will.

There, however, the resemblance ends. For Beethoven does not block our way by asking us to read him in symbols of his own invention. He is subtle, moving, reflective, in a language which we share because he has made it possible for us to share in it. Out of a limited number of musical tones and devices, he has organized his thought and impressed his conception in such a way that his difference is all *in* his art. When we have grasped his meaning something has enriched our lives without dislodging them. Beethoven is as luminously human as he is creatively independent; he can be gay; he parodies; he introduces a little Russian tune to compliment a patron; he is fond of bearish jokes. He is often difficult, but never impossible. He does not challenge man's submission to the natural order; he finds his place in it, and often in such deep wells of serenity, of happiness in his own struggle, that the song that rises from him almost at the very end, in his last quartet, is for a dance. "Must it be?" he wrote on the manuscript. "It must be. It must be." He may have been thinking of something less than man's ultimate relation to life. But the idea that something *must be* is what is most hateful to Blake's mind.

For Blake accepts nothing—not the God who is supposed to have proposed it this way, or the man who is constrained to dispose it in any way he can. Blake begins with a longing so deep, for all that is invisible and infinite to man under the dominion of God, matter, and reason, that he tears away the shell of earth, the prison of man in his own senses, to assert that there is nothing but man and that man is nothing but the highest flights of his own imagination. With his little tradesman's look, his fanatical industriousness, his somber qualities of the English dissenter and petty-bourgeois, he begins with so absolute a challenge to the religion that was dying in his age, and to the scientific materialism that arose in it, that he transcends them both—into a world that is exalted and often beautiful, but of which he alone saw the full detail.

To understand this is to pass up the usual tags. Blake is seeking something which is analogous to mysticism, but he is not in any ordinary sense a mystic. He is very much in the stream of thought which led to naturalism, but he is not a naturalist. It is more important, however, to show what he shares with us rather than with the mystics. Only those who want to make a Blake easy to explain and apologize for, convenient for the textbooks, can see him as a queer and harmless "mystic." As D. H. Lawrence said of his work, "They'll say as they said of Blake: It's mysticism, but they shan't get away with it, not this time: Blake's wasn't mysticism, neither is this." Even at the end, when Blake celebrated Jesus as his great friend and deliverer, we have in "The Everlasting Gospel:"

> The Vision of Christ that thou dost see
> Is my Vision's Greatest Enemy:
>
> . . . .
> Thine is the friend of all Mankind,
> Mine speaks in parables to the Blind:
> Thine loves the same world that mine hates,
> Thy Heaven doors are my Hell Gates.

Christian mysticism is founded on dualism. It is rooted in the belief that man is a battleground between the spirit and the flesh, between the temptations of earth and God as the highest Good. The mystic way is the logical and extreme manifestation of the spiritual will, obedient to a faith in supernatural authority, to throw off the body and find an ultimate release in the Godhead. Christian mysticism is based upon a mortification of the body so absolute that it attains a condition of ecstasy. To the mystic, God is the nucleus of the Creation, and man in his earthly life is a dislodged atom that must find its way back. The mystic begins with submission to a divine order, which he accepts with such conviction that earthly life becomes nothing to him. He lives only for the journey of the soul that will take him away, upward to God. What would be physical pain to others, to him is purgation; what would be doubt to others, to him is hell; what would be death for others, to him is the final consummation—and one he tries to reach in the living body.

Blake has the mystic's tormented sense of the doubleness of life between reality and the ideal. But he tries to resolve it on earth, in the living person of man. Up to 1800 he also thought it could be resolved in society, under the inspiration of the American and French Revolutions. Blake is against everything that submits, mortifies, constricts and denies. Mystics are absent-minded reactionaries; they accept indifferently everything in the world except the barriers that physical existence presents to the soul's inner quest. Blake is a revolutionary. He ceased to be a revolutionary in the political sense after England went to war with France and tried to destroy the revolution in Europe. That was less out of prudent cowardice—though like every other radical and free-thinker of the time he lived under a Tory reign of terror —than because he had lost faith in political action as a means to human happiness. Even in politics, however, his libertarian thought became a challenge to all the foundations of society in his time. Blake is not only unmystical in the prime sense of being against the mystic's immediate concerns and loyalties; he is against all accepted Christianity. He is against the churches,

> Remove away that black'ning church;
> Remove away that marriage hearse:
> Remove away that place of blood:
> You'll quite remove the ancient curse.

Against priesthood:

> And Priests in black gowns were walking their rounds,
> And binding with briars my joys & desires.

Against the "moral law." He denies that man is born with any innate sense of morality—all moral codes are born of education—and thinks education a training in conformity. He is against all belief in sin; to him the tree in Eden is the gallows on which freedom-seeking man is hanged by dead-souled priests. He savagely parodied a Dr. Thornton's new version of the Lord's Prayer:

> Our Father Augustus Caesar, who art in these thy Substantial Astronomical Telescopic Heavens, Holiness to Thy Name or Title, & reverence to thy Shadow. . . . Give us day by day our Real Taxed Substantial Money bought bread; deliver from the Holy Ghost whatever cannot be taxed. . . .

He is against every conception of God as an omnipotent person, as a body, as a Lord who sets in train any lordship over man:

> Thou art a Man, God is no more,
> Thine own humanity learn to adore.

He believes that all restraint in obedience to a moral code is against the spirit of life:

> Abstinence sows sand all over
> The ruddy limbs & flaming hair,
> But Desire Gratified
> Plants fruits & beauty there.

Blake is against all theological casuistry that excuses pain and admits evil; against sanctimonious apologies for injustice and the attempt to buy bliss in another world with self-deprivation in this one. The altar is a place on which the serpent has vomited out its poison; the priest is a blind old man with shears in his hand, to cut the fleece off human sheep. Sex is life, and no one can be superior to it or honestly content with less than true gratification:

> What is it men in women do require?
> The lineaments of Gratified Desire.
> What is it women in men do require?
> The lineaments of Gratified Desire.

Restraint, in fact, follows from the organized injustice and domination in society:

> The harvest shall flourish in wintry weather
> When two virginities meet together:
>
> The King & the Priest must be tied in a tether
> Before two virgins can meet together.

He is against all forms of human exploitation, and all rationalizations of it in human prejudice:

> And all must love the human form,
> In heathen, turk, or jew;

Where Mercy, Love, & Pity dwell
There God is dwelling too.

Against war, especially holy ones; against armies, and in pity for soldiers; against the factory system, the labor of children, the evaluation of anything by money.

In "London," one of his simplest and greatest poems, Blake paints the modern city under the sign of man's slavery, the agony of children, the suffering Soldier and the Whore:

I wander thro' each charter'd street,
Near where the charter'd Thames does flow,
And mark in every face I meet
Marks of weakness, marks of woe.

In every cry of every Man,
In every Infant's cry of fear,
In every voice, in every ban,
The mind-forg'd manacles I hear.

How the Chimney-sweeper's cry
Every black'ning Church appalls;
And the hapless Soldier's sigh
Runs in blood down Palace walls.

But most thro' midnight streets I hear
How the youthful Harlot's curse
Blasts the new born Infant's tear,
And blights with plagues the Marriage hearse.

"Charter'd" means "bound." In his first draft of this poem, Blake wrote "dirty Thames," but characteristically saw that he could realize more of the city's human slavery in describing the river as bound between its London shores. His own place in the poem is that of the walker in the modern inhuman city, one isolated man in the net which men have created. "I wander thro' each charter'd street." For him man is always the wanderer in the oppressive and sterile world of materialism which only his imagination and love can render human. In a more difficult poem, characteristic of his deeper symbolism, he speaks of the world of matter as

> A Fathomless & boundless deep,
> There we wander, there we weep;

In "London," however, the wandering is not a symbolic expression. In the modern city man has lost his real being, as he has already lost his gift of vision in the "fathomless and boundless" deep of his material nature. Blake here describes one man, himself, in a city that is only too real, the only city he ever knew—yet the largest in the world, the center of empire. The city stands revealed in the cry of *every* Man, in *every* Infant's cry of fear. The wanderer in the chartered streets is concerned with a social picture and, in the face of so much suffering, with the social evil that some create and all permit. The extraordinary terseness of the poem stems from Blake's integral vision of the suffering of man and his alienation from institutions as one. His indignation gives him the power of movement; it also leads him into the repetitions which dominate the tonal order of the poem—the *every* cry of *every* Man, the Infant's *cry of fear,* till his tender vehemence swells into the generality of *in every voice, in every ban.*

Every is magic to Blake. Poetically he cannot go wrong on it, for it carries such a kernel of glory to his mind, it points so immediately to his burning human solidarity, that in using it he knows himself carried along by what is deepest to him. The *mind-forg'd manacles,* as central to his thought as any phrase he ever used, follows with a triumphant sweep right after it, and for an obvious reason. For he is one with every voice, every ban, and can now make his judgment. On this fresh creative impulse he leaps ahead to what is so complex, but for him so natural, a yoking of images:

How the Chimney-sweeper's cry
Every black'ning Church appalls;

The young Chimney-sweeper is always dear to Blake, especially when he is condemned to get the soot out of the churches—an impossible task. He is the symbol of the child who is lost. He works among the waste-dirt of the Church, itself black with dogma and punitive zeal, and his own suffering makes it even blacker. *Black'ning* is a verb of endless duration in present time for Blake. In his drawing to this poem, the Chimney-sweeper is shown in one corner struggling before a black flame. At the top of the page he stands in defiance before the blind and tottering old man, the fossilized Church, who seems to be pouring out fresh soot. The walls are the stone blocks of a prison. The whole page is marked, like the turn of the hand on a vehement signature, by a fierce black border. Pictorially and verbally we thus rise to a climax at the word *appalls.* The Church is not appalled by the Chimney-sweeper's cry; the cry of the child, out of the midst of the Church, makes the Church appalling. Blake's thrust is so swift and deep that he characteristically puts the whole burden of his protest, with its inner music, into four words. Every black and blackening Church is appalling, and in every way. The tone of *palls* to his ear, carrying the image of death, the grief and shame that will not rest, clangs with reverberations.

The unhappiness of the Soldier is not that of a man bleeding before a palace of which he is the sentry. Blake means that the Soldier's desperation runs, like his own blood, in accusation down the walls of the ruling Palace. Blake's own mind ran in so many channels at once, his vision of human existence was so total, that it probably never occurred to him that *blood* would mean anything less to others than it did to him. "Runs in blood down palace walls" is what Blake sees instantaneously in his mind when he thinks of the passivity and suffering of the Soldier. Blake is too much abreast of the reality he sees to use similes; he cannot deliberate to compare something to another. And he is equally incapable of using a metaphor with self-conscious daring. He saw the blood running down the ruler's walls before thinking of blood as a "powerful" image. There is no careful audacity in him, the preparation for the humor of T. S. Eliot's

> I am aware of the damp souls of housemaids
> Sprouting despondently at area gates.

Blake's poetic urge, it is clear, was not to startle, to tease the mind into fresh combinations, but to make tangible, out of the wealth of relationships he carried in his mind, some portion of it equal to his vision of the life of man. How swiftly and emphatically he turns, at the first line of the fourth stanza, to

> But most thro' midnight streets I hear

But most stands for: what I have described thus far is not the full horror of London, my city; not anything like what I have to tell you! And he then gives back, in eighteen words, the city in which young girls are forced into prostitution; in which their exile from respectable society, like the unhappiness of the Soldier, expresses itself in a physical threat to another. The Soldier accuses the Palace with his blood; the prostitute curses with infection the young husband who has been with her; the "plague" finally kills the new-born child. The carriage that went to the church for a marriage ends at the grave as a hearse. Nothing can equal the bite of "blights with plagues," the almost visible thrust of the infection. And thanks to Blake's happy feeling for capitals, which he used with a painter's eye to distinguish the height of his concepts, Marriage stands above the rest in the last sentence of the poem, and swiftly falls into a hearse.

These are some of the poem's details, but they are not the poem. For the poem is to be grasped only by the moral imagination, as a shuddering vision of the mind. The title is a city, as the city is the present human world on the threshold of the industrial revolution. We are to read from the title to the last word, from London to its inner death, in one movement of human sympathy and arousal. This, in its simplest sense, is the key to Blake's meaning of vision. Vision is his master-word, not mysticism or soul. For vision represents the total imagination of man made tangible and direct in works of art. And as the metric structure of the poem encloses, in each line-frame of sharply enclosed syllables, the sight of man entering fully into the city with all his being—*hearing* "the mind-forg'd manacles," the harlot's disease *blasting* "the new born infant's tear," so the whole poem carries us along, in a single page, while the border designs meanwhile extend the vision by another art.

Blake was artist and poet; he designed his poems to form a single picture. Trained to engraving as a boy, he invented for himself a method of etching a hand-printed poem and an accompanying design on the same page. Only two of his works were ever printed—his first book, *Poetical Sketches,* most of which he wrote between the ages of twelve and twenty-one, and a long and declamatory celebration of the new world after '89 called *The French Revolution*. Neither of these works was ever published. *Poetical Sketches* was run off for him, with a patronizing and apologetic preface by a Reverend Mathew, who with his wife formed a provincial intellectual society that Blake burlesqued in *An Island in the Moon*. *The French Revolution* was printed by a bookseller, Joseph Johnson, who was the center of a radical circle in London that included Blake, William Godwin, Mary Wollstonecraft, and Thomas Paine. After England became embroiled with France and a reactionary witchhunt set after radical intellectuals and sympathizers with the French Republic, Johnson became panicky and left the book in proof. Some of Blake's greatest poems—"The Everlasting Gospel," "Auguries of Innocence," the lyrics that follow *Songs of Innocence and of Experience*—were found in "The Rossetti Manuscript," which was bought by Dante Gabriel Rossetti for ten shillings from an attendant at the British Museum. Blake's most famous works, *Songs of Innocence and of Experience* and *The Marriage of Heaven and Hell,* along with his Prophetic Books—*The Book of Thel, Visions of the Daughters of Albion, America, Europe, The Book of Urizen, Milton, Jerusalem,* etc.—were done entirely by his method of "illuminated printing." Blake said he got the inspiration for this technique from the spirit of his dead brother Robert, the only member of his family with whom he had common sympathies. This may be true, but it is a pity that Blake had to say so, for it has given people the idea ever since that Blake's visions were of the kind limited to a séance.

Blake's general technique is now clear. He etched his poems and designs in relief, with acid on copper. He corroded with acid the unused portions of the plate—characteristically, this became a symbol in *The Marriage of Heaven and Hell* of the corrosion of dead matter by the visionary human imagination. Each print-page as it was taken off the press was colored by hand. Each copy of a work was planned in a different color scheme. There are probably no handmade books in the world more beautiful. The only models for Blake were, of course, the illuminated manuscripts of the Middle Ages. But Blake worked in an entirely different spirit. The medieval manuscripts, impressive as they are, remain pictorial and remote; they were created by copyists, ornamentalists and pious scribes who worked in a liturgical spirit. Blake's designs are the accessories of a single creative idea. His conception of the beautiful book, as Laurence Binyon said, was one of a complete unity, "in which the lettering, the decoration, the illustrations, the proportions of the page, the choice of paper, surpassed even the conceptions of the medieval scribes and miniaturists." Yet Blake was not aiming at a "beautiful book" for its own sake, or at the kind of isolated luxury product which we usually associate with book illustration by a master artist. To him all the arts were simultaneously necessary, in their highest creative use and inner proportion, to give us the ground essence of his vision and a stimulus to our own. What was most important to him was that he should get all his vision down, through all the arts open to him, in work done entirely in his own person.

Blake's search for unity began in his own hands, with his sense of craft. The symbolic synthesis to be created by his imagination was an image of man pressing, with the full power of his aroused creativity, against the walls of natural appearances. Each page of "illuminated printing" for him was a little world, in which the structure of the poem, the designs on the border, the accompanying figures on the page, the tints of the color, the rhythm of the lettering, were joined together into the supreme metaphor.

The attempt to model some ideal unity in a single work is not unique in itself—it is the symbolic function of traditional religious art, and is to be found in the outer and inner architecture of the cathedrals, the structure of *The Divine Comedy*, and cruciformly printed poems of George Herbert. What is different in Blake is that he is not modeling after any symbols but his own. The symbols always have an inner relatedness that leads us from the outer world to the inner man. The symbols live in the ordered existence of his vision; the vision itself is entirely personal, in theme and in the logic that sustains it. What is before us, in one of his pages, has been created entirely by him in every sense, and the unimpeachable quality of his genius is shown in an order that is as great as his independence, and shows us how real both were. The characteristic of his genius is to lift his unexpected symbols for the inner world of the imagination into a world in which they stand apart from the natural world and defy it. When he designs illustrations to Gray's poems, the magnitude of his vision throws the lines he is illustrating off the page. But what impresses us in their magnitude is not their physical size, but the uncanny spiritual coherence which joins them together and gives them an effect of absolute force. Blake could never "illustrate" another man's work, even though it was pretty much the only way by which he could earn a living. Even if he respected the other man's work, as he did Milton and Dante, he created new conceptions of their subject in his own designs. When he did his twenty-one engravings to the Book of Job, he reversed the pious maxims of the Bible story to show a man destroyed by his own materialism and selfrighteousness. Fortunately, he did not set his Job designs against a page reproduced from the Bible; he selected passages, and wrote new ones, and put both into the scroll-work of his border designs. His vision of Job is entirely his own work, as the Job is indeed the greatest of his "Prophetic Books." Where the words were created by him, as in his poems, the love of the word to the design is only one revelation of man's will to wed the contraries—like the marriage of Heaven and Hell. Blake's conception of union and of the infiniteness of union has no physical status. For him infinity is in man's passions and his will to know; it is a state of being.

Yet what has been designed is bound, much as Blake disliked

all limits. So he carried the force and delicacy of his longing for the infinite into the subtle inwardness of everything he drew. In *Songs of Innocence and of Experience,* he designed his poems in such a way that the words on the line seemed to grow like flower-heads out of a thicket. Each hand-printed letter of script, each vine trailing a border between the lines, each moving figure above, beside, and below the page mounts and unites to form some visible representation of the inner life of man—seen in phases of the outward nature. Yet Blake was not seeking to represent nature; he used it as a book of symbols. When he put down something "natural" and visible on his page—a bramble, a tree, a leaf, a figure moving mysteriously in its symbolic space—the effort seemed to dissolve his need to believe in its separate existence. The acid of the designer's imagination burned away the materials on which it worked. What he represented, for purposes of spiritual vision and imagery, dissolved its own exterior naturalness for him. The natural forms—from the arch of the sky to the stolid heroic figures he liked to draw—became a mold that would *contain* his symbolic ideas of them. This is what makes his gift so beautiful on one level, and often so unreachable on another. He brought a representation of the world into every conception; but he never drew an object for its own sake. He wrote and drew, as he lived, from a fathomless inner window, in an effort to make what was deepest and most invisible capturable by the mind of man. Then he used the thing created—the poem, the picture, joined in their double vision—as a window in itself, through which to look to what was still beyond. "I look through the eye," he said, "not with it."

In short, Blake was not looking for God. He shared in the mystic's quest, but he was not going the same way. But we can see at the same time that he was not interested in natural phenomena, in the indestructible actuality of what is not in ourselves but equally real. Spinoza once said that the greatest good is the knowledge of the union which the mind has with the whole nature. That is an exalted statement, but we can recognize its meaning through the work of naturalists of genius like Darwin, Marx, and Freud. The creative function of naturalism has been to establish, with some exactness, a measure of objective knowledge —whether in the description of matter and energy, man's own life as a biological organism, his economic society, or the life urges which civilization has pushed into a world below consciousness. Naturalism is a great and tragic way of looking at life, for with every advance in man's consciousness and in his ability to ascertain, to predict, and to control, he loses that view of his supreme importance which is at the center of religious myth. Naturalism helps to postpone death, but never denies it; it cannot distort objective truth for the sake of personal assurance; it finds assurance in man's ability to know something of what lies outside him. There flows from its positive insights an advance in man's consciousness of his own power that is more fertile and resourceful than any anthropocentric myth can inspire. Naturalism declares limits, and discovers new worlds of actuality between them. It is tragic, for by showing that man's experience is limited it gives him a sense of his permanent and unremitting struggle in a world he did not make. But the struggle is the image of his true life in the world, and one he deepens by art, knowledge, and love. The quality of tragedy is not sadness but grave exhilaration; it defines the possible.

Blake is not a naturalist; he believes in apprehension, not in being; in certainty at the price of reality. He does not believe that anything is finally real except the imagination of man. He grasped one horn of the classic dilemma—"how do I know that anything is real, since I know of reality only through my own mind?"—and pronounced that the problem was settled. He refused to believe the evidence of his senses that the human mind—however it may qualify or misread reality—is bombarded by something outside itself. We are eternally subjective; but there are objects. Indeed, it would seem to follow from our very ability to correct ourselves that we do measure our knowledge by some source. Our backs in Plato's cave are to the fire; but we know that the shadows on the wall before us are shadows, and not the fire itself. Blake assumed that what is partial is in error, and that what is limited is non-existent. But the truth is that he was not trying to prove anything philosophically at all; his greatness depends not on his conception of the world but on what he created through it. In defense of his own personality, and in defiance of his age, he imagined a world equal to his heart's desire. He refused to admit objective reality only because he was afraid man would have to share the creation.

It is here that Blake has perplexed his readers even more than he has delighted them. The reason lies in his refusal to concede a distance between what is real and what is ideal; in his desperate need to claim them as one. Blake is difficult not because he invented symbols of his own; he created his symbols to show that the existence of any natural object and the value man's mind places on it were one and the same. He was fighting the acceptance of reality in the light of science as much as he was fighting the suppression of human nature by ethical dogmas. He fought on two fronts, and shifted his arms from one to the other without letting us know—more exactly, he did not let himself know. He created for himself a personality, in life and in art, that was the image of the thing he sought.

Like all the great enlighteners of the eighteenth century, Blake is against the *ancien régime* in all its manifestations—autocracy, feudalism, superstition. Though he loathed the destructive reason of the Deists, he sometimes praised it in the fight against "holy mystery." He was fighting for free thought. Yet he is not only a confederate of Diderot and Voltaire, Jefferson and Tom Paine; he is a herald of the "heroic vitalism" of Nietzsche and D. H. Lawrence, of Dostoevsky's scorn for nineteenth-century utilitarianism and self-contentment. Where the Encyclopedists were concerned with the investigation, on "natural principles," of man's place in society and his order in the universe, Blake—who hated the Church as much as Voltaire and was as republican as Jefferson—was concerned with the freedom of man from all restrictions, whether imposed by the morality of the Church or the narrowness of positivism. Like Nietzsche, he considered himself an enemy of Socrates and of the Platonic dualism that became a permanent basis of Christian thought. What Blake said in so many of his early poems Nietzsche was to say in his autobiography: "All history is the experimental refutation of the theory of the so-called moral order of the world." Zarathustra, dancing mysteriously to the bacchanal of Nietzsche's imagined self-fulfillment, is prefigured in Blake's Los, the crusading imagination with the hammer in his hand. And like Nietzsche, Blake writes in his masterpiece, *The Marriage of Heaven and Hell,* with the playful daemonism of those who league themselves with the "Devil" because his opposite number restricts human rights:

> The reason Milton wrote in fetters when he wrote of Angels & God, and at liberty when of Devils & Hell, is because he was a true poet and of the Devil's party without knowing it.

With it there is the stress on heroic energy, on the rights of the superior that cannot be claimed under what Nietzsche called the "slave-morality":

> The eagle never lost so much time as when he submitted to learn of the crow.

Damn braces. Bless relaxes.

Improvement makes strait roads; but the crooked roads without Improvement are the roads of genius.

Destroy, Blake says, all that binds man to decayed institutions. But destroy as well man's obedience to moral precepts that hinder the full power of his creative will to assert, to love and to build. Desire is never vicious in itself; it is only turned to vicious ends when driven out of its real channel. Restraint in the name of the moral code is alone evil, for it distorts man's real nature. It is a device of the rulers of this world to keep us chained. For life is holy. Energy is eternal delight. Jesus is dear to us not because he was divine, but because he was a rebel against false Law, and the friend of man's desire. He defied the Kings and Priests. He was against punishment. He was the herald of man's joy, not of his imaginary redemption. Joy is the only redemption and all suppression is a little death. Humility is an imposture born of cunning. Better wrath than pity. "The tygers of wrath are wiser than the horses of instruction."

> If he had been Antichrist, Creeping Jesus,
> He'd have done anything to please us:
> Gone sneaking into the Synagogues
> And not used the Elders & Priests like Dogs,
> But humble as a Lamb or an Ass,
> Obey himself to Caiaphas.
> God wants not man to humble himself:
> . . . . . .
> For he acts with honest, triumphant Pride,
> And this is the cause that Jesus died.

In *The Marriage of Heaven and Hell,* Blake writes: "Opposition is true friendship." His drive is always toward creative self-assertion, toward man as a free creator. In *A Song of Liberty,* his vision of the old world burning in the fires of the French Revolution leads him to cry: "Empire is No More!"

Let the Priests of the Raven of dawn no longer, in deadly black, with hoarse note curse the sons of joy. Nor his accepted brethren—whom, tyrant, he calls free—lay the bound or build the roof. Nor pale religious letchery call that virginity that wishes but acts not!

So far Blake is a libertarian, an eighteenth-century radical more vehement, daring and imaginative in his conception of freedom than others, but sharing in a revolutionary tradition. Where he becomes truly prophetic and difficult is in his rejection of materialism. He denounces the Priest, in his "deadly black"; but he warns us not to "lay the bound or build the roof" with our anti-clerical freedom. He sets his thought absolutely against rationalism, scepticism, and experimentalism. He is with the Deists so long as they attack supernaturalism—detestable to Blake not because it is disprovable by reason, but because it implies obedience. He is against the Deists so long as they seek to submit the imagination to reason. Rationalism is dangerous because it leaves man in doubt. When the time-serving Bishop Watson wrote, at the request of the English Tory government, an attack on Tom Paine's *The Age of Reason,* Blake scrawled vehement attacks on the Bishop all over the margin of his *Apology for the Bible.*

It appears to me Now that Tom Paine is a better Christian than the Bishop.

I have read this Book with attention & find that the Bishop has only hurt Paine's heel while Paine has broken his head. The Bishop has not answer'd one of Paine's grand objections.

But in one of his most famous poems, he denounced Voltaire and Rousseau as the arch-Deists seeking to destroy man's capacity for visionary wonder:

Mock on, Mock on Voltaire, Rousseau:
Mock on, Mock on: 'tis all in vain!
You throw the sand against the wind,
And the wind blows it back again.

The sand is the dead particles separated by reason from the true unity of the human vision. Man under the domination of reason is to Blake a creature who has lost his integral nature and has become a dead fragment in himself. Separateness is death; doubt is the child of separateness; the portions which man separates by his reason, in the analysis of natural objects, or by thinking of himself as a natural object, are the mocking ghosts of his dead imagination.

This impassioned rejection of all that is analytical and self-limiting in modern thought is central to Blake. It underlies all his conceptions, is the psychological background of his life, and falls, sometimes with a dead absoluteness, between his revolutionary thought and the modern world. It is only when we have understood that doubt and uncertainty stand to Blake's mind as the prime danger of modern life that we can see the main drives of his work, of his personal "queerness," and what led him to the artistic wreckage and incoherence of the later Prophetic Books. Blake's whole pattern, as man and artist, is that of one for whom life is meaningless without an absolute belief. He is like the nihilist Verkhovensky, in Dostoevsky's *The Possessed,* who "when he was excited preferred to risk anything rather than to remain in uncertainty." Freud spoke out of what is deepest and most courageous in the modern tradition when he said that "Man must learn to bear a certain portion of uncertainty." That is a great injunction which it is hard to follow: much harder than the authoritarian faiths of our time, the secular, sadistic religions, the phony ecstasy with which a Hitler's self-mortification is lost in vision of eternal conquest. But Blake is very much a man of our time: one who speaks to us with prophetic insight of our nihilism and insensibility. He was so frightened by what he could already see of it that he found his security only in an absolute personal myth. It is a trait that has become universal politics in our own time. Insecurity has become so endemic, in a society increasingly unresponsive to basic human needs, that men will apparently distort and destroy anything to find their way back to the mystical faith of the child in his parents, the medieval man in his God, and the Nordic in the pagan forest. Blake is peculiarly contemporary in his anxiety, his longing for a faith that will be absolute and yet insurgent, his fear of evidence that will destroy the fantasy of man as the *raison d'être* of the universe. He is as great as Dostoevsky in his understanding of our modern deficiencies; he is as self-deluding as Dostoevsky, who was so afraid of his own nihilism that he allied himself with all that was most obscurantist in Czarist Russia.

This does not make what is central in Blake's work any less prophetic and beautiful. He is not the enemy of society, any more than Dostoevsky was, or the D. H. Lawrence who succumbed to a silly literary Fascism. The very excesses of Blake's myth, like the golden quality in his best work, spring from his impassioned defense of human dignity. Far less than Blake have we solved the problem of restoring to modern man some basic assurance, of giving him a human role to play again. It is the mark of a genius like Blake, or Dostoevsky, or Lawrence, that what is purest and most consistent in his thought burns away his own suffering and fanaticism, while his art speaks to what is most deeply human in us. The distortions and flatulence of Blake's myth spring in part from the very abundance of his gifts—turned in on themselves, with the "fire seeking its own form," as he wrote in *The French Revolution*. Those who distrust reason are usually those who have not enough capacity for it to know why it is beautiful, and slander in advance what they are afraid will destroy their prestige. But there are also those, like Blake and Dostoevsky, who are supremely intelligent, and in whom the audacity and loneliness of genius, not to say social frustration, have led to the distrust of all that will not lead to personal security. Blake had one of the greatest minds in the history of our culture; and more fear of the mind than we can easily believe. He was a genius who from childhood on felt in himself such absolute personal gifts that, anticipating the devaluation of them by a materialistic society, he made sure that society's values did not exist for him. Yet one of his most distinguishable personal traits, weaving through his vehement self-assertion, is his need to defend himself against society.

This is not the view of many people who have written on Blake's life; but with the exception of writers like Alexander Gilchrist and Mona Wilson, who at least sought the basic facts about him, most of his biographers have had no understanding of him. The usual view is that he was a happy mystic, who sat like a gloriously content martyr before his work, eating bread and locusts with an idiotic smile on his face. Blake evidently did enjoy great happiness in many periods, for he was a man for whom life consisted in exploring his own gifts. But there is even more in Blake's total revelation of himself, a rage against society, a deeply ingrained personal misery, that underlies his creative exuberance and gives it a melancholy and over-assertive personal force. He defends himself in so many secret ways that when he speaks of himself, at abrupt moments, his utterances have the heart-breaking appeal of someone who cries out: "I am really different from what you know!" To a Reverend Trusler, for example, who complained after commissioning some drawings that inspiration had led Blake too far, he wrote:

I feel that a man may be happy in This World. And I know that This World is a World of Imagination & Vision. I see Every thing I paint in This world, but Every body does not see alike. To the Eyes of a Miser a Guinea is far more beautiful than the Sun, & a bag worn with the use of Money has more beautiful proportions than a Vine filled with Grapes. The tree which moves some to tears of joy is in the Eyes of others only a Green thing which stands in the way. Some see Nature all Ridicule & Deformity, and by these I shall not regulate my proportions; & some scarce see Nature at all. But to the Eyes of the Man of Imagination, Nature is Imagination itself. As a man is, so he sees. As the Eye is formed, such are its Powers.

This is beautiful; as many of Blake's personal notes, in letters, marginalia, notebook jottings, and recorded conversation, are beautiful. But they are beautiful in the same way, just as most of *The Four Zoas, Milton,* and *Jerusalem* is ugly in the same way—as a series of passionately eloquent self-assertions, so burning in their exaltation that they seem to spring out of deep gulfs of private misery and doubt. That last word is always Blake's enemy. Just as he believed that

He who doubts from what he sees
Will ne'er Believe, do what you Please.
If the Sun & Moon should doubt,
They'd immediately Go out

so he felt the antagonism of the age to his vision to be such a burden that he exceeded what is normal in the human longing for certainty and made his kind of certainty the supreme test of a man. Reading a contemporary work on mental disorder, he suddenly scrawled in the margin:

Cowper came to me and said: "O that I were insane always. I will never rest. Can you not make me truly insane? I will never rest till I am so. O that in the bosom of God I was hid. You retain health and yet are as mad as any of us all—over us all—mad as a refuge from unbelief—from Bacon, Newton and Locke."

Blake never wrote anything more important to himself. If he was mad, it was as *a refuge from unbelief,* and thus with the satisfaction of being firmly placed in the sense of his own value. His terrible isolation spoke in the need to defend his identity; if madness was the cost of this, it at least placed him "over us all." And he was higher than his age and over most of those who lived in it—higher not in a fantasy of superiority, but in the imaginative subtlety and resolution of his gifts; his faith that

> we are put on earth a little space,
> That we may learn to bear the beams of love.

Yet what is so marked in his history is his need to prove to himself that his genius could survive. For he was struggling with his own temperament in a time when society threatened his right to exist.

Blake's need of certainty, whatever its personal roots, is also one of the great tragedies of modern capitalist society; particularly of that loss of personal status that was the immediate fate of millions in the industrial England of the "dark satanic mills." Blake was only one of many Englishmen who felt himself being slowly ground to death, in a world of such brutal exploitation and amid such inhuman ugliness, that the fires of the new industrial furnaces and the cries of the child laborers are always in his work. His poems and designs are meant to afford us spiritual vision; a vision beyond the factory system, the hideous new cities, the degradation of children for the sake of profit, the petty crimes for which children could still be hanged. "England," a man said to me in London on V-E day, "has never recovered from its industrial revolution"; Blake was afraid it could not survive it; the human cost was already too great. He never saw the North of Britain, but the gray squalor of the Clydebank, the great industrial maw of Manchester and Liverpool, the slums, the broken families are remembered even in the apocalyptic rant of *Jerusalem,* where

> Scotland pours out his Sons to labour at the Furnaces;
> Wales gives his Daughters to the Loom.

The lovely poem at the head of *Milton,* beginning

> And did those feet in ancient time
> Walk upon England's mountains green?

is so intense a vision of a world other than the real industrial England that it has long been a Socialist hymn of millions of its working people.

Blake was an artisan; an independent journeyman living entirely on the labor of his hands, dependent on patrons in a luxury trade that was being narrowed down to those who could please most quickly. He lived as near the bottom of the English social pyramid as was possible to someone not sucked into the factories. His London is the London of the small tradesmen, the barely respectable artisans and shopkeepers who were caught between the decline of handicrafts and the rise of mass industry. He had to live by hackwork for publishers, but was so independent in his designs that he was forced more and more to engrave after others. One of the reasons why he delighted to make his own books is that he enjoyed complete liberty as an artist-engraver; they certainly would not have been printed by a commercial publisher. But his own prints went largely unbought. The stray copies of *Songs of Innocence and of Experience* and *The Marriage of Heaven and Hell* that now belong only to the wealthiest collectors were offered, often unsuccessfully, for a pittance. In 1809 he held an exhibition of his pictures, featuring his design of the Canterbury Pilgrims, and offering with it "a descriptive catalogue" that is one of his most personal documents. The exhibition, held under the grudging hospitality of his brother James, was a complete failure.

To measure the full depth of Blake's alienation from his age is impossible. Like Tharmas in *The Four Zoas,* he felt himself "a famish'd Eagle, raging in the vast expanse." But it may help us to see his predicament when we realize that he was an impoverished engraver, without any real class to which he could belong; a libertarian without continuing faith in politics—"something else besides human life"; an unknown Romantic poet and artist who felt suffocated by the formalized tastes of the age; a visionary without religion; an engraver after artists he often despised; a poet whose works were unprocurable. Even in his own trade, engraving, he seemed outmoded in competition with sophisticated craftsmen, especially from the Continent, who advanced beyond Blake's stiff techniques. Blake learned to engrave in a rigid and rather lifeless tradition; all his early training was under the direction of a master, James Basire, who set him to copy Gothic monuments. What makes his art so unique is his ability to design, with great formal inventiveness, his own intellectual visions; technically he was an anachronism even in his own day. He never resolved the twin influences upon his work of Gothic and Michelangelo's heroic grandeur. His human figures are always distinguished by a somnambulistic quality: they are mechanical actors in the spell of a tyrannical stage director. Their look on the page is always one of watchful waiting; they are symbols of ideas and states of being. Blake satisfied his own conception of design, but he very rarely satisfied anyone else. Naturally he resented more successful fellow-artists; particularly in oil portrait, for which he had no skill and which symbolized to him the effort of society artists to paint with ingratiating "realism."

It is no wonder that Blake's writing so often sputters out into furious protest against a world that would give him neither a living nor a hearing. In his own mind he lived in "a city of assassinations." He was a man who could be easily cheated; when defrauded by a shrewd "art-publisher" of the day named Cromek, he took out his revenge, after Cromek had brazenly hinted that it was easy to take advantage of him, since he was "one living in the wilderness," by writing in his notebook:

> A Petty Sneaking Knave I knew—
> O Mr. Cr(omek), how do ye do?

But his ability to hit back ended in his notebook. He hated Sir Joshua Reynolds—the ruling light of the Royal Academy from which engravers were excluded; the genial and obliging portraitist of the ruling aristocracy, the complacent Augustan mind counseling artists to follow the rules. But all he could do about it was to note his hatred of Reynolds and his intense opposition to the latter's theories in the margins of Sir Joshua's *Discourses*.

> Having spent the Vigour of my Youth & Genius under the Oppression of Sr Joshua & his Gang of Cunning Hired Knaves Without Employment & as much as could possibly be without Bread, The Reader must Expect to read in all my remarks on these Books Nothing but Indignation & Resentment. While Sr Joshua was rolling in Riches . . . (he) & Gainsborough Blotted & Blurred one against the other & Divided all the English World between them. Fuseli, Indignant, almost hid himself. I am hid.

Henry Fuseli was a Swiss-born artist, famous in London, who liked Blake and was one of his few friends. He was successful, as

Blake was not, and Blake seems to have exaggerated Fuseli's artistic solidarity in his joy at having found a friend in his own craft. Fuseli once said that he found Blake "damned good to steal from."

The vehement marginalia that contain so many of Blake's deepest resentments—against Bacon, against Reynolds, against Bishop Watson and Wordsworth's "atheistic" love of nature—are an obvious symbol of his protest against society. Not being part of it, he put his dissent into the margins. What is not so obvious, however, is that much of his vehement struggle to assert his independence was based on his marriage. The dissenting and small tradesman's class into which Blake was born was one tributary of our Puritan culture; on Blake it imposed poverty made drearier by genteel conformity. Nietzsche, the lonely professor of Greek, became drunk on the vision of the all-conquering male, but the fantasy was his basic sex experience. Lawrence dreamed all his life of a sun-filled Mediterranean world, full of literary Indians and impossibly hospitable women, whose chief virtue was that they lacked the self-righteousness of Presbyterian miners and school-teachers in Nottingham. Blake in most accounts of his life is portrayed as the ideal husband, who taught his illiterate Catherine how to read, and even to see visions when he did. There is little doubt that he was the ideal husband; and apparently he could not stand it. Catherine Blake became the perfect amanuensis, to the man even more than to the artist. She even learned to write and draw so much in his style that her known contributions to his work would otherwise be indistinguishable from his own. She was the ideal wife of his artistic and intellectual alienation; she was the perfect helpmeet in his social and economic desperation. She starved with him, believed in him, and even saw visions for company. If visitors were shocked by the lack of soap in the Blake household, she explained that "Mr. Blake's skin don't *dirt!*" If Blake became completely indifferent to the lack of funds, she would gently remind him of the state of things by putting an empty plate before him for dinner.

Catherine Blake was an ideal wife; her only fault, apparently, was that she was not a person in her own right. The fault was most assuredly not in her but in Blake's annihilating need of her. He made an adoring servant out of her, and then evidently found that he longed for a woman. All the stories we have of them add up to very little, and those who drew upon her and Blake's friends for reminiscences after his death felt such veneration and excitement before their recovery of a neglected genius that they prettied up his domestic life as much as possible. But we do know that he proposed to her at their first meeting when, complaining that a girl had spurned him, she said: "Then I pity you." "Do you truly pity me?" he asked, in pleasure. Whereupon he found that he loved her. Yeats, who helped to doctor up the truth about Blake's life as much as anyone, thought this a lovely story and that they lived happily ever after. Unfortunately, Blake's own writing shows that he was tormented by her jealousy and that he thought marriage was the devil.

It is not necessary to find malicious confirmation of this in the famous story that he wanted Mary Wollstonecraft to join his household for a *ménage à trois*. Mary Wollstonecraft was a noble and deeply intelligent woman, more than a century ahead of her time, who believed in women's rights and took them. She was a tragic and courageous woman, far more attractive than the complacent bluestockings of London highbrow society, and much more interesting than her husband, William Godwin, or their daughter Mary, who became Shelley's second wife. She was the English type of the great Continental heroines of feminism, from George Sand to Alexandra Kollontai. But though Blake was a member of the same intellectual radical group, headed by Johnson the bookseller, it is not hard to imagine how incongruous she must have looked at his side—Blake, who was the imperial visionary of his meager household, but in the London world a curious and threadbare crank. A liaison between John Wesley and Isadora Duncan would not have been more strange—indeed, Wesley was a worldly and aristocratic figure; Blake was a lower middle-class drudge, more of a Wesleyan than Wesley himself. But he seems to have been of the type that makes history, partly because he is not very happy at home.

Blake's "immoralism" (a silly word made necessary by the fact that *moral* lies like a fallen giant across our discourse) is of two kinds: lyrical and poignant expressions of human longing, and a dark obsession in the "Prophetic Books" with sex as the battleground of human struggle and revolt. And however narrow and pitiful the experience from which his own search for fulfillment sprang, there is no doubt that in its psychological truth, its tenderness and passionate support of human dignity, Blake's writing is one of the great prophecies of the love that is possible between man and woman. He is not a writer of "erotica"—the honeyed crumbs of those who have no bread; he rages in his notebooks, but he is never sly. The very status of the dirty story in our society reveals a conception of sex as something one puts over on the conventions. It is the great betrayal of human sincerity. Blake's fight is against secrecy, unnatural restraint, the fear of life—the distortions in the personality that follow from deception and resignation to it. There is implicit in all his attacks on the "moral code" an understanding that gratification is impossible without true union. In this, as in so much else of his thought, Blake painted not only the immediate consequences of a reactionary morality based on outward conformity—the anxieties, the subtle hostilities, the habit of lying. He also foresaw the danger that is exactly present in our modern eroticism, which has the same relation to the failure of love that totalitarian solutions have to the failure of society. When we compare Blake with an artist like D. H. Lawrence, or an oratorical rebel like Henry Miller, we can see how much the obsessiveness, the cringing over-emphasis on sex in the most advanced modern writing is due to the inability of these writers to treat sex naturally in the whole frame of the human organization. As the dirty story pays homage to puritanism, so our modern eroticism wearily proclaims that the part which has been dislodged from the whole shall now be the key to all experience. The limitations of eroticism have exactly the same character, in life and in art: it divorces sex from human culture. As medieval men despised the body for the sake of the spirit and perhaps lost both, so we tend to forget that the body is above all a person. Every reaction in favor of some suppressed truth overshoots the mark. Hence, too, the dreary primitivism of so much advanced writing—as great a lie about our human nature as the genteel writing of the past.

Blake is not free of the characteristic modern obsessiveness; he was no more free than we are. But he always knows exactly what he is. His theme is always the defense of the integral human personality. His principal virtue is that he does not make a virtue of "frankness"; he is concerned with basic human desire, fear, longing, resentment; with the innermost movements of a human being in the world. He describes, in his great song cycle, the gulf between Innocence and Experience; he feels an inexpressible solidarity with those who are forever in it. For he knows that innocence and experience are not the faces of youth and age, but "the two contrary states of the human soul." He writes as a man, not as an "immoralist." One of the reasons why he is so supreme among those who have written of childhood is that he sees it as the nucleus of the whole human story, rather than as a state that precedes adult "wisdom." If he is afraid for the child, he pities the adult. In experience there is always the longing for "unorganized innocence: an impossibility"; in innocence there is the poignant foretelling of experience, which is death without the return to confidence and vision. Blake is utterly without cynicism. He never makes the characteristic modern mistake of devaluating a prime experience; he never throws out love with the love-affair. We may not agree with him that desire is infinite; we can never be sufficiently grateful to him for insisting that it is never cheap.

Blake is serious about sex, as he is serious about the child; and for the same reason. For he knows that as sex is the buried part of our civilization, so the child is the buried part of the man. His faith in the creative richness of love has the same source as his feeling for the secret richness of childhood: his ability to see through the dead skin of adulthood. He would have understood very well that our "child-psychology" shows the same guardedness toward the child that modern love and marriage reveal between men and women. The same guardedness and the same fear: for we "handle" children from the same negative fears and out of the same lack of positive participation and sympathy. Blake would have seen in our pedagogic carefulness the effort of caution to do the work of the imagination. In his own time, when children were regarded as miniature adults, or as slaves or pets to those who ruled by their maturity, he showed that a child is not an abbreviated version of the adult, but a different being. In our time he would have seen that the distance between a parent and a child is usually the distance between the parents as lovers. For him sex meant enjoyment framed in wonder: the full play of our life-striving beyond all the distortions inflicted by respectable society and cynical experience. By the same token childhood was also a lost world—calling to us from our buried life.

> Piping down the valleys wild,
> Piping songs of pleasant glee,

On a cloud I saw a child,
And he laughing said to me:

"Pipe a song about a Lamb!"
So I piped with merry chear.
"Piper, pipe that song again;"
So I piped: he wept to hear.

Innocence is belief and experience is doubt. The tragedy of experience is that we become incapable of love. The tragedy of childhood is that we inflict our lovelessness upon it. Blake's thinking is always organic; it is always directed to the hidden fountains of our humanity. Having never lost the creative freshness of childhood, he challenged experience with it. Having, as I believe, no real love-affair of his own, he had it with childhood. In any event, he had no children of his own. He was a man who had to believe fully, at the highest pitch of being, to live at all; and he loved childhood because it was native in its certainty. Human sensibility was so precious to him that he was ready to discard all its natural trappings to preserve it. Blake never deals with history, with the process and its reality; his search is only for the central and forgotten sources of human feeling, imagination, solidarity. To be certain of them, he conceived the world over again in the image of his desire. But it is like our desire, even if it is nothing like our real world. And our desire is always a portion of the reality we have, as it is always a shadow on the reality we have not. That is why Blake at his best is enchanting even in the smallest proportions—in fact, it is difficult to read him with the usual continuity, so much does he fill our minds at each step.

The central subject of *Songs of Innocence and of Experience* is that of the child who is lost and found. In its symbolism, it is the great theme of all Blake's work—the "real man, the imagination," that has been lost and will be found again through human vision. In Innocence, the little boy loses his father in the night, and God the Father leads him back to his weeping mother. The child is lost to its guardians, for in Blake's mind the child's nature is beyond the parents' comprehension, and is alone in a world the parents cannot enter. The grief of the child is also the loneliness of the soul in its sudden prison of earth; he is protected by God the Father. In Experience, however, the little boy who demands of the priest the right to assert his own thoughts and desires is "burn'd in a holy place." The little girl who enjoys love, without shame or fear, is suddenly confronted with the earthly father whose "loving look, like the holy book," drives her into terror. One little girl is lost and yet found in Experience, however; for she enters lovingly into the world of the passions, where she lives in freedom from the "wolvish howl" and the "lions' growl."

Experience is the "contrary" of innocence, not its negation. Contraries are phases of the doubleness of all existence in the mind of man; they reflect the unalterable condition of the human struggle. As hell can be married to heaven, the body seen by the soul, so experience lifts innocence into a higher synthesis based on vision. But vision is impossible without truth to one's deepest feelings. A lie is "the negation of passion." Life is thought and creation; it is to be had only in its fullness, for the "want of thought" is death. To enter fully into life we must go through the flame of disbelief, kill the fiction that man's desire is lawless and evil. In Innocence

> Mercy has a human heart, pity a human face

In Experience

> Cruelty has a Human Heart
> And jealousy a Human Face;
> Terror the Human Form Divine,
> And Secrecy the Human Dress.

The Human Dress is forged Iron,
The Human Form a fiery Forge,
The Human Face a Furnace seal'd,
The Human Heart its hungry Gorge.

That is what experience is for: to bring us from God the Father to the God that man alone creates. Experience is not evil; it merely shows us the face of evil as a human face, so that we shall learn that the world is exactly what man makes it, and that its ultimate triumphs occur within his understanding.

In the world of Innocence the child speaks to the lamb and marvels in its soft and bright goodness, over which stands the Jesus who is himself a lamb. In Experience we stare into the fiery eyes of the Tyger and think ourselves lost in the "forests of the night." But the Tyger is the face of the creation, marvelous and ambiguous; he is not evil. When Blake cries, in the most moving single expression in his work,

When the stars threw down their spears,
And water'd heaven with their tears,
Did he smile his work to see?
Did he who made the Lamb make thee?

he does not find the thought abhorrent. But he does not answer the question; he keeps it as one, where a religious man would answer it consolingly. Never is he more heretical than in this most famous of his poems, where he glories in the hammer and the fire out of which are struck the "deadly terrors" of the Tyger. Blake does not believe in a war between good and evil; he sees only the creative tension presented by the struggle of man to resolve the contraries. What has been created, by some unknown hand, is a fiery furnace into which our hands must go to seize the fire. "The Tyger" is a poem of triumphant human awareness; it is a hymn to pure being. And what gives it its power is Blake's ability to fuse two aspects of the same human drama: the movement with which a great thing is created, and the joy and wonderment with which we join ourselves to it. The opening and closing stanzas are the same, for as we begin with our wonder before the creation, so we can only end on it. It is the living eternal existence; the fire is, so long as we are. That is why Blake begins on the four great beats of "Tyger! Tyger!", which call the creation by a name and bring us in apprehension before it.

The poem is hammered together with alliterative strokes. *Frame* is there,

> What immortal hand or eye
> Could frame thy fearful symmetry?

because he wants *fearful* as well.

> In what distant deeps or skies
> Burnt the fire of thine eyes?
> On what wings dare he aspire?
> What the hand dare seize the fire?

begins the questioning. Blake goes straight to the poles; we are in the presence of a creation that can be traced from distant deeps to skies. What sustains the verse in our ear is the long single tone in which are blended the related sounds of *burnt, fire, thine, eyes.* By natural association—from the burning fire to the topmost eyes of the Tyger—and through the swell of the line, these words also form a natural little scale of four notes—a scale that ends in the crash of the question-mark. Blake's mind is darting between the mysterious unseen *he,* the maker of the Tyger, and the fire in its eyes. The fire is central to his thought, so much so that it eclipses the maker as a person and turns him into the force and daring with which he creates. Blake does not write "He"; he is far more interested in the creation than in the creator. But so great is this creation that the creator grows mysterious and powerful in its light. What is so beautiful in the second stanza is the leap from the Tyger to the creator. Blake goes from the fire to the creator's wings. This is not because he has an image of a celestial being with great wings, but because the fire could be created only by someone lifted on topmost wings. Blake is as astounded by the creator as he is by the Tyger—and in the same way, for both are such revelations of absolute energy. The emphasis on the creator, in the last line of the second stanza, is thus on *dare*.

We are now in the midst of the creation—or rather, of the great *thing* being created. The hammering, twisting, laughing strokes with which the creator works are not more decisive than Blake's own verse hammer. As usual, he has leaped ahead of us, and begins on a new question; a question that begins with *And* because it is like a man taking breath between hammer strokes:

> And what shoulder, & what art,
> Could twist the sinews of thy heart?
> And when thy heart began to beat,
> What dread hand? & what dread feet?

The creator's shoulder, with terrible force, twists the sinews to make the Tyger's heart. *Twists* is powerful enough; but there is joined to it in Blake's mind what is "crooked" and off the main path for the genius-creator. The shoulder twisting the heart together has turned the creator's back away from us, even as we imagine him at his work. The hammer strokes now go faster and faster; the creation is so swift and final with each blow that Blake's mind rushes after the fall of the hammer, the movements of the creating hands and feet, the beats of the new heart. The poem now moves to the rhythm of the great work. Yet the poet must know whose dread hands and feet, working together before the anvil, could create this. Where does the creator's body and tools end and the Tyger begin?

> What the hammer? What the chain?
> In what furnace was thy brain?
> What the anvil? what dread grasp
> Dare its deadly terrors clasp?

The chains ring in the sorcerer's workshop. The questions now dart from the heart to the brain with the same instantaneous force with which brain and heart are being made. But *where* is this being done? Where is the furnace in which the fire of consciousness is being poured out into the Tyger's brain? What, in space and time, could even hold the Tyger as it is being created? Blake never answers, for the wonder with which he asks them is the wonder with which he beholds the Tyger. But he leaps ahead, in the last phrase of the third line and the whole fourth line after it, to create the image of so dread a power that it can grasp the terrors of the Tyger. It is the long courageous movement with which the clasp is made—a great hand moving into the furnace to bring the Tyger to us—that gives the creation its final awesomeness. Blake creates this by the length of his question. Between the dread grasp and the clasp that holds the terrors in its hand is the movement between the creation and our being witness to it. Technically the thing is done by leaving a distance, a moment's suspense, between the end of the third line on *grasp* and the hard closing of the stanza on *clasp*. The assonance of those two words, like bones rasping together, joins us to the thing. The terror is in our hands.

But when Blake asks,

> When the stars threw down their spears,
> And water'd heaven with their tears,

Did he smile his work to see?
Did he who made the Lamb make thee?

he has no answer—least of all the comforting religious explanation of the division between the Lamb and the Tyger. The stars throwing down their "spears" join in the generation. But did he smile his work to see? *Did he?* Blake's answer is to bring us right back to the Tyger. He has no moral, and he will not let us off with anything less than our return to the fact that the Tyger exists—a fact that includes all its ambiguity and all our wonder and fear before it. The poem ends on the upbeat of man's eternal question of the world: where is its moral order? Blake offers no answer; he asks his question with the "fearful symmetry" of the creation straight before us.

Blake does not let us off with any conventional religious consolation; *nor does he let the creator off.* Had he believed in God, the contraries which are presented to man's mind by experience would have been easy to explain. The Christian explains them by the Fall—by that "happy guilt," as Augustine put it, which left man with a sense of original sin which only religion can cleanse away. Blake is utterly opposed to this: man never fell, and there is no prime evil in him to redeem. For him the contraries exist not because God willed it so in his punishment of man's transgression—could a just God punish man for "following his energies" and for showing curiosity? They exist because man's gift of vision is blocked up in himself by materialism and rationalism. Every man, by the very nature of life, is engaged in a struggle, against the false materialism of the age, to find his way back to perfect human sight. Man is not a sinner—he is a weary traveler lost under the hill, a material "spectre" looking for his "spiritual emanation." He is looking for his human center. Man cannot help getting lost when he deludes himself that he is a natural body subject to a natural society, obeying the laws of a natural God.

> Do what you will, this life's a fiction
> And is made up of contradiction.

But vision restores his human identity. With the aid of vision, and through the practice of art, man bursts through the contraries and weds them together by his own creativity.

Blake's Prophetic Books are his attempt to explain how the contraries arose. They are his Greek mythology, his Genesis, his Book of Revelations. Blake is not Diderot or Stendhal; he does not take man as he finds him. He is a Bible-haunted English dissenter who has taken on himself the burden of proving that man is an independent spiritual being. This required the refutation of all existing literature. The tortured rhetoric of the Prophetic Books is not a lapse from taste; it is the awful wilderness into which Blake had to enter by the nature of his staggering task. This was to give man a new Bible, and with it a new natural history; a new cosmogony, and with it his own version, supplanting Hebrew and Greek literature, of man's first self-consciousness in the universe. But this is not all he tried to do in the Prophetic Books. No one in his time, after all, could escape the influence of realism. To Blake the myth-maker the age required a new Bible. As a contemporary he could hardly escape the inspiration of neo-classical drama, of the historical chronicle, and even of the psychological novel. His Prophetic Books are in fact an attempt to create, on the basis of a private myth, a new epic literature that would ride the currents of the age. His chief model was *Paradise Lost,* and *Milton,* he tells us, was written because Milton came back to earth and begged him to refute the errors of his own epic. But Blake had an eye on Greek tragedy as well, and the Book of Job, and *The Divine Comedy.*

Blake was not a *"naif,"* a "wild man" piecing his philosophy together from "odds and ends" around the house. He was a very learned man who felt challenged and uneasy by what he had learned. One of the reasons why he labored so hard to create a new literature equal to his own vision is that he could never free himself of the models others had created. When we look at his first poems in *Poetical Sketches,* we can see solemn imitations of Shakespeare, Ossian, Gray, and Spenser; his first beautiful songs move slowly away from neo-classic form. His tracts, *There Is No Natural Religion* and *All Religions Are One,* imitate the geometrical order of philosophic propositions that was the carry-over from mathematics to natural philosophy. *The Marriage of Heaven and Hell* is a parody of sources to which Blake was deeply indebted for his form: Genesis, the Proverbs, the Apocalypse, and Swedenborg. The Prophetic Books are an attempt to create a new classical literature, after all the sources. Nothing shows so clearly the tremendous inner conflicts in Blake as the ghosts of other men's books in his own. It is impossible, for anyone who has studied the Prophetic Books carefully, to see him as an enraptured scribe singing above the clouds. His visions in these books were an attempt to force down his own uneasiness. He could find his peace only by creating an epic world so singularly his own that it would supplant every other. He never succeeded. His task was beyond all human strength and all art. He created myths endlessly and represented them as human beings in endlessly energetic and turgid postures of struggle, oppression, and liberation. *But he never gave up the myth.* The "mad" Blake, whose wildest sayings furnish so much biographical chit-chat about him, was the man who still believed the myth long after suffering and alienation had dulled in his mind the objects it represented. Without the myth he would have been entirely lost, intolerably isolated. So he went even further—John Milton believed in it, too; and—the significant last chapter of Blake's thought—Jesus was above all a Blakean.

The last Prophetic Books are a jungle, but it is possible—if you have nothing else to do—to get through them. What Joyce said so lightly Blake would have repeated with absolute assurance—he demanded nothing less of his readers than that they should devote their lives to the elucidation of his works. Yet there are whole areas of the first Prophetic Books that represent Blake's art and thought at their purest; the illuminated designs, even to a fantastic jumble like *Jerusalem,* are overwhelming in their beauty and power. To labor over works like *The Four Zoas, Milton,* and *Jerusalem* for the sake of intellectual exegesis is against the whole spirit of art. Where Blake does not write poetry, he orates; and when he orates it is "the will trying to do the work of the imagination." Yet his rhetorical resources were so overwhelming that they flow like hot lava over the stereotypes of the myth. He obviously felt so little the consecutiveness of his "argument" that in at least one copy of *Jerusalem* he allowed misplaced pages to remain where they were. His concern is not with the coherence of his theme, but with his need to get everything in. Even within the assumed order of the myth the characters lose their symbolic references when they do not transfer them among each other. They came to represent so much of Blake's private life as well as his public vision that he interrupted himself at regular intervals to preach against jealousy and the domination of man by woman.

Blake was never jarred by the tumult of all the conflicts he revealed in his Prophetic Books. His loneliness as a man and thinker was so overwhelming that he took his gifts as the measure of human insight. He was a lyric poet of genius and a very bad dramatic poet; but he suffered from the illusion that his poetic gift was also a dramatic and representational one. The gift of creating character is inseparable from an interest in history. Just as the novel owes its principal development to the modern consciousness that society is man-made, so the ability to create character is impossible without an understanding of men in relation to other men; in short, of man as a creature of process and conflict. Blake's characters are names attached arbitrarily to absolute human faculties and states of being. The name of the character may have a punning or derived relation to the faculty he represents, as Urizen is the god of this world and its sterility who is "your reason," or Orc, Blake's first hero, may have been derived from *"cor,"* or heart. So Albion is the central figure of man, "the eternal man," and Enitharmon is the "universal" woman. But when Blake sets them to orating against each other, their nominal identity is only the line which he must desperately hold on to to bring up the deep-sea fish of human passions, errors, lamentations. The figure of Urizen is an oppressor; Orc is the spirit of visionary emancipation; Los, who comes in later, is the spirit of time working to rejoin man to his lost unity, and the "Eternal Prophet." Through them, and many other characters, Blake is seeking to explain how man lost the gift of vision. Urizen is the false God, the Satan who separated himself from the prime unity and set in motion the divisions in man, the search after the analytical and the inhuman.

Blake is not interested in character. His figures are the human faculties at war with each other. He is trying to explain, in the form of a new Genesis, how the split in man occurred, and to show the necessary present struggle of man to unify himself back to an integral and imaginative human nature. He is also raging against all those who would hold him in—from the analytical God of Newton to the scepticism of Voltaire, from the successful painters of the day to "the shadowy female," who torments man by jealousy. But since he has no interest in history, the beginning, the present, and the future dissolve into each other. What was begun in error is suffered through error now. He is fighting his own sorrows even as he is trying to impose the massive structure of his hazardously built myth onto the contemporary world: to bring himself to us, and the England he actually lived in. Hence the bewildering jump from Old Testament names to English streets, cities, and counties, in which Blake's own cries were never heard:

O dreadful Loom of death! O piteous Female forms, compell'd
To weave the Woof of Death! On Camberwell Tirzah's courts,
Malah's on Blackheath; Rahab & Noah dwell on Windsor's heights,
Where once the Cherubs of Jerusalem spread to Lambeth's Vale.
Milcah's Pillars shine from Harrow to Hampstead, where Hoglah
On Highgate's heights magnificent Weaves over trembling Thames
To Shooter's Hill and thence to Blackheath, the dark Woof. Loud,
Loud roll the Weights & Spindles over the whole Earth, let down
On all sides round to the Four Quarters of the World, eastward on
Europe to Euphrates & Hindu, to Nile & back in Clouds
Of Death across the Atlantic to America North & South.

Hence, too, the poetic atrocities:

In torrents of mud settling thick
With Eggs of unnatural production

Which is dreadful, but only a paraphrase of the noble rant which deafens and dulls us all through the later books:

But in the Optic vegetative Nerves Sleep was transformed
To Death in old time by Satan, the father of Sin & Death:
And Satan is the Spectre of Orc, & Orc is the generate Luvah.

Blake cannot get away from the materialist trappings, the naturalistic "spectre"; no one can, and his collapse as an artist in the later Prophetic Books is due to his effort to *dispel* the natural forms by a mythological explanation of them. He created his myth to contain his defiance, as it were; when he found it insufficient, he let it supplant life itself. On the subject of God, he even borrowed a thought from the Gnostic heresy, as he was indebted to the Jewish Cabala for his vision of the man who anciently contained all things of heaven and earth in himself. The Gnostic heresy is one the Catholic Church understandably rooted out in furious alarm—for it held that the world was dominated by Satan. It is not hard to understand how comforting this thought must have been to Blake. If this world is a mere deception, and all its natural appearances a masquerade through which man must look for spiritual vision, it is because the "real" God has been supplanted by Satan. So all spiritual vision leads us back to the "real" God, who is now Jesus. Blake's Jesus is the defiant iconoclast, the friend of artists and revolutionaries. When one reads *Jerusalem,* one thinks of Nietzsche, who when he went mad signed himself "The Crucified One," and of that old cry from the defeated—"Thou hast conquered, O Galilean!"

Blake does not "yield" to Jesus; he creates Jesus in his own image.

> The Son, O how unlike the Father! First God Almighty comes with a Thump on the head. Then Jesus Christ comes with a balm to heal it.

But not before he has shown us the inner thread in his snarled Prophetic Books—which is the lament against his own "selfhood" and the appeal against the Accuser, "who is the God of this World." It is impossible to read Blake's vehement and repeated cries against the "Accuser" without being moved by the tremendous burden of guilt he carried despite his revolt and independence. The "Accuser" is Satan, who rules this world, which is "the Empire of nothing." It is he who tormented man with a sense of sin; who made men and women look upon their own human nature as evil; who plunged us into the cardinal human heresy, which is the heresy against man's own right and capacity to live. The "Accuser" is the age in which Blake lived and it is the false god whose spectre mocks our thirst for life. It is the spirit, to Blake, of all that limits man, shames man, and drives him in fear. The Accuser is the spirit of the machine, which leads man himself into "machination." He is jealousy, unbelief, and cynicism. But his dominion is only in you; and he is only a spectre.

The Accuser is the prime enemy, yet he is a fiction; he need not exist. But Blake fought him so bitterly that he acknowledged how great a price he had paid for his own audacity. What was it that made him long at the end, above everything else, for "forgiveness"? What was it he had to be "forgiven" for?

And now let me finish with assuring you that, Tho' I have been very unhappy, I am so no longer. I am again Emerged into the light of day; I still & shall to Eternity Embrace Christianity and Adore him who is the Express image of God; but I have travel'd thro' Perils & Darkness not unlike a Champion. I have Conquer'd, and shall go on Conquering. Nothing can withstand the fury of my course among the Stars of God & in the Abysses of the Accuser. My enthusiasm is still what it was, only Enlarged and confirmed.

We do not know—his only name for his "guilt" remains "selfhood"—that is, the full force of his individual claim to self-assertion. Blake was a prophet who was not delivered by his own prophecy. But if he succumbed at all to the "Accuser," he did more than anyone else to expose him. If he failed at the complete harmony to which all his own thought is directed, it is because man, though he is a little world in himself, is little indeed when measured against the whole of a creation that was not made for him alone—or for him to know everlasting certainty in it. Blake's tragedy was the human tragedy, made more difficult because his own fierce will to a better life prevented him from accepting any part of it. Laboring after the infinite, he felt himself shadowed by the Accuser. That is the personal cost he paid for his vision, as it helps us to understand his need of a myth that would do away with tragedy. But as there is something deeper than tragedy in Blake's life, so at the heart of his work there is always the call to us to recover our lost sight. Blake was a man who had all the contraries of human existence in his hands, and he never forgot that it is the function of man to resolve them.

Men are admitted into Heaven not because they have curbed & govern'd their Passions, or have no Passions, but because they have cultivated their Understandings.

Six

TURGENEV AND THE NON-RUSSIANS

Ivan Turgenev was the first Russian writer to be widely read outside his country, and it was through him that Europe discovered there was a Russian literature—which was promptly identified with his exquisite and elegiac art. Today, ironically, he seems of all the great Russian writers the least characteristic: a superb artist, one of the finest in the history of the novel, but hardly one who reminds us of the fierce involvement in the whole human situation, the overwhelming naturalness, that keep Dostoevsky and Tolstoy at the center of our thinking about the world we now live in. I can see why Henry James found it so easy in 1878 to include an appreciation of Turgenev in *French Poets and Novelists.* This is not because Turgenev's art is "French" and of course it is not. It is rather that James saw a new dimension of feeling in Turgenev to which he could enthusiastically respond but which was still so much like his own concern with purely personal situations. James could not know how different Turgenev was in this from other Russian writers.

Turgenev, unlike Tolstoy or Dostoevsky or Chekhov, does not write about Russia as if it were the world itself; he does not take it for granted as the great arena of human existence. Though he loved Russia, he preferred to do so from a distance. And though he wrote famous tributes to his native tongue, and even said, with a defensive violence, that a writer who used any language but the one learned in childhood was a scoundrel, the fact is that he was able to dispense with Russia, to convert it into a "background" to his tales of personal frustration—something the other great Russian writers never did.

Like Henry James, Turgenev could look at his own country from both sides at once, could even be bored by it. But while it has been traditional for American writers to be bored by America, or to abuse or to escape it, one can hardly think of many Russian writers who were so bored by Russia, who were so easily disillusioned with it. And it is this quality in Turgenev that perhaps explains why, though the center of his art is always firm, and often very beautiful indeed, there is felt all through his work an atmosphere of tepid resignation, of lyric sadness, of disenchantment, of some irrevocable disillusionment with men and affairs, and Russia itself.

This is not true of Turgenev's most robust work, *A Sportsman's Sketches,* but it is of *Fathers and Sons.* Extraordinary and heartbreaking as this book is, it is nevertheless not dissimilar in *tone* from *On the Eve, Smoke,* and *Rudin,* or the long stories, "A Quiet Spot," "First Love," and "Diary of a Superfluous Man," all of which point up Turgenev's melancholy, his lack of inventive power, and even the curious suggestion he sometimes gives of some deep inertia inside himself. These are not the qualities that taught Hemingway so much when he read *A Sportsman's Sketches,* but they are precisely those which from the beginning led to the Turgenev vogue in Europe.

Today Turgenev's "civilized" and "European" art seems no longer in the forefront of Russian literature, but behind it. Even Chekhov, the Russian writer most superficially like Turgenev in tone, insisted that the frustration of his characters came out of the inertia and backwardness of Russia in the nineteenth century. Chekhov's characters are frustrated by the world they live in;

Turgenev's by themselves—their special mark is always the sad autonomy of human love, its final impossibility in a country that afflicts them, but which they do not recognize as their destiny. Russia is a background to their quiet ordeal; it is not, to their conscious mind, of the ordeal itself. If it had been, Turgenev's art would not have been quite so exquisite, so closed off by its own perfection, so resigned—so much, in a word, the kind of art Henry James found it natural to admire.

Turgenev is the great poet of the doomed love affair—doomed, because the characters sacrifice everything in life to love, and yet know from the beginning that it is unnatural; that seeking everything from love alone, they will never get anything from their love itself. Even *Fathers and Sons,* with its famous nihilist hero, Bazarov, the arrogant young doctor from whom a whole generation of Russian intellectuals formed its idea of emancipation, now seems curiously unrelated to the intellectual and political battles of a century ago. It emerges simply as an elegy on all human frustration. Bazarov's many speeches in defense of positivism, his naïve worship of science, his opposition to "poetry"—all now have an effect of parody.

It is as if Turgenev, in forecasting this new type of Russian hero, had actually rendered him absurd at the same time, for Turgenev cannot take Bazarov's ideas, or any ideas, very seriously. But Bazarov's hopeless quest of Madame Odinstova, his unvoiced despair at ever being able to win her, his unconscious suicide, when he allows himself to be infected by a patient dying of typhoid—these make the real story, these are closest to Turgenev's heart, as it is this hopelessness that creates the marvelous effect of a slow irrevocable curve, from life into death, with which the story draws to a close.

Similarly, one might define Turgenev's subject as the fatality of love. Something always goes wrong; the lovers know in advance that it will, and nevertheless they persist. Perhaps it is the idea of fatality they are in love with. In *Smoke,* Litvinov's hopeless love for Irena—the usual Turgenev *femme fatale,* with her trance-like astonishment at being unable to love anyone in return —is genuinely felt in a way that Turgenev's heavy satire against the Russian fops and pretentious "liberals" at Baden-Baden is not. In *Rudin,* a devastating portrait of the young Russian intellectual of the period, it is Rudin's inability to love that makes the story so harshly effective. In *On the Eve,* Turgenev's most admired heroine, Yelena, actually finds love with Insarov, but of course he dies as promptly as possible.

Still, it is precisely in this conviction of slow, inevitable frustration, of aimless drift and passage in human affairs—the "smoke" Litvinov saw from his railway carriage, symbolizing the impermanence and ennui of human affairs—that Turgenev finds the extraordinarily precise yet lyric details with which he describes the Russian countryside. Stroke by stroke, the Russian woods and streams emerge with incomparable beauty as that inner world his characters hope to win, and cannot. For they never realize how little they are committed to it as theirs; how much, beyond all their frustration, it still speaks for what is enduring—in their love itself.

Seven

EDMUND WILSON: THE CRITIC AND THE AGE

In *The Shores of Light* Edmund Wilson has collected ninety-seven of his pieces—most of them were published in the *New Republic* when he was its literary editor—and has reworked, annotated, and arranged them so as to give us "a literary chronicle of the 'twenties and 'thirties." Ordinarily, few of us would take at one blow from any critic—no matter how much he had suppressed, put in, rewritten, and polished—ninety-seven book reviews and essays. But Edmund Wilson is not like any other critic: some critics are boring even when they are original; he fascinates even when he is wrong. And the book itself is unusual, to begin with, because not since Randolph Bourne and H. L. Mencken have we had another critic whose back pieces could so naturally and still so vibrantly bring forth a vanished age.

The book opens with a memoir of Wilson's great Princeton mentor and lifelong friend, Christian Gauss, who died in 1951 while returning from a memorial service for the remarkable Austrian novelist Hermann Broch; it closes with a long, unashamedly tremulous elegy for Edna St. Vincent Millay, who died in 1950. Between these two half-open gates of memory, Wilson's old essays—their jollity subdued, as we read them, by our knowledge of what lies ahead—take us over old American ground, from Woodrow Wilson's premonitory failures as president of Princeton to the bankruptcy of Greenwich Village; from the emergence of young Mr. Hemingway, touchingly grateful for his first intelligent notices, to the Hemingway who succeeded Jack Dempsey in the popular American mind as the type of fearless brutality; from the decline of vaudeville to the final systematization of imbecility in Hollywood; from the *New Republic* of Herbert Croly and Edmund Wilson to the miseries and inanities of proletarian literature. This is a book of many deaths, it seems; it is, in fact, its own retrospect. He brings us up to a period whose basic conviction is that no man is any longer his own master; it reaches back to those Vergilian shores of light—*"in luminis oras"*—to which every living form aspires, and which a remarkable generation of writers once identified with the personal liberation of every chafed, suppressed, and rebellious human being under the American sky.

Reading these pieces thus involves us in a web of recollection—the usual Proustian setting that puts Wilson's criticism in motion. There are deeper critics, more modest critics, critics less hidebound by indifference to abstract thought; there is no other critic who so evenly and so hauntingly writes criticism as a work of art. *Should* anyone try to create criticism as an art? The answer is that Wilson cannot help it. The key words of fashionable criticism today are "form," "sensibility," "difficult," "proper," "tact"; his are "grasp," "solid," "vivid," "focus," "lens"; he is a writer among writers, *the* writer who has taken on the job of explaining them to the world. Writing always from that other shore of memory and good English usage, where the great novelists were still on the parlor table and there were Americans still detached enough from our "commercial ideals" to see the country in focus, he has always to grasp out of time lost, out of the books misread by other critics, the whole figure of the writer in his age, and to present this subject as a new creation. He has to show his subject as a character in a story and each book as an action; he has to find what is most permanent about a writer yet may be not so much in the writer as behind him, in the force of the age that is backing him up; he has to make a point each step of the way and to show a case all around; he has to do it solidly, in his own style, gathering up all the details into one finally compact and lucid argument, like a man whose life hangs on the rightness of each sentence.

Even in these old pieces—so unexpectedly genial yet already prim in their effort to see behind every writer to the proper standards—all the fascination of Wilson's writing starts from this tensely balanced effort to seize, to control, to portray, to consummate. What he does not put under his lens—he allows you to infer—is perhaps not worth making clear at all, and so absorbed do we get in Wilson's compulsion to make order that it may not immediately occur to us, unless we are cooler to such writing than we should be, that there may be another side to the story—that verse is not "a dying technique" and Edna Millay not a great poet; that his theoretical formulations are often gross; that books may be entirely as unique as authors are, and so are not always to be compared with the books on which Wilson formed his taste. How hard it is, indeed, to remember that any judgment of a book based too dynamically on the character of the author is unsure, for our notions of character are set to fixed horizons; a real book revises all the conditions by which we judge it.

Yet these lapses and limitations do not matter, not while we read; we are taken up, we have been involved, by one of the greatest of living writers, in man's enduring effort to gain a meaning and to control his experience. In fact, this overpositive taste, these impertinences of our American pragmatism are—like the sentimentality of Cummings, the bitterness of Hemingway, the floridity of Faulkner—what our author creates with. Would you have him doubt his old thesis that verse is a dying technique? Then we would lose such a point as only Wilson can make (the great novelists from Flaubert to Joyce taking up the tasks left behind by the classic poets); we would lose that characteristic passage here—*se non è vero, è ben trovato*—in which, appealing against hermetic poetry to our natural sense of what literature should be, he cries out that "modern life seems to have had the effect of driving the old kind of lyric feeling, which used to embrace the world, into the depths of the private consciousness; and the deliberate formulas and attitudes derived from the study of external reality which the younger poets are trying to impose on their poetry have a way of yielding nothing but rhetoric. Who knows that we may not, in the long run, have to depend on our dreams for lyrics?"

Were Wilson another kind of critic, we might even lose his disposition—it is at the very center of his criticism—to picture intelligence as a hero struggling against an age that threatens the humanity of all. When one turns from the Wilson who in 1931 insisted that "American radicals and progressives . . . must take Communism away from the Communists" to those intellectuals who now exploit the names of two famous libertarian magazines of the 'twenties in order to push the most reactionary men and causes in America, it is frightening to see how far we have come —under cover of the literary charades and academic triviality which our criticism has become—from the democratic affections that once held our writers together. For Wilson—who years ago was quick to see a peculiarly amoral historian as "a symptom of the decay of Great Britain," who in a literary article published in the Soviet press reminded the Russians that there are "moral obligations that make themselves felt in spite of everything," who in 1937 saw how much Auden gives us a sense "of the slackening of the social organism and the falling apart of its cells," who said that Lytton Strachey's portrait of Elizabeth was "slightly disgusting; it marks so definitely the final surrender of Elizabethan to Bloomsbury England"—a literary critic is first of all a man and a citizen, a man who would be as ashamed to take the side of power as to write a bad sentence.

Eight

THE PAINFULNESS OF D. H. LAWRENCE

Richard Aldington's *D. H. Lawrence: Portrait of a Genius But . . .* is largely a personal biography that emphasizes the difficulties of being Lawrence's friend, is conventional in its thinking, and betrays a rather entertaining impatience with its subject. The petty and coyly equivocal subtitle is a fair introduction to the book. On the one hand, Mr. Aldington is scornful of those who hounded and maligned Lawrence during his lifetime; on the other, he certainly enjoys showing the man up.

Since anyone picking up the book will suppose from the qualifying "but" in the title that Mr. Aldington feels some reservations about Lawrence's genius, it is a little confusing to be told at the beginning of the preface that the title was so constructed because this is what *other* commentators have been saying about Lawrence; that they admit he had genius but imply that genius is not much to have, or that it cannot make up for his faults. At this point, I assumed that Mr. Aldington was going to expose the shallowness of this view, and that he had mimicked it in his title, especially since the epigraph of his book is Jonathan Swift's bitter but certainly well-justified complaint that "When a true Genius appears in the World, you may know him by this Sign, that the Dunces are all in Confederacy against him." I was mistaken again, for, as is made clear at the end of the preface, the "but" *is* Mr. Aldington's. Though he claims that he wishes merely to show "what sort of a genius" Lawrence was (why could he not simply have indicated this in his title?), the whole tone of the book reveals that he is quite antipathetic to Lawrence. I suspect that the slyness of the title serves both to hint of this and to conceal it. This is a roundabout way of doing things and makes me wonder how Mr. Aldington can be so lofty about the "dunces" who opposed Lawrence when he supplies them with so much ammunition.

Mr. Aldington knew Lawrence long and well; like all Lawrence's friends, he is obviously still fascinated by that violently intense, radiant, and often intolerably dictatorial personality—this is his second book on the subject. And he is naturally so amused and irritated by the reverent cults that have gathered around Lawrence's memory that it is easy enough to see why he should wish to write a detached and sensible book about the man. However, the rather over-demonstratively "normal" tone he takes on Lawrence's abnormalities does not get him into the depths of his thought. It leads him to say many shrewd and catty things, and is amusingly snobbish (in the fashion that is now affected more even by England's emigrant writers than by its Conservative Opposition) on Lawrence's lower-class secrecy about money and his "char-woman" mania for cleaning up every Italian villa and Mexican hut he ever lived in. But such personal notes do not really help us to understand what "sort" of genius Lawrence was; they only tell us that he was peculiar and complex, which we knew.

Of course, Lawrence must often have been poisonous to be with. Mr. Aldington's book shows all the signs of a long-endured exasperation. Those who never knew Lawrence can gather well enough from the nastiness and downright sadism in even his happiest books just how difficult he was—how wildly and juvenilely insistent on his own point of view he must have been with all comers (the point Mr. Aldington likes to stress), how remorselessly he could inflict his vision of himself as the intelligentsia's Führer on those who did not submit instantly to him (and on many who did submit). Yet, after all, Lawrence has been dead for twenty years; there is by now a sizable literature (much of it by Lawrence himself) on the whole racked story of his upbringing in a miner's cottage, his obsession with his mother, his marriage to Frieda von Richthofen, his compulsive travels, his quarrels with his friends, his cult of the sexual mystery, and all the rest. There can be very few facts in Mr. Aldington's account that have not appeared before. But Lawrence still bothers him; he admires him but wants to take him down. And this is what gives the book its interest and—not always because of Mr. Aldington's own cleverness—its humor, for he goes to strange lengths to score a point off Lawrence whenever he finds the opportunity.

A particular example is Mr. Aldington's account of Lawrence's early controversies with John Middleton Murry and Bertrand Russell. Though he usually likes to sound a blunt, plain-spoken man with a healthy suspicion of intellectuals (he speaks in one place of "that quasi-philosophising which now passes as criticism" and in another of "self-appointed critics"), he is so glad to demonstrate Lawrence's emotionalism in argument that he honors Murry as a "philosopher"—because he had studied philosophy at Oxford—and then says in weak scorn of Lawrence's "mystical" position, in reporting Murry's inability to understand it, "And if a philosopher cannot understand a new philosophy, who can?" Similarly, in comparing a passage from Lawrence with Russell's work in general—for no ascertainable reason, except to take Lawrence down again—he describes the first as "detached sayings or paragraphs, usually though not always heavily charged with symbols; quite different from the beautifully formed abstract thought, rounded and complete, of his one-time friend, Russell." This means more than Mr. Aldington realizes, for it implies that any artist is always put in the shade by any philosopher and that Mr. Aldington himself has a predilection for "beautifully formed abstract thought," which I doubt.

It is by such pettinesses that Mr. Aldington reveals how much he is still irritated by Lawrence. Yet he is not unfair to Lawrence's work, for he pays many sincerely felt tributes to the man's marvelous creative spontaneity, his naturalness, his uncanny feeling for landscape. He does try to be objective, by methodically listing Lawrence's creative achievements and by stressing the blatant contradictions of his character. But Lawrence's general painfulness keeps erupting, and Mr. Aldington keeps trying to confine it to the man's discordant personality. His view is not long enough. For that painfulness is an unmistakable quality of twentieth-century genius, of genius as a force in itself —a genius that has learned to discomfort, to threaten, to shock, in order to assert the creative principle against the increasing unawareness of how much inner freedom contemporary man has lost. Lawrence's anxieties, obsessions, and rages do not explain this painfulness; it is found in many "healthier" talents, like Picasso, Bartók, and Faulkner. Even more pressingly in Lawrence's case, it is the painfulness of a writer who was always sounding the alarm against the self-suppressiveness in Western culture, who warned that people would finally bring the whole house down if they could not obey the truth of their own feelings, and who has been horribly vindicated by the anti-humanist temper in Europe today.

Mr. Aldington constantly invokes this prophetic and painful element in Lawrence but never comes to grips with it. In some part, of course, this is because he still identifies Lawrence's work with the avant-garde of thirty years ago and has not noticed that Lawrence's kind of creativity points directly to the passionate sense of outrage which so many Europeans feel about their lives now and which is the most haunting note in their postwar literature. But essentially it is because our popular literary biographers believe that "objectivity" means bringing a great subject down to their level. Lawrence once said that man "has his excess constantly on his hands." Mr. Aldington has had Lawrence's excess on his hands now for many years, and obviously it *is* painful—so painful that he never once works his way through Lawrence's principal ideas but remembers that the queer fellow once took red wine with bouillabaisse.

Nine

THE JOURNAL OF HENRY DAVID THOREAU

Many writers have kept journals—the habit is almost an occupational necessity. It was in America once a characteristic literary and moralistic exercise by no means confined to New England Puritans and seems to have become a favorite literary practice in France. Some writers, like Emerson, have kept their journals as a "savings bank" for future work; some, like Dostoevsky and François Mauriac, in the form of newspaper polemics; some, like Amiel, as an apology for their failure in the world; some—André Gide is now the most fascinating contemporary example—have kept theirs as artful public confessions, and, in the usual self-conscious twentieth-century way, with more emphasis on their longing for sincerity than on the truth itself.

But even among writers' journals—and usually, with the exception of dry business-like records like Benjamin Constant's and Arnold Bennett's, each is as interesting as the man who kept it—Thoreau's must stand in a special place. For his journal—now reprinted for the first time since the edition of 1906 long out of print—is not merely the record of a life lived almost entirely within. It is the life itself. Thoreau's Journal was not a hide-out for his lacerated soul, not altogether what he and others have most used it for—the storehouse out of which his published books would come. It was the thing he lived in, the containment of his love—and therefore had to be as well-written as a prayer or a love letter. "All that a man has to say or do that can possibly concern mankind," he found himself writing in 1854, "is in some shape or other to tell the story of his love—to sing; and, if he is fortunate and keeps alive, he will be forever in love. This alone is to be alive to the extremities." This is where he sang, sentence by sentence; the journal took its "shape" from the manner of his love.

Actually, the Journal bogs down after the middle volumes into disjointed nature notes of whose barrenness even as scientific information he was well aware. But it is the unflagging beauty of the writing, day after day, that confirms its greatness among writers' journals. It is not natural for a man to write this well every day. Only a man who had no other life but to practice a particularly intense and truthful kind of prose could have done it —a man for whom all walks finally came to end in the hard athletic sentence that would recover all their excitement. Other writers have been lonely, and have learned to accept their loneliness; have felt yearnings toward God that their distrust of churches could not explain; have dissected their solitary characters down to the last bearable foundation in human self-analysis; have, at least in the privacy of a journal, scored off at last the obtuseness of their neighbors, the insipidity of their contemporaries and the unfeelingness of the age. And of course all writers of memorable journals have made characters out of themselves; you have to be thoroughly suffused in yourself before you can break away and take a good look back. Thoreau did all this, and something more. For in and through his Journal he finally made himself a prose that would fully evoke in its resonant tension and wildness the life he lived in himself every day.

The Journal was begun when he was twenty, a few months out

of Harvard, and noted that someone (Emerson?) had asked him: "What are you doing now? Do you keep a journal?" "So I make my first entry today." He concluded it thirty-nine manuscript volumes later, in 1861, when his last illness made impossible those daily afternoon walks that were the sustenance of all his literary work. The first volume, whose opening pages suggest the commonplace book he must have kept at college, is earnestly packed with quotations from Latin, Greek and German writers, his early poems, and those tiresomely sententious aphorisms and "analogies" between nature and man's spiritual life in which he was still consciously modeling himself after Emerson, but which were always to be the weakest and actually least characteristic element in his writing. But soon the journal settles down into the pattern of those walks—"to Conantum," "to Fair Haven," "to Walden"—on which he kept field notes he later carefully rewrote and extended into his Journal.

There is very little in it of how he earned his living—as a handy man in Emerson's household, as a pencil maker, as a lecturer; something more, in the middle volumes, since the occupation was so congenial to him, on his experiences as a surveyor. Nor is it from the Journal that you would learn that he interrupted his stay at Walden to go to jail for a night because of his refusal to pay a poll-tax to support the Mexican War; or that it was he who rang the bell of Concord's Town Hall when not even the sexton would do it, to announce Emerson's discourse in 1844 on the emancipation of the slaves in the West Indies; or *whom* it was he ever loved—only that he had so ideal a conception of friendship and love that no genuine experiences could ever have satisfied him. From time to time there are shrewd, rather too self-righteous, sometimes disdainful, but not altogether unaffectionate notes on his neighbors in Concord, on the farmers around, on the Irish emigrants, and on the rebellious characters who managed to get down a good deal of strong liquor even in those godly days. Occasionally there is a touching glimpse of the bareness of the American scene in those years—"villages with a single long street lined with trees, so straight and wide that you can see a chicken run across it a mile off." One of the most moving refrains in the Journal is his hunger for music—"I would be drunk, drunk, drunk, dead drunk to this world with it forever." And though it is the fashion these days to exaggerate Concord's hospitality to the arts, it is made clear by the Journal that if Thoreau made so much of the music in the telegraph wires, "the telegraph harp," as he so lovingly calls it over and again, it was because there was not much other music to listen to. "I have lain awake at night many a time to think of the barking of a dog which I had heard long before, bathing my being again in those waves of sound, as a frequenter of the opera might lie awake remembering the music he had heard."

But by and large the Journal is the attempt to shape into words the vision he took back from his walks, a testing-ground for his art, and a commentary on the journal itself—that is, on the necessities of his character. What he sought from those walks he very consciously defined to himself in 1857, after twenty years of the Journal, in one of those sentences which are so heartbreaking in their truthfulness, for when you read it you realize not only that he has said everything he means, but that he has put his whole life into that sentence. "I come to my solitary woodland walk as the homesick go home."

In this same passage, however, he added with his usual canny awareness of the type he represents in history, "I suppose that this value, in my case, is equivalent to what others get by churchgoing and prayers." As a statement of the facts, this is altogether more deft than accurate. Though Thoreau was genuinely and even profoundly mystical, God did not occupy his mind to that extent; it was writing he cared about first, not a belief. But what such nimble and all too often repetitive analyses of his character point up so sharply is that he spent much more time painting himself as Concord's leading crank than on following to the depths the stunning originality of his nature.

Contrary to the usual belief from Emerson and Lowell on, that Thoreau was too intractable, "not enough in touch with his fellow man," I would say that the great fault in his writing, and indeed the real pathos of his life, is that he was all too aware of what other men would think of him. Had he not been so, he could never have written *Walden,* which is exhilarating precisely because of its defiance and far more self-dramatizing than even *Leaves of Grass.* But Thoreau had an even more deeply original quality to him than *Walden* reveals; you see it in the Journal over and over again—a quality that was perhaps best described by the French mystical writer Simone Weil when she said that "attentiveness without an object is prayer in its supreme form." Only the very purest and most solitary writers have had the gift of such attentiveness; to be alive entirely to the creation itself. But for many reasons, not least of which was the fact that Thoreau was so much the end of a tradition that he had to retrace it for himself, he went to nature as his formal vocation, a background to his quest, something that would support his picture of himself. "Nature" itself was not his chief interest; he was so entirely subjective that he distrusted scientific method even when used by others. But he was looking for a subject; that is, for an opportunity. And of course he could always find a subject in himself. But by constantly dwelling on how different he was, he tended to become uncharacteristically smug about who he was.

Still, without these excited daily inroads into the fields, Thoreau could never have found the measure for his prose. It is a prose, like Hemingway's and Faulkner's, that most characteristically defines the American in literature. We have had greater or at least more comprehensive writers, but none who with such deep intuition grasped in their solitariness the secret of the wilderness, of the legendary unoccupied Western lands, the very tone of man's battle in America against empty space. Emerson had given the call. It was Thoreau who went out and tried it: who wrote as if a sentence were not even true unless you heard it first ring against the ground.

Ten

THE ANGER OF FLAUBERT

Not long ago, there appeared in new translations three works by Gustave Flaubert—a volume of *Selected Letters,* edited and translated by Francis Steegmuller; his last, unfinished novel, *Bouvard and Pécuchet,* in a translation by T. W. Earp and G. W. Stonier, with an introduction by Lionel Trilling; and the supplement to this encyclopedic satire on the two retired clerks who tried to find the solution to every human problem in books—the *Dictionary of Accepted Ideas,* translated for the first time into English by Jacques Barzun.

Now, there are very good reasons for these editions: Flaubert's marvelous letters are still too little known in English, *Bouvard and Pécuchet* has never been adequately translated before, and up to now the *Dictionary*—the collection of clichés and current smugnesses that Flaubert recorded with such passionate scorn all his life and used as a source book for *Bouvard*—has seemed almost untranslatable. From one point of view, then, this sudden re-emergence of Flaubert comes in answer to a need. Mr. Steegmuller, who had already used the letters so well in his *Flaubert and Madame Bovary,* has now been persuaded to do a cross-section of this enormous correspondence; Mr. Barzun, whose mother tongue is French, has been "making it a special game of his own, over a number of years"—his publisher tells us—

"to find the exact English equivalent for each 'accepted idea' Flaubert recorded," and "has documented here our own inanities. . . . Together with Flaubert he has produced a very contemporary self-portrait of the middle-class philistine, as present today as when Flaubert railed against him." The translation of *Bouvard,* by two British critics, is reinforced with a long introduction in which Mr. Trilling places the book in the tradition of Rabelais, Cervantes, and Swift and argues against the usual view that it is a satire on bourgeois culture. So far, so good; we have needed these works, and here we have all these expert translators and distinguished critics to give us Flaubert again. The works are presented virtually in conjunction, and Mr. Trilling's introduction ties them together for the American public, for whom some portion of its unfulfilled needs is at last fulfilled. Flaubert is available.

But why at just this time? Is it merely a coincidence that Mr. Barzun had a private interest in translating so curious and difficult a work as the *Dictionary,* that Mr. Steegmuller was commissioned to translate the letters, that Mr. Trilling happened to be interested in a book so little known here as *Bouvard and Pécuchet?* Or do these three very different works have a common value and interest for us because they are all by Flaubert? And why Flaubert at all, just now? Why is it that at a certain moment some writer out of the past, some acknowledged classic whose greatness and permanent value have been taken for granted, who is part of the history of the race and a symbol for certain virtues, unexpectedly becomes important to us? It is never his art as such that first sends us back to him, for art is always wrapped around a point of view, is felt *as* a point of view, and makes it clear; it is always some particular angle of vision, some blunt prejudice about life, the very tone of a man's voice, to which we are attracted again. Suddenly, out of the hundreds of writers, and *their* points of view, to whom we might profitably return at this particular moment—Rabelais's earthiness, Emerson's purity, Goethe's universality—suddenly it is Flaubert to whom we instinctively respond, who brings out of us something that has badly wanted saying, and who, having given his whole life to a particular vision, reappears before us as a hero. But what is it of Flaubert that we so desperately need just now? Is it his portrait of the "middle-class philistine"? Is it his belief that art should be endowed "with pitiless method, with the exactness of the physical sciences"? That "an artist must be in his work like God in creation, invisible and all-powerful"? Is it the "selflessness" that Mr. Trilling considers the real theme of *Bouvard,* and indeed of Flaubert's life? All these things must be in our minds as we read him, and they add up to something more than a literary method and a moral lesson.

If there is one basic experience to be gained from these books, it is of Flaubert's anger. The most telling entry in the *Dictionary* —amid so many that indicate the fury with which Flaubert set down the inanities, stupidities, vulgarities, and pretensions of his contemporaries—is "ORIGINAL: Make fun of everything that is original, hate it, beat it down, annihilate it if you can." And the overwhelming impression one gets from *Bouvard,* a brilliantly desolate work, is of the mountain of books and the oceans of folly over which Flaubert could labor in order to spew forth, in all its detail, his contempt for the ideas of his age. But it is in the letters, the magnificent letters Flaubert dashed off after his torturing daily stint was done, that his anger is most compelling. To read these letters is to see a man bursting with the eloquence of rage—rage against the conventional opinion, against contemporary intellectuals, against all the political ideas of the day, against shoddy writing passed off as the real thing; against the materialism of the working class, the brutality and smugness of the middle class, the emptiness of the aristocracy. He thought them all "bourgeois," "a being whose mode of feeling is low."

He scolded his boyhood friends when they became successful and complacent; he lashed back at those who urged him to get his books out quickly ("When I make an appearance," he retorted, "it will be in full armor"); he lectured Guy de Maupassant, whom he regarded almost as a son, for his whoring and laziness ("A little more pride, by God!"). He was furious with his mistress, Louise Colet, for showing around poems she wrote in order to get back at her ex-lovers, and he could be made "rabid"—the word, Mr. Trilling reminds us, is Flaubert's own—by a book, a phrase heard in the street, an article, an opinion. In short, everything in modern life that can annoy, lacerate, and outrage an unwearied conscience and a triumphant mind and a perfect integrity; everything that nowadays we are so used to and that only the most heroically unrelenting effort can resist *all* the time; everything for which, in order to fight it, a man will pay the final price in loneliness and unremitting labor, Flaubert fought gladly, fought constantly. "I can no longer talk with anyone without growing angry, and whenever I read anything by one of my contemporaries I rage."

It is all too easy, however, to believe that Flaubert was angry only with his age, that he felt the debasement around him on our own level of sophisticated dislike for "popular culture." One may feel, as I do, that in *Bouvard* he recorded too literally his contempt for modern ideas, that he expects us to read his *Dictionary* of platitudes with a smirk of self-satisfaction—and at the same time see that he sometimes trains all his fire on current stupidities only because he despairs of being understood. A writer like Flaubert can feel his own exceptionality so keenly as to dislike everything in sight. The *Dictionary* sometimes sounds like Mencken's disdainful examples of "Americana," and *Bouvard* can be taken as an invitation to look down on everyone but ourselves. But these works also point to a feeling of suppression, of some final exasperation, that has set itself up not only against the slogans and catchwords of culture but against culture itself.

This constant sense of his own struggle is what counts with Flaubert. But the struggle is not simply with the conventional opinions of the time; as he himself knew, one can reach a point in the longing for originality where everything sounds like a cliché, where one dare not open one's mouth for fear of sounding like everyone else. It is a struggle against some bitter necessity in the artist's position, against that vision of the "abyss" which more and more in the centuries since religion ceased to have its old authority, art has tried to bridge. It is in the letters that you see that Flaubert's anger has a deeper source than the complacencies and lies and stupidities of popular opinion, the vulgarities of his age, the self-seeking of his contemporaries, and the apathy of his friends. This is the anger of someone who, with all his pride—and Flaubert could have said, as Joyce did of himself, that he had discovered he could do "anything" with language—nevertheless felt that he was not fully getting his say.

Flaubert's anger is extreme, not because other men of the same stamp have not felt such anger but because he was struggling with the final human powerlessness to lift art itself up to a height that would have the effect of absolute permanence, that would give some unmoving, unyielding embodiment to what he saw. The gap between human mortality and the nonhuman ideal; the desire to give the effect of lastingness, hardness, unchangeability to one's works; a man's need to round out his puling little days, his nervous, fretful efforts, his everlasting concern with himself, into something that would have the permanent splendor of the gold and the ivory Flaubert loved—this is what makes his anger in his letters so profound and moving an expression not merely of our general quest for immortality but of the artist's aim to show in the actuality of his work the possible joining of his life to eternity. Flaubert took on himself everything that can cause spiritual anguish, from the unworthiness of the daily round to the broken arc of life itself, and then hurled himself, with all his force, into the breach.

This is what makes Flaubert one of the heroes and renders these letters so remarkable, above all, for their consistent passion. A letter is usually notable because it consists of a single affirmation, of a predominating idea; it is an occasion on which a single note is struck, on which one exclamation, a prevailing mood, *makes* that occasion. What is so amazing about Flaubert's correspondence is that he talks on the highest level all the time. He rushes into each letter with the same fight, the same brilliance, the same exultant, unwearied militancy. In the small hours of the night, long after his excruciatingly careful day's work is done—it sometimes came to a page a week—he suddenly tears loose in these letters, and, dashing them off quickly, burningly, scathingly, he constantly astonishes us with the high pitch of his spontaneity, with the fact that he never "relaxes," never wants chitchat for its own sake, but is always a "frantic idealist," as he says, charged and ready to burst, his mind gathering from the deepest hours of the night exactly the tone of truth a man needs to talk to himself in.

Anger is a great quality, a classic quality, and one rarely evident today, for what most people feel just now is usually resentment and bitterness, the telltale feelings of people who consider themselves imposed on, who know that they are not getting their due, who feel *small*. Flaubert's anger, on the contrary, is that of a powerful caged beast (how often the image of the lion recurs in his work), of a man who, feeling his strength to the uttermost, is continually outraged by the meanness, the self-seeking, the lowness, the vulgarity around him. It is because he feels his strength—unlike most of us today, who feel only our weakness—that he is so magnificently angry. It is because of the very excess of his love, of his wonderful natural idealism—that which a great writer possesses almost with the air he breathes—because of the very *insatiability* of his gift, that he is so continually enraged. It is because he wants to unite, as every great writer does, the life of reality with the life of imagination, and precisely because he is not a "realist" in the cheap modern sense of someone who has wised up to the limits of human experience and has decided to make the most of his opportunities.

Flaubert knew that for someone like himself there could be nothing but this need to unite the life of imagination with the life of reality, and that it is the gap between them that causes the greatest pain. But, exasperated and torn by the human situation itself, he tried to specify in the greatest detail what *this* side of "reality" is like—as if he were seeking not so much to transcend reality as to exhaust it, to drain it, to follow its thread to the very end of the labyrinth. No wonder that he was fanatical, that he constantly railed against the complacent, that every letter was a great shout raised in the faces of the unfeeling. He was unable to live with "reality," and he was unable to write about anything else.

But to have this vision makes everything else fall into place. "And besides," he wrote in the midst of *Bovary,* "after reaching a certain point one no longer makes any mistake about things of the soul." This is the real meaning of Flaubert's anger. And it is a classic anger, the anger of prophets and heroes, the anger of someone who knew that what makes a writer great is exactly his impatience with life itself—which does not live up to the ideal and cannot be fitted to the great idea, to the vision beyond life that, if it makes life seem unworthy and insufficient, also creates the only vision by which a man can stand away from pettiness.

Eleven

FITZGERALD: AN AMERICAN CONFESSION

F. Scott Fitzgerald's *The Crack-Up,* as everyone now knows, is a collection of personal essays, letters, notes and tributes to Fitzgerald by several leading writers, some of them his best friends. Its main feature is the account of his "crack-up" in the middle 'thirties, which Fitzgerald reported in such a way, and planted in such a place, *Esquire,* that it would serve as a sensational confession and release, yet present the minimum of facts on what had happened to him.

If this seems a cold disparagement of a document that was written out of such intense personal suffering, do not put it down to a lack of fellow-feeling on my part, or to a disregard of the courage and moral firmness with which Fitzgerald sought to resolve his tragedy. The essay is a haunting footnote to the inner history of America and of American writing in our time; but it is important not for what it says but for what it reveals—and Fitzgerald, whether he knew it or not, sought to reveal as little as possible. As a personal document it has a vivid painfulness, made tolerable and even esthetically smart by that softening and diffusing glamour which Fitzgerald scattered like a fine gold dust over everything he wrote; it is not moving. Yet it describes so acute a sense of loss on the part of a marvelously talented writer at the height of his career that we may wonder why it does fail to move us—when so much that is casual, fragmentary and even fantastically blind in the personal literature of our time can move us deeply. The answer obviously does not lie in Fitzgerald's situation; it never does in the *situation;* but in the way he addressed himself to it, in the lack of some complete sincerity with which to describe it.

It was as urgent for Fitzgerald to report on his breakdown as it was for him to withhold some essential portion of its meaning from himself and from us. The confession itself, with all its defiance of the repressive and the death-dealing urbane in our culture, is rarely a way of leading us to the truth. On the contrary, it may be the best possible device for not revealing it. In that sense Fitzgerald's essay is not a portion of some meditated autobiography, but belongs with those facile canny professions of guilt which are so rife in our personal conversation and our love affairs, in appeals to God or the psychoanalyst to restore our lost innocence, or in novels like Charles Jackson's *The Lost Week-End*. The other side of our professional American optimism is that well-known personal explosion and unconscious defiance, serving to make the self unavailable, which we so familiarly call the "breakdown"—a deeply pathetic but cumbersome form of evasion which is as common in our society as the void slogans of uplift and irresistible material progress, and which proceeds directly from them, by a commonplace human reaction and exhaustion. Just as the alcoholic bouts in Jackson's book were a device by which to avoid exploring the initial loss of confidence which led to the hero's need of amnesia, so it is characteristic of us to charge ourselves with any guilt so long as it will put distance between us and the concrete reality it is easier to suffer than to understand. The sense of guilt is apparently more than the residue in our racial unconscious of some ancient defiance of parental and divine authority, Freud's theme in *Totem and Taboo* and *Moses and Monotheism*. It also serves as the most immediate weapon by which the intelligence practices some duplicity against that part of itself which can assess the elements of experience with candid objectivity or clear self-assertion. It is the inbred weapon, the little dagger of the soul, by which we make ourselves literally in-valid when we wish to remove ourselves from an intolerable situation. It is the device by which we suspend thought under the name of morality.

At the same time guilt, which is the excuse for the "breakdown," relieves its paralysis by serving to create a false eloquence. It is not only a form of evasion but a field of discourse. By "admitting" that we are guilty we often plan to shock, to reap the vibrant advantages of having gained some dramatic singularity. By our admission we suddenly command that authority which women who feel themselves unloved exercise over their men. The shrew is always an aggressor, and the guilty take advantage of their "honesty" and the show of some awful social courage to dominate the situation. We are all of us so bred in false humility that we rarely permit ourselves to see that its counterpart, aggressive guilt, serves its unconscious purpose by leading us to a false drama; that it breaks publicly through the sterile inner world of introspection, perplexity and remorse.

There are confessions and confessions, and undoubtedly none ever lead us to that real and absolute "truth" about ourselves which is the greatest of all the fictions our rationalism reads into the nature of life and experience. Psychology is always less true than art, and even the most acute clinical psychology is limited, by its concern with disorder, to a small branch of human physics. But there are confessions, like Dostoevsky's *Notes from Underground,* which at least seek to describe as much of human anxiety and realized unworthiness as is consonant with the duty of every being to defend and assert his particular existence. There are confessions, like Melville's letters to Hawthorne, which are parables of "the infinite task of the human heart," and which do not deliberately withhold what is "ugly," but affirm that which is most true. And there are confessions, of the current and commonplace American kind, which are not instruments for a deeper search of reality, in us or life itself, but a subtle form of rebellion—the deepest motive of its rebellion being resistance to the actual solving of a problem, for that would call for a different order of thinking. Suffering is always proportionate to intelligence, and is often an escape from intelligence. Fitzgerald's is of this kind; and that is why it is not moving. One feels in reading it that something is being persistently withheld, that the author is somehow offering us certain facts in exchange for the right to keep others to himself. It is as if he were playing with his own tragedy; which does not make the tragedy less deep. It is merely that *The Crack-Up* is as careful as it is mournful, as shrewd as it is despairing, and as mechanically well-written as the experience it purports to describe was lawless and afraid.

Persistently withheld, but not deliberately. It was in the very nature of Fitzgerald's mind to sculpt the contours of experience in such a way that the light falling on them, from his own ready charm and vivid perception of tragedy, would suggest some content they did not represent. He had learned early in his career—not with *This Side of Paradise,* which was juvenile, but with his first intensive stories of the jazz age and *The Great Gatsby*—that his talent was colorful rather than deep, immensely resourceful in suggestiveness and blending, and that it was futile for him to try for more. Life, or at least the America and tourist France of the 'twenties, appeared as a succession of brightly lit scenes whose significance emerged not from the frank and frontal realization with which he could mold them—the idea-giving power—but from the prompter's quickness with which he underscored the scenes. The emphasis was always on the immediate light irony of some human encounter, the placing of the characters to each other in such a way that they were silhouettes of a mood, quickly inserted into a scene and as quickly releasable from it. The living rhythm of the work was in the movement of the filmy curtain through which he saw it. Everything had to be faintly and deliciously supported on a lightly running river of little golden words. Just as the story of *Tender Is the Night* was heartbreaking without ever being definite, too thickly suffused, for all the delicacy and grace, in the unmistakable glare of the American Mediterranean, so in *The Crack-Up* even the most awesome admission of personal bankruptcy and irretrievable loneliness had to be subtly bent to sound good, to put a subtly diffusing eloquence between the emotion and the fact.

Yet what comes through, so far as one can break through the walls of an experience so coated and painted and glamorized, so heightened and modulated by the strategy of a mind that sought grace at any price, is a very American confession, an unrealized but agonized revolt against certain basic American patterns by which Fitzgerald knew himself to be imprisoned. Success was the grinning idiot's face that haunted him even when the boyish dream of power had gone away. He had begun so easily, so lightly, we thought; success had been the logic of good looks, good luck, the best of good schools in a social sense, good friends who admired him yet could be his "intellectual" conscience, like Wilson, if he needed one—he always felt intellectually inferior. But the success had a kind of subtle mockery about it; he could not tell anyone how deliberately he had to fight for it, how pressingly he needed it. The good fairy who showers gifts always does so with some final reservation to remind us that life is a coil of many springs and never a straight road. To Scott Fitzgerald she gave talent as a weapon rather than as a gift; it was to be a means to success rather than the content of some ultimate human success in itself. And the meaning of that success was always interpreted by others, by the high and glamorous Eastern world into which he had not been born. He did not want it so, but he could not read it otherwise. In the heady days when they were all just out of the army, he had the feeling whenever he joined his friends at the Plaza bar that he was the hero of some social struggle—with a poor room in the Bronx—of which they knew nothing. The girl who dismissed him because of his poverty was the end even of his writing. "If I stopped working to finish the novel, I lost the girl." He releases these facts by tacit admissions and fretful questionings, as much ashamed to discuss his social ambitions openly as he was occasionally ashamed of the ambitions themselves. From the first he was haunted by the feeling that he was always missing out on the real thing, at the Plaza bar or in the world of the novel. Yet it was the high world, of Princeton classmates and officers' training camps, the Plaza and the Ritz, the great city "O glittering and white," that was the real symbol for him. He was *not* what his threadbare fashionableness proclaimed or even what his good looks could persuade; not *really* Princeton, or really an "intellectual" either, like his good friends Edmund Wilson and John Peale Bishop. He was Minnesota, and with a name and a need off the common Anglo-Saxon track; a young man laboring under the tyranny of ambition who had had to stand apart from the Scandinavians at home whose blonde girls he secretly adored. He was not easily up to Princeton or New York. Literature, then, was a way of getting back, of getting in, just as he had to console himself at college for an illness that had kept him from the presidency of some club by "taking a beating on English poetry" and for not getting overseas during the war by making Amory Blaine a second Faust. Even in the worst period of his breakdown "the overseas cap that was never worn overseas" was a bitterly recurrent wound, and it is repeated in this confession by an important American writer threatened with spiritual death at forty.

In fact, he was Gatsby. It was for him, not for that ambiguous ghost impeded by a German immigrant name and a gangster's loss of social power, that the green light burned at the end of the dock—that symbol in the book of the true success, the ultimate home. It was he who wanted Daisy, "glowing like silver, safe and proud among the hot struggles of the poor," Daisy whose voice so fascinated Jay Gatsby because it had "money" in it. Since he was Gatsby, and could never really admit the fact into the course of the novel, he made a bargain with himself. He would make Gatsby an object of rich historical pathos, but a kind of anonymous figure, and easy to patronize, to whom the cool amused narrator of the book (Fitzgerald himself, as we were led to think) would not seem related. He could create Gatsby only at the price of never admitting that he *was* Gatsby, just as he could develop as a writer only by disguising the fact that he thirsted for immediate goals, for that impalpable social world where people derived their self-importance by osmosis from each other, and in which a writer could be accepted, for what came after he had done his writing.

The Great Gatsby concludes with a murder; and the true murderer of Gatsby is not the crazed garage owner whose wife was Tom Buchanan's mistress, but Buchanan himself, the stupid and vicious stockbroker. It was as if Fitzgerald was describing the subtle death of the will that he felt threatened by, in the form of the ultimate violence and disrespect leveled by the very rich against the truly poor. He hated the rich, for they had fascinated him too well—"they are not as we are," as he said to Hemingway. Dick Diver complains to Mary North in *Tender Is the Night:* "You're all so dull," and Mary rhapsodically flies back: "But we're all there is! . . . All people want is to have a good time, and if you make them unhappy you cut yourselves off from nourishment." And Fitzgerald obviously believed that too, which is why he hated them even more. His notion of society, after all, was not much different from Cholly Knickerbocker's. When he read the first chapters on Michelet from Wilson's *To the Finland Station* he expressed appreciation of everything in them but the immediate content of Michelet's revolutionary interests. And when his daughter complained of some school jealousy or exclusion which humiliated her—as he could never forget how often at college he had lived on the verge of humiliation—he advised her to read the chapter on The Working Day in *Das Kapital*. "The terrible chapter . . . and see if you are ever quite the same."

Yet because the rich "were all there is," he came at last to identify them with evil. It was the revenge he played on them for having thought them life's romance. Tom Buchanan kills Gatsby; Daisy becomes as essentially vulgar and inhuman as her husband; the tennis-champion whom the narrator of *The Great Gatsby* would like to love is revealed as a pathological liar; Nicole and her sister in *Tender Is the Night* fashion Dick Diver's ruin. Nicole herself rounds out the ultimate portrait of her class. She escapes madness only by parasitically marrying the psychiatrist hero, but she gives him nothing except the subtle moral bribery of her wealth. When his own decline begins she almost absent-mindedly deserts him, after a gay little taste of adultery with a wealthy athlete, and the story concludes with Dick robbed of his home and children, his work and his dream of love. Standing on their beach one last hour before he leaves, Dick renders Nicole and her set a last ironic homage by making the sign of the cross over them, as Ahab said: "In the name of the devil!" The rich "are all there is," the diabolic life-force, and Dick could at least acknowledge it before he departed broken from them.

"Books are like brothers," Fitzgerald wrote in one of his notebooks. "I am an only child. Gatsby my imaginary eldest brother, Amory my younger, Anthony my worry, Dick my comparatively good brother, but all of them far from home. When I have the courage to put the old white light on the home of my heart, then. . . ." He never did put "the old white light on the home of his heart"; he was an only child and his heroes were not quite himself, only subtle and glamorized disguises. The conflict that tore him, however, appeared in the romance of goodness struggling against evil in *Tender Is the Night.* Dick Diver, Dick Dare: the boyish American pilgrim, the old childhood hero, who went out to see the world and had many adventures. In our childhood he dared; in the true life of maturity he had to dive under, to encounter the face of evil at the bottom of the sea-floor, the other continent. And when he came home, it was a broken victim; evil had done its worst, paralyzing him into dependence; the good die very young, before their actual deaths. Dick Diver's failure is not the failure of a man, but of an idea.

So in Fitzgerald's own life the conflict sharpened as his art developed and grew in graceful concentric loops around it. What he had wanted so long no longer had any real value for him when he could get it, but nothing in his life or work had prepared him to be superior to those instinctive goals. When the conflict reached its most acute stage, in "breakdown," he really wanted to get away from it altogether; to be relieved by a psychic suicide. But it was impossible to get away altogether, it never is while we live; and he found he could survive by a kind of bitter parody of art for *his* sake, of the noble if deficient Jamesian device of making life nothing, of giving "all" to discrimination and art. To James, who had survived his own kind of conflict through a more compulsive and *learned* talent, a talent that gained immense authority and structural harmony by actual expatriation and by escape, through family tradition and wealth, from the success-mongering of his time, the task was lonely but not impossible, narrowing but not paralyzing. Fitzgerald, whose actual intelligence was never equal to his talent, and whose talent was always greater than his experience, went another way—frantically, spitefully determined not to give in, to condemn the class he had always most deeply admired in short spasms of distaste. The revolt, ironically, was against experience, the cumulative tasks of living, himself. He who had never given himself freely to art now said: "I must continue to be a writer because that was my only way of life, but I would cease any attempts to be a person—to be kind, just or generous." Or the last, deceptively boastful confession: "I have now at last become a writer only."

These years in which he was brought to the final and intolerable stage of his conflict were also his Hollywood period; a period when he either could not write or would not sell; when he made a living from the smooth-paper magazines and from film scripts. He did not despise either medium, on the contrary; he was merely impatient because they would not come up to him, to serve him willy-nilly as he still needed to be served or reclaimed as an artist. There is a note in one of the letters about his campaign to interest a producer in "Babylon Revisited," with Shirley Temple as the daughter. There are notes on producers, who always emerge before us as fundamentally more decent and more likeable than the professional writers, from Nunnally Johnson to Dorothy Parker, who had "gone left." We feel in reading these letters of his last period that he had really found an unexpected principle of identity in Hollywood. The passing humiliations, of another kind than the ones he had suffered as a young man—for they humiliated his social inferiority, and Hollywood pinched his pride as craftsman—must have occasionally been awful enough; but it will not do to imagine Fitzgerald wearing his heart out in conflict with Hollywood. In a sense, he had been writing movies all his life, and their facile prismatic genius, their remoteness from real statement, were not of too different an order from his own. With other writers he tended to be preternaturally humble, as before Hemingway—"Ernest who speaks with the authority of success; I speak with the authority of failure"; Ernest along his "solid gold bar"—or inattentive. In Hollywood he could dip his little golden brush into waters of whose depth he was never afraid.

Most of all, in Hollywood he found Monroe Stahr—the sad, skilled, burned-out genius of manipulation who was as much the refracted image of himself at forty as Gatsby had been at twenty-five. Stahr is unquestionably the greatest of Fitzgerald's achievements; even in the half-pages of the unfinished *The Last Tycoon* he has a depth, a variety of human color, that was missing from the young dancers of the 'twenties, the nostalgia of Gatsby, or the arbitrary innocence of Dick Diver. Stahr was a man whose true life was all *inside;* who was a success in the worldly sense and yet above success; an artist of gravity and importance and immense responsibility, but one who did his work casually and quietly; he was occupied with a tragedy. It was important to Fitzgerald to create Stahr; it was even more important for us to have him. For no very good American artist had ever taken the movies seriously enough before. Dos Passos in *The Big Money* caricatured and mauled Josef Von Sternberg, and the caricature remains a caricature. Fitzgerald did something deeper and more enduring. Out of the very heart of the American dream, at the topmost pinnacle of American success, he plucked an alien, a "mere" producer, a Jew, and gave him back to us as one who might have been with White-Jacket and Huck Finn, Lambert Strether and Sister Carrie. And if the success did not bring home "the old white light" of the heart; if Monroe Stahr stood among tinsel miracles; what would? What had? Fitzgerald had found *mon semblable, mon frère;* he gave him everything for a while; and suddenly he died.

Twelve

WE WHO SIT IN DARKNESS

THE BROADWAY AUDIENCE AT THE PLAY

To have great poets, you must have great audiences, too.
—Whitman

If you love the theater; if you have at least once in the darkness of a theater known what it is to have your mind changed and your senses aroused by that dialogue between man and man on the stage which can be reproduced and enlarged in the inimitable immediate bond between actor and audience, then between members of the audience—the chief impression that a round of Broadway playgoing leaves on you is the overwhelming, secret, embarrassed apathy of the audience itself. Despite the great crowds jostling each other to get into the latest hits, the social éclat that now belongs to anyone who has managed to see *South Pacific* or *Kiss Me Kate,* despite the pure delight of anticipation that will seize any audience as the lights are lowered and the curtain begins slowly to rise, the atmosphere at a Broadway play these days is so inherently dull, distracted, so unrelieved by anything the audience actually expects of the play itself, that if you care for the theater you do not know whether to be outraged more at the theater owners, producers, playwrights, and critics for joining in such a cheat, or at the audience for being such sheep.

The Broadway audience today does not even know what it is missing. It hopes it will be entertained, it expects at least to be surprised. But if neither entertained nor surprised, it does not know whom or what to complain of; or if it is right to complain at all. For having, on the whole, waited so long and paid so much to sit in a plushly uncomfortable New York theater for the pleasure of watching a "production" whose chief distinction, in the fantastic economic setup of Broadway, is that a great many harried and ingenious people have gone to such limitless expense and trouble actually to get the thing on the boards, the audience is at once too proud of itself for being there at all and too submissive to some living person's eloquence or fabulous sexual appeal, to complain. It is almost enough for itself that it is there (any experience of the living theater in America today being still rare and "old-fashioned" enough to provide an added social consideration); that it has got in; that it has won some small advantage it can prove in conversation.

Surely not the conversation at intermission time in the lounges, or after the play, or in some last poignant effort to recall to the stage a person or a scene that has just given us so much pleasure, which we identify with all deeply felt experiences in the theater. Nothing, to my mind, so characterizes an evening today in most Broadway theaters as the self-consciousness one sees and hears between the acts; the bewilderment, restless boredom, the nervous satiety of people who have been patient and uncomfortable for a reason they cannot quite justify; the rush, as soon as the curtain is down for the last time, still "to make an evening of it"—and with good reason, since the experience that the tired disenchanted day-time self expected of the theater in the evening has not yet begun.

What *is* the experience of the Broadway audience today at the play? What is it that happens, or rather doesn't happen, to that great crowd of tired, hopeful middle-class people in the dark that explains the irritability and over-conscious discomfort that are felt in New York theaters like an emanation of stale warm air?

To begin with, the audience remains entirely parallel to the life on the stage, the stage to the audience. It is as if they were two vaguely estranged and even possibly hostile entities that must under no circumstances get any nearer each other than they have to. I am not sorrowing over the lack of "audience participation" —that old, cheap, and indeed sinister trick which developed in the agit-prop theater workshops of the Weimar Republic so many totalitarian techniques for the swaying of Hitler's audiences. It is enough, here, to point to the incredibly bad, neurotic, too often simply inaudible, diction of so many young actors and actresses today.

This would seem to come not so much from bad training, since most of them get no training at all, or only the most shallowly "professional" one; but from the fact that they do not know on what level to pitch their voices, *whom it is they are addressing from the stage*. They obviously have no picture in their minds of the audience except as a great shapeless mass, and certainly not of the inherent differences within it.

It cannot be said that most American actors now play up to the gallery; they seem hardly to know that a gallery exists. With what relief does the audience at such a trivial piece as *The Velvet Glove,* or at such claptrap as S. N. Behrman's *I Know My Love,* comfortably settle into its seats, knowing that from such dependable old hands as Grace George, Walter Hampden, and the Lunts it will at least hear every word spoken with relish, with grace, and with the old-fashioned actor's enjoyment in his own presence. This heightened self-enjoyment, something announced to an audience by the very way an actor walks onto a stage and occupies it, can actually be sent back to him by the audience's delight, and then usually communicates itself to the supporting players. It can now be seen only in the last of the old circus and music-hall stars, like Bobby Clark, just as half the fun of watching the Marx

Brothers in the movies lies in their direct unashamed eagerness, learned from how many hilarious evenings in vaudeville, to force themselves on the attention of every last man, woman, and child in the audience. But to do that, you have to believe that the audience is in the theater to get an experience it expects nowhere else. Most performers on Broadway today give one the impression that they are as little interested in the theater as an institution as is the audience itself.

The quality of speech on the stage is, of course, the surest indication of what relations actually exist between the performers and the audience. Whether or not the fine edge and always slightly patronizing clarity of British "educated" speech would seem to have been developed, as I think it was, from long centuries of practice in giving orders to servants and the lower orders generally, the British actors in T. S. Eliot's *The Cocktail Party* have the peculiar effect on the audience of surprising it that people so "affected" in their speech can be interested in religion or ideas generally. Hence the incoherent resentment one sees and hears in the audience against the play, from a fear of being taken in; which is quite apart from all serious criticism of it. But the peculiar inaudibility of so many new American performers would seem to come not only from the lack of continuous theater practice which most European actors have, or from the lack of a common standard of American speech; but even more, from their obvious unrelation to the audience. And this begins, I believe, in the fact that the audience does not make enough claims on the actor, that its polite bewilderment, its passivity, keeps him tense and unprepared, but without the final tension (something that escapes even seasoned European actors on Broadway) that is always so marvelous on the stage when everything in your sight and hearing is on the same dramatic pitch.

Properly, the audience is either the third element present to the actor's mind in every dialogue, or it is a great crowd of strangers looking on—it does not matter how friendly, enthusiastic, or indifferent; they will still be strangers. But to overcome that strangeness, the audience must be at home with itself in the theater, something I have not felt in a New York theater for years. The members of the audience must have some bond with each other greater than the social chic and sexual provocativeness of the new Empire fashions. And there must be some outspoken enjoyment of a beautiful line, if and when it comes, for its own sake alone. Though here, however, the audience is perhaps not entirely to blame, since it is usually straining so hard to hear what is being said at all.

Perhaps the deepest reason for the inaudibility of the performers in such "serious" American items as *The Member of the Wedding* or *Come Back, Little Sheba,* is the fact that the characters are solitary people who do not expect to be overheard by anyone. In the last few years the American drama, like the American novel of the 'forties, has turned sharply against the very language of social protest. The only vague, wistful vapors left of it are now in the movies (*Pinky* and *Lost Boundaries* have shown that it is possible to make successful films about Negroes, so long as they are mostly white and look entirely so), and in those large, abundantly relaxed "musical plays," like *South Pacific* and *Lost in the Stars,* which redeem the social guilt the American middle class discovered during the war about its racism. But through the unexpected success of Tennessee Williams, young American playwrights have discovered, just as young novelists have discovered in Truman Capote, that their authentic subject is American loneliness—which is dramatized in the neurotic, the child, the Negro, both man and wife in *Come Back, Little Sheba,* and in every last character in *The Member of the Wedding.*

The extraordinary number of children now on the New York stage is itself an indication that Broadway has at last fallen back on the introspectiveness that has dominated highbrow American fiction in the last decade. And of course children on the stage do not speak too clearly, to a whole audience, in the old-fashioned actor's way, without appearing unnatural, unbearably cute, or even intentionally monstrous. The latter is precisely the point intended in *The Innocents,* that bad movie they have made of Henry James's *The Turn of the Screw,* for the ironic title underscores the remarkable wickedness and homosexual insolence of the young Miles, as played by David Cole.

This characterization, as it is written into the play and as it is performed, bears no resemblance whatever to the extraordinary, shy, and pitifully confused young boy in James's story. But obviously it is meant to be a parody of some British homosexual avant-garde poet, and to sting the audience into having a satisfying moral reflex of dislike. But where the child's speech is largely indistinct, for the excellent reason that he is truly a child (like the little boy in Carson McCullers' *The Member of the Wedding*), one realizes that the pressure on the stage of our familiar American loneliness has made impossible the old, ideally dramatic relations between actor and audience. For here the dialogue on the stage itself is not so much heard between the actors as it is overheard. The child speaks to the Negro, the adolescent heroine to the child, the Negro to the poor, the father to his daughter, as if each were always alone, and had no confidence that he could understand the other or be understood. So that something blurred, always touching, yet inherently elusive—human solitude as a fact in itself alone—is shown on the stage before which the audience feels like an amazed onlooker. It may catch memories or echoes of each human being's private ordeal, but nothing that is in any dramatic sense its own. It responds by pity, not by recognition. There is no *situation* to enter into. The life of the theater is action, reciprocality. Here there is no action—there is only character, and in the characters themselves nothing but their passive suffering—

that element which Matthew Arnold said was not a subject for poetry, and is even less so for the stage.

Hence the grateful emphasis that the audience puts, amid all these human silences and obscurities, on the individual performer rather than on the character played; on the performer divorced from the play—which is the most familiar response of the audience in a Broadway theater. For if there is no action and not even the hope of action; if the performer, in what is finally his own solitude on the stage (in a play that does not *move*), must try by any means to elicit some response from the audience, then ironically the inherent sensitivity of such a play as *The Member of the Wedding,* far from transmitting to the audience an experience of human despair, will simply become the occasion for an actor's personal triumph. The tremendous effect that Ethel Waters has on the audience at *The Member of the Wedding*—and very justly, for she is the one fully rounded human being on the stage—is nevertheless due to the freedom she enjoys *from* the play. And we respond so gratefully to her own abundant humanity precisely because we, too, have not been taken up by the play, have not been absorbed. So that in some unexpected release from our unadmitted perplexity or boredom, we fix on her. Alas, on her only as *the* Negro, the great Negro mother, as if even the performer whom we love for herself alone, especially when we cannot love the play, were, still, only the embodiment of a race or class or type.

It is perhaps in some such terms that we may understand the Broadway audience's wistful, over-susceptible, yet coldly self-conscious submission to the performer rather than the play—perhaps even *against* the play. I am not speaking here of what happens at such obvious "vehicles" as *Detective Story,* which is an offensive piece of trash held together by loud screams and yells from Ralph Bellamy; or *I Know My Love,* which would be inexcusable if the Lunts were not there to play that happy married couple, the Lunts. But rather, of what happens to the audience at *South Pacific* looking on at the now celebrated love affair between Mary Martin and Ezio Pinza. This is a love affair which seems to take place between races or generations rather than between individuals, and it is conducted in so tumultuous an atmosphere of American largesse, know-how, sex appeal, and achingly liberal good-will toward all those darker and older races which are not so rich, happy, and beautifully careless as ourselves, that I have not in years heard from the stage so ringing an indication of what Americans think of themselves in relation to the world they have just learned is more than half theirs.

The audience at *South Pacific* never forgets that it is present at a fabulous occasion. Everyone in the theater feels this. It is the only really joyous, or at least deeply excited, audience I saw this season. Fabulous because of the planetary American success of the play, which everyone wants to see, which wins all the prizes, which is an obviously complicated American industrial product of the highest ingenuity, but is also extremely liberal—not cheap, but benevolent toward everything and everyone in the creation. Fabulous because we are there, and so feel ourselves, along with the charming people on the stage, fortune's darlings from the first. Fabulous because there arises from the sex-starved Navy men in the Pacific, like the blast from a steel mill, such a rip-roaring, hungry, idolatrously adoring hymn to the American woman that if we ever had any doubts about American power in the world, we lose them at *South Pacific*. If we ever had doubts about what we were fighting for, we lose them here, and can instantly answer Pinza's weary "European" question—I know what you Americans are fighting against, but what are you fighting for?

We were fighting for love. We were fighting for Mary Martin. In sight of that enchanting girl, so sophisticated, yet so natural;

so independent and obdurate in her search for the real thing, yet so kindly and dignified a comrade to every American mother's son three thousand miles from home—she who is every GI's ideal girl friend, but reserved in her American naturalness and good sense for the older, graver, deeper European soul of Ezio Pinza—we rejoice in ourselves, in the immediate human advantages our power can give us, and see in that love affair on the stage the meeting of the continents, of the races, of the traditions. For if Mary Martin represents American goodness and naturalness, Pinza embodies that maturity we Americans know we still need to complete us, to round out the shock of our power with a song straight from the heart, a hymn to the human affections.

Curiously, this was the great theme in Henry James—the meeting between America and Europe, between the power of innocence and the depth of wisdom. And it is more true at *South Pacific* than at *The Innocents,* or at *The Heiress* some seasons back, that Broadway no longer lags culturally behind the world of Henry James; that it, too, has taken our American perplexity, and virtuousness, and inner liberalism, out into the world. But Henry James was too pessimistic, perhaps too morbidly conscious of what the world did to Americans, rather than of what Americans could do for the world. Whereas when Nurse Mary Martin, our fabulous American miss, truly fortune's darling, "the heiress of all the ages," skips round and round in her delight, singing "I'm in love, I'm in love, I'm in love," the audience knows that with no other people could war be such an occasion for the discovery of human sweetness, of love, of the most radiant happiness. And is itself in a perfect frenzy of delight, and, for once, can go home fulfilled.

Thirteen

THE LOST REBEL

When Ellen Glasgow, the Southern novelist, died, in 1945, she left in manuscript an intimate memoir, *The Woman Within,* which she indicated was to be brought out only when it could no longer embarrass the principals. "But," she requested her literary executors, "do not destroy it." No one saw the manuscript during her lifetime. She refused to allow a copy to be made, and she kept it in brown envelopes inside a briefcase that was locked, marked "Private and Personal," and stored in her safe-deposit vault in Richmond. She left instructions that the manuscript was never to be entrusted to the mails, and that if anything happened to her, the executors were to come to Richmond and take charge of it. Once, after the executors had visited her and heard her read one small passage from it, she put the manuscript inside still another envelope, marked it "Original Rough Draft of Autobiography," and added "Only Copy. Preserve Carefully."

The pains she took to preserve the book and to shield its contents are easily explained. At the age of sixty, Ellen Glasgow was not only a distinguished novelist, with a great body of work already in existence and a still growing reputation, but also almost the last of what had once been a large and well-known Virginia family. She still lived in the famous gray house at 1 West Main Street, a house that had a picture-book magnolia tree outside it; she was, in fact, a leading Virginian, with a famous social tradition behind her. And despite the great body of work, the growing reputation, the admiration of certain critics; despite the famous gray house at 1 West Main Street (which anyone in Richmond could have told you about); despite the tradition, and all the rest, Ellen Glasgow was an agonizedly unhappy and isolated woman, who, when she began this book, was as desperate as she had been when, in her childhood—this was the most vivid memory of her life, and it colored all the rest of it—she had been terrified at seeing in the sunset "a face without a body staring in at me." She was as excruciatingly sensitive as she had always been; she was alone in the house where once a family of twelve had lived; she suffered constantly from nervous depression and had once half-consciously tried suicide; and she was deaf, and had been more or less so since she was a girl.

This, then, is why she wrote the book—to speak out for once, to cry out, as she had never done in her novels, though at their best they mock the ignorance and unfeelingness and smugness of her own class. This is the book of a great sufferer who inside that gray house felt all her life the emotional bitterness of someone who has never had her due, who knows that life has deprived her of her rights, who could still record meticulously, like an adolescent, that her mother had let her down by dying. If there is something moving in all this, there is something pitiable about the unrelenting way in which she returns to her theme in remark after remark that was wrung out of her for this book: "My big sisters, of whom I was terribly afraid," "I was still a child when I learned that an artificial brightness is the safest defense against life," "Why was it people made you do things that would break your heart always?," "But I knew at seven, as well as I know now, at sixty, that the happiest time of my life was already over, that I had crossed the bridge between childhood and the grown-up years when you have to have trouble, I told myself, and more trouble as long as you live."

This is the refrain, the purpose of the book, told as the history of a family. Ellen could never feel that she had much sympathy at home except from her mother, who became ill, a "nervous illness," and was away from Ellen a long time before she died. The father was an industrialist and a cold Calvinist of the old school—he even ran an ironworks, like the harsh father in an old-fashioned novel—who could be moved to tears by a sentimental work of fiction but never by his children. Though his son Frank found that riding was the only thing that could cure his terrible insomnia, his father ordered him to stay home on the Sabbath. Eventually, the brother, like all the other members of the family Ellen cared about, came to a tragic end. Even her deafness, she felt, had been passed down to her by the family. On every score, wherever she looked, she considered that she had grounds for complaint. Of the ten children—Ellen, born in 1874, was the ninth—two had been born before the Civil War, and one of the constant refrains of the book is the distance and cold antagonism Ellen felt in her older sisters, especially Emily, who frankly appears over and over as an enemy. On discovering Ellen's first literary efforts, she derisively read the verses out loud to her friends; she hid books that Ellen wanted to read; she retrieved from the local postmaster a letter Ellen had written their mother, ill and away from home, telling how Emily had got rid of a favorite pet. When Ellen moved out of the family circle, in 1911—for good, she thought—she left manuscripts of her novels, and a number of letters she treasured, on the top shelf of a closet. In 1916, she returned to find that "my housekeeping sister had burned every manuscript and every letter, and that the highest shelves of the closet had been scrupulously scrubbed and cleared of all literary associations. . . . At the time I was too ill to care or to feel annoyed; but I can wonder, as the years pass, whether that particular incident could have occurred anywhere except in the South, where, throughout the centuries, valuable records and innumerable interesting diaries and letters have been treated as so much waste paper."

In short, this is the story of a family as told by the proverbially sensitive and younger child in it, and it is above all the story of a schism in a family. "And a man's foes shall be they of his own household." We do not get very much of this, which is the real note and the best, in Southern writing any more; even Faulkner, who portrayed family antagonism to perfection in *The Sound and the Fury,* and who in the old days suffered from it himself, long ago gave up this kind of youthful rancor, while Southern writers have been treating us for years to that sweet young sufferer who is the principal figure in Tennessee Williams' plays, and who lives amid her fantasies, her glass animals, in a little world of silent yearning. The deepest characteristic of Southern writing is the contention with the past, the struggle with the gods of the household. As Ellen Glasgow records her efforts to write, her need to keep her writing secret, the contempt her family felt for it, the passion in the South for "sweet stories," and the wonderful remark made to her by a close friend (that she was dying to read one of Ellen's novels but couldn't find anyone to borrow it from), one catches a note, and more than a note, of what is best in the formal but sprightly satire of her work, with its bright variations on a climate where "social charm prevailed over intelligence." Even the great love affair of her life, with a married man, which lasted seven years and gave her her deepest happiness, is only a prelude, in this book, to her strange but often hilarious liaison of twenty-one years with a Virginia lawyer and politician whose pomposity, as she describes it, belongs on the stage, and who, when he busily headed a Red Cross mission to Rumania during the First World War, spent much of his time making eyes at Queen Marie—an affair reported here with catty but understandable malice and amusement.

In any event, even so mildly illicit an affair as Ellen Glasgow's turned, among the F.F.V.s, into a slightly overdrawn farce. And the rebel who had had to keep her first novel a secret, who felt that no one around her could understand her, who knew that she lived in a culture utterly without ideas, surrounded by the hostility and indifference of her family, found herself, it is obvious in this book, writing it in her private night, now that everyone else was dead, like a woman who is shrieking but cannot be heard. This is the real pain of the book, that it recounts a rebellion which in a sense came to nothing, which could never find anything in Virginia itself to rub off against, which could give her no ally. One of the most touching things about her first love affair is that the man seems to have been one of the very few in that society who could understand her work, who felt any real sympathy for her. And it is this that makes Ellen Glasgow's struggle appear more like self-protection than a writer's open fight, for it describes a rebellion that got lost amid the vapors and the teacups, with only James Branch Cabell in Richmond for friend, and a secretary in the house who, as Ellen complained, felt no interest in what she wrote. This final loneliness is, after all, the story of what happened to Ellen Glasgow the writer, whose novels, though they figure respectably on the shelves, possess too little real force and nowadays serve mostly those tiresome spokesmen for gentility, like J. Donald Adams, who are always warning us against modern literature.

She was a lost rebel. But so, when you think about it, were even better writers of her generation, such as Cather, Lewis, and Anderson, and so many others of the next generation, who also ended bitterly, feeling that life had strayed away from them, that the new generation—which, after all, is their generation—had betrayed them. This is an attitude to which Ellen Glasgow, as she makes clear in several tedious passages, was not averse. Can it be that the real content of so many American books has been just that first rebellion, against Winesburg and Main Street and Richmond, and that once liberation is won, there is nothing much left except the personal pain? Can it be that this tendency to rebel only against one's family, one's town, one's own, so as to open the door, explains why "there are no second acts in American lives," why American writing is so short-lived? This, it is obvious, was Ellen Glasgow's tragedy, and she certainly did not rebel very much.

Fourteen

KAFKA

There are undoubtedly great writers in our time whom we cannot immediately understand, either because they challenge us too deeply or are simply too much in advance of us. But there are also great writers whom we would rather not understand too well, for we can not live with them and our usual compromises at the same time. Franz Kafka, who during his lifetime had almost no public and certainly sought none, seems to me the case of a contemporary genius whom we too easily term mysterious because we are unwilling to admit that he is in a certain sense unbearable.

This fact has been clouded by the general disposition to make Kafka the last word in the cabala of advanced art and theology. *The Kafka Problem,* an anthology collected from the interpretations of thirty-five European and American critics, presents every possible point of view about Kafka, but is unified by the assumption that he is only a little less difficult than the physics of the atom bomb. In the face of anything so overwhelmingly exegetical as *The Kafka Problem,* the very format of which is suggestive of the higher theology, the reader is understandably terrified. Kafka would have taken the book as another instance of his distance from humanity; too many readers, misjudging the character of his mind from such a book, will be only too happy to leave him to the experts. And this is too bad, not only because so many of the critics repeat each other, each in the language of his special interest (not excluding Barthian theology and the party line), and so are unnecessary; but even more because there is a universal experience to be gained from reading Kafka which many of these critics do not even suggest. It is even easier to read Kafka than it is most of his critics. *The Kafka Problem* is the last word in the annotation of works which are as peculiarly organic as a great lyric; exegesis can go no further, except to disappear. No doubt there is something to be learned about the confusion of contemporary thought, if not about Kafka, from the zeal to exploit him in so many directions. But the book as a whole is a weariness to the mind and flesh, for it is an accumulation of all the efforts to present Kafka as a problem rather than as an experience.

Now Kafka is difficult, as only a great writer can be, and we certainly need elucidation of his work. But the difficulty is not resolved, it is not even named, by reducing him to a system of symbols. It lies in our ability to accept and to share his sensibility; to take him for what he is, a writer who saw the world from below, and meant what he wrote to be the bottom-most vision of reality. Kafka is difficult not because "he really meant" to say this or that about the nature of contemporary experience, but because he saw in his private and contemporary agony that part of us all which is more real than the public "reality." Just as religious doctrine can be a way of muffling the religious ache in people, so Kafka saw below man's institutions and formal learning the essential unappeasable loneliness of man in the universe, man's longing to know the meaning of his existence and the unbreaking struggle with his own nature. We do not like to face those facts in themselves, and in reading Kafka we immediately assume that the world he presents is constantly a reference to something other than itself. This is why we find him difficult, for we are always trying to find out what hidden suggestion is buried in his work.

Hence our desire to explain him, for our purposes, rather than to experience him. For to take that experience undistractedly, to see it for what it is, is to admit that his vision is real.

What was that vision? It is best indicated in the maxims and diary notes that are printed at the end of *The Great Wall of China,* an important collection of his stories and parables. In the great novels, *The Castle* and *The Trial,* Kafka's conception of man and the world is dramatized into enormous fables, and it is only in their total character, with every portion of the narrative kept firmly in our minds, that we can grasp his meaning. But in the notes that accompany *The Great Wall of China* Kafka sought to compress his thought into sayings, and if we study them attentively we can almost feel their meaning expand and coil around us in witness of Kafka's unglossed perception of man's fate in the universe. One note reads: "We were fashioned to live in Paradise, and Paradise was destined to serve us. Our destiny has been altered; that this has also happened with the destiny of Paradise is not stated." Another: "One must not cheat anybody, not even the world of its triumph." Still another: "There are questions which we could never get over if we were not delivered from them by the operation of nature." In one place he says, "You are the problem. No scholar to be found far and wide." In another, "From a real antagonist boundless courage flows into you."

There is only one parallel to such writing, and it is to be found in the work of a man who could not bear to say all he felt, and soon embraced the Church: Pascal's *Pensées.* When Pascal says, "Man does not know in what rank to place himself. He has plainly gone astray, and fallen from his true place without being able to find it again. He seeks it anxiously and unsuccessfully everywhere in impenetrable darkness," we are immediately in the world of Kafka, who said: "There is a goal, but no way; what we call the way is only wavering." The crucial difference between them is that Pascal defined this state—the phrase in our time is "metaphysical anguish"—as an inescapable fact in moral science, a condition preliminary to the seeking of grace, an avenue to God. "Console thyself, thou wouldst not be seeking me if thou had not already found me." Pascal bet on the Church; it had to be true; he could not bear it otherwise.

Kafka bears it; he insists on it; there is a goal but no way; there is a problem, but no resolution; there is only an eternal search. What he gets into his sayings immediately, as his novels unfold it, is the haunted quality of existence—haunted by man's own mystery unto himself. To face him openly is to see that he is talking directly about that inner portion of consciousness which is unbreakingly the judge of life. That portion is not simply the stream of consciousness, where we silently quarrel with things we must outwardly accept, and it is not simply the realm of anxiety or sickness. It is that sense of ourselves on earth whose captive wing we occasionally get into poetry. It is in another realm that equi-distance between nature and immensity that leads us not only to create gods but to believe in them. What is intolerable in Kafka is that he throws no comforting bridge of doctrine across for us. What is beautiful in him is that he takes us gravely, and with the most meticulous seriousness, into a world which is exactly, in all its proportions, true to our inner experience. With his meekness, his humor, his kindly gravity and scrupulous accuracy, in a German marvelously lean, firm and clear, he presents as a fact, as a simple adventure, man's search for his own meaning.

Someone said of Kafka that he has the great quality of genius in that his integrity seems something given rather than something for which he struggles. It is in his own lack of surprise, in the immediate unity of his perception, that he captivates and troubles us. For Kafka has the purity of those who see the world in such an inclusive metaphor that we cannot quite believe in it, and prefer to break it up, to see what it "really means." When we paraphrase Kafka, or comment on him, we extract the theme of his work and try to use it for our special purpose. But it is exactly the quality of his work that he accepts his fate as a measure of the human condition. What makes Kafka so difficult is not so much in what he says, line by line, as in his inability to let himself off, and hence us as we read him. And the symbols he discovers for himself are not so much tools as they are an inescapable embrace of the world. The world for him is an impossible struggle to reach the castle of grace; is a trial for crimes we do not even know we have committed, whose precise character we can never learn; is like "clambering up a steep precipice, as steep, say, as you yourself seen from below." For Kafka is peculiarly that writer who believes himself the contemporary man of sorrows and is willing to bear all our burdens—they all seem to him so true. Standing at the extremity of human isolation, conscious of himself as an eternal solitary, a Jew, a poor clerk in the prisonhouse of the modern industrial bureaucracy, a cipher in the Central European maze of nationalities, he yet challenges us through and through, and defies us to say that the nightmare is not real. But "defies" is too strong a word. Kafka does not defy any one or any thing; on the contrary, he notes us as we go our way "over a rope which is not stretched at any great height but just above the ground. It seems more designed to make people stumble than to be walked upon."

An imagination like Kafka's is marked by an ability to dissolve the world in his symbols without losing it. It is not easy to define such an imagination, or primary gift; it is the functioning in one man of all that unorganized relationship to the world which is released in poetry. But one of its greatest characteristics is a gift of surrender; the creator yields to his inference about the world and recasts it in the light of his symbol. In "Metamorphosis," a long story rather than a novel, a young clerk wakes up one morning to find that he has been transformed into "some monstrous kind of vermin." He is not dreaming it; his metamorphosis is only too real, and the life of his family is deeply changed by the fact. Regarding him with horror and shame (what will the neighbors say?) they make him a prisoner in his own room and prisoners of themselves, to watch over him and prevent disgrace. They hate him and would like to get rid of him, but some perplexity as to what original and human portion of their son and brother remains in the "object" keeps them from proceeding against it. At the same time they cannot bear living with it and miserably shutting themselves off from the world, humbling themselves before the servant and lodgers, live as if the dreadful event were a punishment upon them. The clerk, in his strange metamorphosis, has lost none of his human feelings and understands only too painfully what is going on. But he cannot communicate with the people; his humanity is reduced to experience of the most painful helplessness and isolation. In a fit of rage, the father—unable by any other means to convey his hatred of his son—throws an apple at him, which is embedded in the skin. This the son must bear as a tangible realization of the horror he has aroused in his own family, and after futile efforts to gain their love or sympathy, dies —virtually, Kafka makes us feel, because life is insupportable. The family is overjoyed by the event and feels released.

Here, even more than in the novels or in the parable about man's effort to reach God which Kafka wrote around "Investigations of a Dog," the main story in *The Great Wall of China,* the inviolate quality of Kafka's symbolism is shown. The sufferings of the clerk in "Metamorphosis" do not proceed from the "dreadful event"; the metamorphosis is itself an expression of the clerk's distance from his own family, of the difficulty at communication with one's own, the loneliness that can be deepest in one's own family. The subject of the story is just that passive and dumb humanity which is associated, as in a dream, with debasement. The genius of this story is that which transforms a figure of speech ("You treat me as if I were an animal!") into a parable of the inner distance between human beings. To Kafka that inner distance is so real that it becomes filled with men in the shape of beasts. They do not cease to be men because they are beasts; the only expression of their human alienation is that which converts them into beasts.

So firm is this understanding in Kafka, and so richly is it forged into new terms by his imagination, that it is curious to see in Max Brod's biography an effort to stress his "healthy" side, his will to a normal life, as if to absolve him of undue eccentricity. Max Brod was Kafka's great friend, and as Kafka's executor declined to burn the unpublished manuscripts, as Kafka requested in his will. His biography is the primary source of our knowledge of Kafka's personal life and character, and is invaluable to any one at all interested in the mind of this Czech-Jewish genius. But it shows, for all its important first-hand records of Kafka's life, more jealousy for the reputation of the friend than boldness in defining the imagination of the writer. Nothing is lost by admitting how close Kafka often came to absolute despair and breakdown, and efforts to "normalize" his personality, as it were, miss the point. What is central to Kafka is not his longing to be like others, which Brod stresses, but his ability to accept his torment as a guide to the human condition. Kafka spent a large part of his life as a minor official in an insurance office in Prague, and it is moving to read how little time he had for his writing, how hard he had to fight for the leisure and tranquillity with which to compose. But what is most striking in this connection is how spontaneously and freely he could write when he had the chance. At the peak of his first creative effort he wrote in exultation: "All things can be put into words, all one's ideas, even the strangest, find a great fire ready for them in which they are consumed and reborn." Such a faith is not found in the "normal" world, and while one can hardly doubt that genius pays a bitter price for it, it is not one that needs apology.

Fifteen

THE JOURNAL KEEPER

A recent volume (1914-27) of André Gide's *Journals* contains such frank declarations on his famous "immoralism" that it will obviously be looked into for its scandal. At the risk of neglecting elements that have certainly not been of minor importance to Gide, I should like to discuss this book—surely the most remarkable journal ever divulged during an author's lifetime—from another angle: its revival of the journal as a work of art and a spiritual document.

Gide is now seventy-eight, and he has been keeping a journal since he was eighteen or nineteen. He began it as a literary exercise and once wrote that he kept on with it to give himself practice "in writing quickly." He has always tested his life and ideas on it, and he has probably never written a sentence in it without shaping it for publication. Like all writers' journals, it has been a "savings bank," in Emerson's phrase, for future work. Such books are dictated as much by prudence as by self-fascination, and it is hard to say of many passages in this one whether Gide was lamenting his life or rehearsing a passage for some unwritten book, since for a writer so consumed by literature there is a constant injunction not to lose a shred of experience. Even in his moments of severest agony, Gide has never forgotten to write well; when a careless passage is forced out of him, he usually instructs himself to repair it. There is probably a good deal of his real life that he has sacrificed for the point and leanness of that amazing style that has been the admiration of even his enemies and his recompense for a certain thinness of imagination. Yet I am sure that Gide has given himself to his journal more freely than to any other book, or idea, or passion. Begun as an exercise, kept up in illness, in travel, in flight from work and as a constant stimulus to work, with many a grumble against its tyranny over him, it has become not only his best book but the symbolic center of his life—its armory, its apology, its supreme justification. If he has surprised himself by living so long, surely one reason has been his unwillingness to finish it.

Journal keepers are a strange breed, and with all their faults are less given to complacency than most people. There have been many writers greater than Gide who kept inferior journals, and many who were incapable of the journal's traditional complaints of failure. It is absurd to imagine Balzac writing a journal (what for?) as it is to imagine Amiel writing anything else. The Goncourt brothers kept one as a gossipy history, and it has survived their novels; Tolstoy seems to have kept his largely to complain of his wife, who kept one against him. (They exchanged them occasionally.) Emerson, Hawthorne, and Thoreau thriftily incorporated large sections of theirs into their works; Melville started one on his voyage to Palestine, when he was half out of his mind and eager to keep himself going against the day he would write again. Perhaps, to carry on a journal in our time, a writer must have a certain vital anxiety about himself and a realization that his personality is his chief literary resource. The great journal keepers have been extreme Protestants, brought up to account for every minute of their time to a watchful God—our early literature is crammed with them—and Frenchmen, in whom the introspective rationalism of their literary tradition has encouraged the keeping of *cahiers*. Gide is both Protestant and Frenchman, and more, a human being who from early childhood realized that he was "different" and that he could find freedom and consolation only in that dialogue with oneself of which every sincere journal consists.

The continual interplay of these elements makes Gide's *Journals* unique. He is a writer whose real gift has always been for the modeling and modulation of his personal experience rather than for any central originality as a thinker or artist, and in these notes all his ability for moral speculation and the abrupt *pensée* is turned on himself, his work, his friends, the cockpits of literary Paris, and his longing for God. One never knows from passage to passage where the burden of his concern will fall next—whether it will be on himself as a "sinner" who needs to flout the outward law but is afraid that pleasure unhinges him for work, or on his superlative keenness for spotting weakness or falseness in his own writing and that of everyone else, a gift that is sometimes indistinguishable from his desire to write a masterpiece that will redeem him from the gnawing sense of his personal unworthiness. He is either noting scraps for future work, or reproaching himself for wasting time, or getting back at critics, or mourning over his sins, or encouraging himself to sin (those Greeks!), or trying unanticipated flights of thought to get the most out of himself, or finishing salon conversations in which someone else, it is clear, got the upper hand. The book is his confessor, with his ever-present Bible his only spiritual tool, for while he venerates Jesus, he is unable to believe in any church, Catholicism being "inadmissible" and his ancestral Protestantism "intolerable." It is also a register of all his reading (he is as careful to make a notch for each new book read as was Justice Holmes or John Quincy Adams), of his progress at the piano (he cannot play if anyone is listening), and of letters to unfriendly critics that he will never mail. The journal is even a character in his life and work. We find him addressing it as his taskmaster, his conscience, the shadow of that outer world he hopes to escape when he enters the journal's happy chaos. When he is idle elsewhere, he can be busy here; when he is writing, or even unexpectedly happy, he complains that he notes in this book merely his bad days—will history misjudge him? But only the journal is adequately flexible and easy to contain all his contradictions; only its privacy will force him to the bottom of his own mind. A good deal like Eliot's Prufrock, he is constantly asking himself "Do I dare?," and, having dared, he attacks his failings with Puritan indignation. He is an unresting student—even after he had reached seventy, he was still memorizing long lists of German words, and he later incurred the wrath of the party-line patriots, who already disliked his views on Russia, when he revealed that he had been studying his beloved Goethe during the Occupation of France—but even here he sadly comments on his inability to rely sufficiently on himself; all those books he must finish are only a way of getting him "ready" for his work. His greatest wish has always been to let himself go, to confess the heresies of his mind and his sexual cravings to the limit. But two injunctions stand on opposite sides of him—the command of Jesus that a man must "lose his life" in order to save it, and the ethic of supreme liberation he worships in the Greeks, in Blake, Keats, Goethe, and Nietzsche. It is interesting to note that his passion for Socrates was not shared by Blake and Nietzsche—*he* needs them all. He would like to "renounce" his life, and, in a famous passage written in 1916, during his religious crisis, notes his wistful belief that "it is in perfect abnegation that individualism triumphs . . . self-renunciation is the summit of self-assertion." Yet, like another La Rochefoucauld, he notes with his little smile that "vice" is "more imperious than any duty." Actually, he has never expected liberation but has characteristically sought the literary text for liberation. If he had achieved the Greek ideal, he would never have defined so correctly, and with typical French *justice,* the limits within which man actually lives. He would like to be both free and good, and, failing both, has compromised by being honest. He is not noble and does not pretend to be. There is many a feline thrust at Francis Jammes (too cloying), at his friend Paul Valéry (makes too many demands on his intelligence, is almost inhuman), at Paul Claudel (too self-righteous, like so many Catholics he knows). And there is a particularly cold portrait of Marcel Proust, whose boldness about his own homosexuality shocked Gide; we are not surprised, in a later passage, to find him peevishly criticizing Proust's syntax. Yet, with all this, he never allows us to forget that, despite everything he feels lacking in his own life and talent, he is a European and that his great tradition has been to translate every experience into an idea.

What is it that drives a man to keep a journal so long? Each writer starts with his own need, but surely the reasons are always the same—the struggle against death and for time, the need to use one's life to the uttermost. Recording one's days somehow saves them from extinction, and if one is a writer, there is always the hope that they will be reused in the tasks that lie ahead. There is nothing so moving in all Gide's works as this struggle with himself to maintain the victory over life. "I cling desperately to this notebook," he writes in one passage. "It is a part of my patience; it helps keep me from going under." In another: "It is time to learn once more to prefer the events that choose men to those I should have chosen myself." The journal is thus an accounting of necessity and a training in necessity. He notes that Briand's secretary, whom he dislikes, is the perfect type of climber: "He succeeds by means of patience, of minute economy, of hygiene." Add "moral" before "hygiene," and this "minute economy" becomes the very pattern of Gide's own journal. Even as he is repeating to himself Jesus's command to "lose" one's life, he is saving his in little ways, improving it, sharpening his mind on the classics, and constantly turning the whetstone of his style. It is this unremitting search for self-correction and self-purification, by a succession of small efforts, that reveals the essentially religious source of the journal. To this must be added the candor of a man who knows that he will always stand outside conventional society; and this would give a special pathos to his book if he were not always able to use up the dead matter of his days in other work. Work fills every gap, and if he cannot work, he must tirelessly analyze why. It is not until one has lived through so many days of Gide's life that one realizes how much modern man has replaced faith in another world with work in this one. Gide is never so Protestant as when he is counting up every minute of his time, and never so modern as in his belief that work will fill the spiritual vacuum. But if the ideal success has escaped him, there is always his journal. And so, consuming his life, he still has it.

Sixteen

THE SOLITUDE OF PAUL ROSENFELD

Reading *Voyager in the Arts,* a collection of tributes to Paul Rosenfeld, whose sudden death in 1946 cut off so astonishing a history of single-minded devotion to the arts in America, has been a curious and often moving experience for me. I knew him very slightly, had a deep affection for his work, but not always the strongest admiration, yet perhaps more than I had known, depended on him for a certain atmosphere and cultural loyalty. It therefore comes with something of a shock to see from these many tributes how little I had realized what the life of an independent critic of Rosenfeld's seriousness means in our present literary culture, and how peculiarly isolated, to the point of the deepest distress, a writer with his particular gifts could become. So many writers usually hostile to each other have found a common ground in their feeling for him that one has almost the sense of their forming a protective ring around his name and work, as if to make up for the bleakness of his last years. And perhaps involuntarily, they have joined to write a deeper history of our literary life than any critic has done. For going over his life and work here one cannot help feeling, as Edmund Wilson has said here in a particularly fine and affectionate tribute, "dismay and disgust at the waste of talent in the United States." It is ironic that the "community of temperament" that so many American writers miss, and that Rosenfeld certainly lacked in the widest and most imperative sense in the last years of his life, has been created here to honor him after his death.

So much of the material in the book is new to me that I can see how casually, like many writers of my generation, I took his services for granted. In my own case, oddly enough, I always went to his work with such instinctive sympathy that I was actually more conscious of his faults of style and the defects of his impressionistic method than of his value as a force in our criticism. We somehow read with the most grateful attention those writers who are most distant from us. From the day his *Port of New York* first introduced me to certain modern American painters and composers, I knew how much I owed him and even how much I would continue to rely on him. Yet I often found myself more aloof from his work than from many critics who are morally repugnant to me.

There were many reasons for this in the form rather than the spirit of Rosenfeld's work. But a deeper reason surely is the split in our present literary consciousness; permanently symbolized, I often think, in the influence of a writer like T. S. Eliot, who has continued to dominate the thought of two generations without ever being fundamentally challenged for his reactionary social-religious doctrine. The revolt against "softness" and "romanticism" in literature has carried with it a fear of the humanistic moral passion that is still the great heritage of our romantic and democratic past. And to this, in an age of increasing depersonalization and the outward hardness that conceals personal anxiety, has been joined the peculiarly contemporary fear of "mere" personal expressiveness. In our day the real princelings of criticism have been those who can manage, in some way or other, to sound like impersonal experts, and for whom the work before them is always an occasion for technical analysis or some sovereign re-definition of our lot. In one sense they have even set themselves up as rivals to the works before them, and have sought by their expertness to replace them with their own. This is not always difficult, and it is not entirely due to the presumption of critics. We live in a time when an overwhelming sense of having come to the end of a period in man's total history has put a premium on intellectual revaluation rather than on the literature of "real" experience. But it certainly leads to arid intellectual pride, and even, as there is no lack of examples around us to prove, patronage of artists themselves.

Rosenfeld's approach to art was so modest as to be, from this contemporary point of view, "naive." I agree with Lewis Mumford that there is no critic in our time who "approached the creations of other artists with so little envy and so much love, and who sought so insatiably for the moment of esthetic creation, as if, by surprising the artist at work, he might unlock the mysteries of life itself."

He grew up in one of those German-Jewish households of the early 1900's in upper middle-class New York that gave all their hopes to Culture, and particularly to the romantic doctrines of nineteenth-century German music. Among the last things Rosenfeld worked on was a translation of Robert Schumann's musical criticism, and in this sense he ended his career as he had begun it, transplanting a familiar sense of the human mission of art from the moral ruins of Germany to America. Up to 1929 Rosenfeld enjoyed a private income, and it is clear that he absorbed in his youth a kind of automatic social optimism and easy personal security that never prepared him for a period like that after 1930, when art in his sense of a religious vocation became a "tool" for politics or scientific analysis or even a cult with which to fill the spiritual vacuum. With his fine personal generosity and enthusiastic love of art, the Whitmanesque glow of *The Seven Arts* and the Stieglitz circle in New York, he could think of no finer career for himself than as a critic who would be a worker for the arts—above all, for particular artists. His personal friendship with artists and his struggles for them as a writer were intimately joined. Like James Gibbons Huneker, but with infinitely more delicacy and secure personal knowledge, he moved easily between music, painting and literature. He thought of himself, in Waldo Frank's phrase, as "a listener"; or as Wallace Stevens has put it, a "shaper"—someone who delighted in listening to and shaping back certain fundamental experiences, and who sought in the lyrical tides of his own prose to communicate his enjoyment to others.

How much Rosenfeld's work meant to many workers in the arts is made clear in this book by tributes not only from friends like Mumford, Waldo Frank, Edmund Wilson and Louise Bogan, but by unexpected appreciations from writers like Robert Penn Warren and several young composers. Yet his writing seems to have irritated many people in the last years. I have been wondering, while going over some of his essays in the light of this collective portrait, if his real fault was not that he took his personal experience of art with such passion that he simply embarrassed. It is taken for granted today that good writing is always "clean" and machine-made writing—writing that is happily uncluttered of all excess, complications of self, mere sentiment. Our new ideal in prose has been shaped by the sentimental toughness of our hard-boiled fiction, the jealousy of scientific "exactness" and the processing mills of our mass-circulation magazines, which have had to shape their product to the million. Rosenfeld's style was peculiarly that of an independent and an "amateur." He wrote in an effort to find the deepest personal associations in himself with the work before him. This meant struggle and even a kind of personal unashamedness that he did not mind leaving on the surface of his work. I will not say that his writing always satisfied me; there were confusions in its texture that suggest the transposition of musical tones into words. But it was inevitable, given his need to search out every work for its inner meaning in his own experience, that he should write with a guileless sincerity and a certain unconscious religious faith in the service of criticism that have simply gone out of fashion. We have more "flawless" critics today, but none, in Marianne Moore's lovely phrase, who are so "biased by imagination," none who are so ready to give themselves away to particular artists. And somehow, expert as they are, they are never so ready to tell us what a particular work of art can mean to our living.

Seventeen

FROM AN ITALIAN JOURNAL

He ought to have a hundred hands to write,
for what can a single pen do here. . . .
—Goethe: Rome, 1786

Florence, June 11, 1947—The night man at the hotel desk is a wizened, fatherly hunchback, with a face that belongs with the insignia of little keys fastened to the lapels of his official frock coat. In the hot and windless summer night, while millions of little green insects buzz around the flickering street lamps along the Arno, he bustles behind the bar, amused at our thirst, gently lifting stoppers from decanters and bringing up green and purple bottles from some mysterious cellar bin under his feet. An old magician doing his act for spellbound children, he first pours out a little of this and then a little of that, pretending to look amazed at their instant transfusion, and as he squeezes the soda over the highly colored surface, cries out *Eccola!*—but with a patient solicitousness that says plainly that while nothing will relieve our thirst if we insist on it so impatiently, he will go on inquiring into bottle after bottle, if we wish.

The lounge is an old family parlor, with the rubber plant on a lace doily over the upright piano, heavy brass-framed pictures of hunting dogs and "The Stag at Eve," and old copies of *The*

Illustrated London News. A withered English blonde sits in one corner, reading *The Times,* and from time to time calls across the lounge in a piercing "Oxford" accent, recounting to another *inglese* her difficulties with the Italian law, "so unnecessarily complicated." She has come back to reclaim a house bought before the war. In another corner a man with the burned-out face of Oswald Spengler: completely bald, shaven head, rock-like Prussian military skull, burning little eyes, a fierce wide scar running across his left cheek and deep into his neck like a singed envelope. Junker face, haughty with suffering: he never looks at anyone, and prowls around the lounge smoking cigarettes out of a long jeweled holder.

All signs and instructions are first in English, then in French, and occasionally underwritten in Italian. The atmosphere is that of a provincial British hotel in an eternity of Sundays, though *they* "no longer come to us as they used to. They, too, are passing through difficult days." Americans, of course, are wonderful—so gay, so young, etc.; but the manager's daughter, whose English is impeccable B.B.C., complains with a little pout that her friends laugh at her—"my accent has become a little coarse"—since the GI's were here.

To the left the Ponte Vecchio; to the right the provisional iron structure that has replaced the Santa Trinita. The gallery that led from the Uffizi Gallery to the Pitti is broken in the middle; on both sides of the Ponte Vecchio a jagged heap of ruins, lit up under the solitary street lamp, has that crumpled, uncovered look of scenery the minute the footlights are turned off. In the daytime the ruins look peculiarly incongruous, a tabloid headline in an illuminated manuscript, against the round towers and the slender cypresses, each cluster of them supreme on its hill. The Germans were on one side of the river and the Americans on the other; hard to think of Florence being fought over on this street.

At the noon hour an old man in an old boat, moored in the middle of the Arno just below our window, patiently dredging up mud from the bottom, hour by hour, which he as patiently packs up on every side of him. Across the way a little boy swimming off a little delta that has formed in front of his house. A scull shoots by, propelled by a young man in tights and blazer and wearing that smart little beard—Dino Grandi, Italo Balbo—why did I think it was worn only by Fascist aviators and ambassadors? Just below the embankment, on the other side of the river, the familiar whitewash slogan we saw on every wall coming down from Genoa: *VOTATE PER IL P. COMUNISTA CHE VI DARÀ PACE LAVORO LIBERTÀ.*

June 12—Ran into P., who was born in New York of Italian parentage and originally came here before the war to finish a medical course. An ex-GI and, of course, armed with the precious green passport: which will do for us what Roman citizenship once did for St. Paul. He gets around familiarly in American army circles from Leghorn to Pisa and has the friendliest relations with the brass. With the tough-faced pal who is saddled on us every time we see him, he is engaged in some elaborate financial exchange deal that obviously pays off (the lire today 650 to the dollar; some weeks ago it was 900). They go around Florence with great wads of lire stuffed into one of those vertical leather zipper bags that are sold at home for packing a bottle of whisky into a suitcase. The pal, who might be an extra in a gangster film, is bursting with prosperity; explained things to me with a condescension that did not hide his awe at my ignorance. Funny to see him standing under the statue of Lorenzo the Magnificent, the latest *New Yorker* in one hand and that moneybag in the other, looking like an Oklahoma Indian who has just discovered oil.

P. is a sensitive guy, and a little pathetic—the medical degree is indefinitely postponed, and his life at the moment is simply that of a British planter self-exiled to Kenya, piling it up for the wife and kiddies at home. He wants to make what he can in this crazy period and then clear out. Yet despite some vague efforts to dissociate himself slightly from his pal, at least in our eyes, there is no doubt that he is having the time of his life. The thing's absolutely unreal: he's way up there, in that new American world in Europe. After years of being a nobody at home, and no doubt a "Wop" to the Gentiles, he is now making the most of his Italian-American background, dines with generals, and with the best will in the world, patronizes the old country. Actually he does not seem to like the Italians very much—says they "simply have no character," and with a certain intellectual disapproval outlines the black-market situation to me, specifying that the government does not govern, that the whole economy rests on private buying and selling, and that the political situation is absolutely hopeless, divided between the priests and the Commies. Personally, he assures me, he is a democratic socialist, and rails against Nenni for surrendering the Italian Socialist Party to the Communists. But this with a blasé, mocking air, as if to say: what can you expect of these people? Funny to think of him among the smart American promoters and finaglers who are here to pick up some easy money, for with all his amiable commercial guile and know-it-all air, he really *hates* Italy for letting him down, morally, so hard. Isabel Archer and Christopher Newman and Hemingway's tough American ingénues: somehow the pattern never changes. How *could* Europe be like this? Still, caught in between the two great blocs, a vacuum has been created here, which obviously some natures do not abhor. There's money in it. Yet notice how these two American types, P. and his pal, respond to their opportunity—the pal frankly a good deal of a mug, indifferent to those who cannot play it smart; P., with his typical American intellectual's contempt for politics, yearning for democratic socialism, but meanwhile unable to forgive "Europe" for destroying his personal illusions—which, if he had saved them, would have left his wife and kids at home in a precarious situation. What a difference from those old British traveling salesmen, with their contempt for the natives and their quietly expert managerial ways!

June 13—In the great Duomo, Santa Maria del Fiore, above the altar in the choir, Christ hangs supine on his cross, but wearing a golden crown that is much too large for his head. His knees are upraised, as if he had been struggling with death, and the paralysis had struck him where he fought; but his whole body slopes downward with a weariness in which I feel the weight of the ages. Every line of him is cast in pain, renunciation, and silence. Yet here he is Christ the King, and so named not by his enemies in mockery, but his own Church. At the foot of the altar, a young monk sweeping the red cloth and smoothing out the breaks in the carpet. How strange it is to pass behind the altar and, looking down the whole length of Christ's poor, bent figure, twisted into the deepest suffering and hopelessness, so forlorn above the ornate altar—how strange to realize that the sculptor perhaps overdid it—see that here he looks not a king but a scarecrow, and that the crown which is so large for his head expresses not so much amazement and homage before him who undertook so much, as the condescension of authority to its own figurehead.

The faces of young monks, like the faces of young girls in the climax of adolescence—both meeting in the same corridor, but the one going back as the other goes forward.

June 15—Sunday—Nenni spoke this morning in the great "town square," the Piazza della Signoria. By ten the Lungarno was jammed with workers walking or riding along to the meeting in trucks—the old men a little sedate, buttoned up into frayed jackets despite the blisteringly hot day; the youngsters cheering, singing, and gaily waving their red flags. The girls looked wonderful. Everyone says that they have been liberated since the war, and they certainly look it as they come tearing along on their bicycles, flapping their sandals against the pedals, with their long, black hair streaming behind. A band trotted along blaring out the Garibaldi hymn and *Bandiera Rossa*. It was all like a light-hearted Sunday excursion en masse—the sun sparkling on the river and the long white sheets hung out of the windows; uncovering depth on depth of green out of the trees. Staggered with sun, drunk with light. I feel these days as if my body had grown taste buds all around it, and every cell were eating at Italy without getting its fill.

At the meeting itself the beauty and unexpectedness of the scene were so overwhelming that at first I could hardly give attention to what was being said. In an angle of the enormous square two contrasting structures—the Old Palace (really the City Hall) on one side; startlingly unaged, its gay and arrogant tower suddenly rearing itself with a kind of deceptive lightness up from behind the row of battlements. On the other the Loggia dei Lanzi, crammed with statuary, set below the Palace like a sideboard at a great feast of stone. There is about the Palace at one side a curiously scalloped and rippling effect, as if the architect had omitted some base to its rhythmic structure and then made it up—with what triumph and ease—in the upward leap of the tower, which gives that exhilarating effect of humor in its own authority. (And in fact something was omitted, for I learn that the architect was forbidden to use any of the ground that had belonged to the hated Ghibelline family of the Uberti.)

The speakers held forth from the Loggia. We stood in the center of the square, near the tablet that marks the place of Savonarola's execution. If one tired of Nenni or the meeting, one could always regale oneself with the Palace, the centerpiece of Neptune, and the reproduction of Michelangelo's David which stands just before the door of the Palace. Nenni must have felt as if he were discoursing from the Florentine Acropolis; there were little compliments and expressions of pride on addressing the citizenry from that celebrated place. He stood behind a loud-speaker, his arms toiling furiously with the conventional Italian vigor, but his face impassive as an owl's under his heavy spectacles. A dumpy little man, bald and round, looking like a union boss at a convention, sweating away, while behind him "The Rape of the Sabine Women," "Hercules Slaying the Centaur Nessus," and Cellini's Perseus—the bloody sword in one hand and with the other majestically holding aloft, with his cool and savage gravity, the head of Medusa. Yet no doubt even Lorenzo the Magnificent must have looked dwarfed and a little mean in that mighty piazza, or Savonarola haranguing the Florentines on their immoral ways—for the whole effect of the Piazza della Signoria is to create in an instant the civic and aesthetic presence of a great city-state. There is something in the ensemble formed by the Palace, the Loggia, the Neptune and the David, the color and weight of the stone, the very historical imagination embodied in a European square, that makes the impervious surface of a fully completed thought. With the imprint still on us of those cramped, functional cities created purely out of commercial relationships, we enter into this piazza with a disbelief almost stronger than our pleasure, as if we were of another race from those who built *this;* as if, with its obvious indifference to anything we might think of it, it could vanish the minute we turned our backs on it.

Not the place, I would have said, for a tired old Social Democrat leading a "popular front" rally. Certainly everything about Nenni himself is commonplace, and brings up thoughts of those battered but crafty relics of the Second International who have decided, after years of futility, to float to success on the Stalinist wave of the future. L. finds Nenni's stubbornness on the Communist issue typical of the Romagna—Mussolini's region—and draws many parallels between their attitudes toward Italian Socialism. But why make it a question of personal traits? Nenni is only another expression of the long, inner defeatism of European socialism, and obviously scared by the prestige and the mass base the Communists built up during the war. According to P., who recently talked with him, Nenni's pro-Communist line is a gamble. Privately Nenni says: "Sooner or later the Russians are going to take over. It's in the cards. I'm for us to become a Czechoslovakia rather than a Poland or Bulgaria." The Communists dominate the largest section of the working class—if the Socialists separate themselves from them, Nenni says, what happens to their mass base? Half the workers in the Milanese factories hold cards in the C.P. Probably the greater part of the crowd this morning was Communist, to judge from the yells and cheers that went up whenever Nenni flattered the party. Yet I noticed that easily the most popular part of his speech was his strong declaration that Italy should remain neutral in any war between Russia and the U.S. Nenni has to keep a lot of people happy at once.

R. drove us out to Settignano to see the Bernard Berenson villa, *I Tatti*. In the courtyard, which might have been the entrance to one of the retreats at which the storytellers in the *Decameron* flourished during the plague, there was a row of neat little lemon trees, each set in its black bucket with finicky care. The lemons all drooped in a plane, exactly at an equal distance from the ground—with what immense and induced art it was not difficult to imagine. The elaborated niceness of the symmetry introduced me to Berenson's mind even before I met him.

The butler seemed uncertain whether to admit us, Berenson

being away, but Leo Stein,* Gertrude's brother, whom R. knows slightly, came out of the library and offered to show us around. Stein is a tall, gentle, gangling old man, now seventy-five, who looks like a Jewish Uncle Sam—very rustic, nervous, deaf, but full of talk and little wisecracks, all of them delivered in such a flat, uncompromised Middle Western twang after his thirty or forty years of Italy, that it was strange in that braided garden to take in his mussed, blue serge suit and hearing aid, the knapsack over one shoulder. He sounded out like the authentic voice of Allegheny, Pa.

The Berenson house very beautiful and quietly massed with treasures, but almost too exquisite to walk in. It is like a private chapel raised to the connoisseur's ideal experience, where every corridor and corner has been worked to make a new altarpiece, and where the smallest detail reveals the mind of a man who has the means to reject all intrusions of mere necessity. He has shaped the whole with an inflexible exactness of taste that is just a little chilling. Curiously, its greatest effect is not so much to lead you to its pictures as to shame you into a fresh realization of how awkward, soiled, and generally no-account life can seem compared with art. In the dim light of the shaded corridors those Sienese saints gaze past you, lost in their own dream of time and interred in an oily gloss—their faces tortured with thought and goodness, and somehow *away,* bearing your praise and awe with equal indifference. What golden and mysterious fish!

I noticed how jumpy Stein became when we stopped too long before some pictures. Of course, showing his friend Berenson's house must have been a bore; he had been in and out of the place for years, and comes almost daily now to work in the library. Yet I was a little surprised, knowing of his life-long concern with painting, to hear him confess that it was not the work

* He died later in the summer, some weeks after our meeting.

of art that mattered to him so much as the mind of the painter. He is very much preoccupied with all sorts of psychological questions and told us that he had just (at seventy-five) finished psychoanalyzing himself. The devouring interest of his life was to discover why men lie. This is something that evidently touches him very deeply. While he had been showing us pictures and rooms with a certain irritation, and made affectionate, mocking little digs at Berenson's expense (their rivalry is famous), he suddenly, in Berenson's study, went off into a long discourse about psychology and the need for scientific exactness in determining character. He spoke with a kind of uneasy intensity, as if he had been held in on this topic for a very long time, and wanted our understanding with or without our "approval." It was of the greatest importance to him, this practice of lying; it would be a key to all sorts of crucial questions, if only he could get his hands on the solution; it was, you might say, at the center of human ambiguity. As he went on he would look up at us every so often, pull irritably at his hearing aid, and grumble: "What? What? You think what? I can't hear you!" riding impatiently over us and his deafness for standing in his way, and rearing up against our passing comments with a loud cry, very moving in an old man, which seemed to come straight from the heart: "It's important! It's the big thing! No one looks these facts in the face! Animals can't lie and human beings lie all the time!"

He was, however, very happy these days; had got over a bad illness and was just publishing a new book* in the States; there was a lot of work ahead of him. He talked about his writing with a mingled anxiety and enthusiasm, as if he were just starting out on his career; though very frail, he gave the appearance of a young writer speculating dreamily on all the books he is going to write. I should have caught on sooner, but didn't until

* *Appreciation: Painting, Poetry, and Prose,* 1947.

we went into Fiesole to have a drink: he had always suffered from a bad case of being Gertrude Stein's half-noticed elder brother, and now that she was dead probably felt liberated to go on with his own career. His resentment of her shone through everything he said. Talking about their childhood in Europe, when they had been trundled around by a father "who didn't think we could get any kind of decent education in America," he remembered most how Gertrude had always lorded it over him. "But you know," he said simply, "she was the kind who always took herself for granted. I never could." And one saw that she had dominated the situation when they had decided to make their lives in Europe. "She always took what she wanted! She could always talk her way into anything! Why,"—discussing her pioneer collection of modern paintings—"she never even *liked* Picasso at first! Couldn't see him at all. *I* had to convince her. And then she caught on and got 'em for practically nothing." After all those years, the bitterness rankled, keeping him young. How often, I wonder, has he been approached only as a lead to his famous sister, and this by people who haven't the slightest knowledge of his interests? It must be this, added to his long uncertainty about himself, which lends that strangely overemphatic quality to his interest in "facts." Facts—the masculine domain of elder brothers humbly and grimly toiling away at *real* things, like aesthetics and psychology, where Gertrude, the mother of them all, took the young geniuses under her wing and, always the last of the feminists, did as she pleased—even to putting the English language in her lap like a doll, and making it babble out of her inscrutable naturalness and humor. *She always did as she pleased.* Strange to see him now, at his age, going back and back to the old childhood struggle. They had transferred the cultural rivalry in that prosperous Jewish family to Europe and worked it in and out of the expatriate life, making of Paris and Florence new outposts for an old ambition.

Rome, Oct. 28—Berenson. I had missed him in Settignano, but went to see him today at his hotel just off Trinità dei Monti. It was very cold, and he sat in a corner of the sofa with a rug over his knees, precise as one of his own sentences. Eighty-two: delicate little *élégant* with a little white beard, very frail, an old courtier in his beautiful clothes, every inch of him engraved fine into an instrument for aesthetic responsiveness and intelligence. He spoke English with such purity and beauty of diction, blandly delivering himself of his words, one by one, that he might have been putting freshly cracked walnuts into my hand. He took me in quickly, quietly, absolutely. "Your name is of course Russian and no doubt you are a Jew? There seem to be so many young Jews writing in the States these days. How is that? Quite a difference from my time!" "Oh! and is there much anti-Semitism in the States these days? Oh!" He was extremely attentive; it was all, one was left to gather, a distant but not uninteresting fact to him, himself a Jew, "born in Lithuania, in the Jewish aristocracy, the old gentry," and taken at a very early age to Boston. Being a "Jewish aristocrat" has probably always been his *carte de visite* in the outside world, from President Eliot's Harvard to Henry James's London, as it was so immediately a way of dissociating himself gently from any possible entanglements he may have incurred by interesting himself in American Jewish life. To be a Jewish aristocrat does not diminish one's foreignness, but transfers it to another plane—like that Negro who went South with a turban on his head and was welcomed everywhere as a foreign potentate.

He reads everything; there was even a copy of that shabby little *Rome Daily American* on his lap when I came in, and it is curious how incongruous he makes anything so typically journalistic and American look in his presence, so unbroken is the effect of elegance he gives to any room he sits in. Every day he goes through at least one Italian, French, Swiss, and English newspaper; takes all the reviews and magazines, even *Time.* It was all out of an intense curiosity in the political behavior of the human animal. Remembering his extraordinary library, one had a picture of him at *I Tatti* as another Voltaire at Ferney, a kind of European intelligence office—yet subtly remote from the pressure of events, each of which he put away in some chamber of his apparatus for meditation. He kept coming back to Henry Miller, whose works he knew fully, and whom he detested. He vaguely shared my admiration for that moving long story in *Sunday After the War* which recounts Miller's return to his parents' home, but with this thought under consideration he turned Miller into a dreary historian of the imponderable petty-bourgeois bleakness of Brooklyn rather than the "cloacal" and confused rebel he had just dismissed. He said "cloacal" in a way that made me see all the refuse coming up from the bottom of the Tiber and gathering itself into the collected works of Henry Miller. And of course I shared in the general illusion that Kafka was a great writer? "There is a very small light of reason burning in the world," he said reflectively. "Mr. Kafka tries to put it out." He had exact, firm judgments on everything that crossed his path; his years, his fortune, his snobbery, and his taste have given him a freedom in getting past conventions that is highly stimulating if not very satisfying—it is as if he were surveying the present from a point removed in sympathy; I miss that quality which alone makes a thinker interesting, his commitment to the living. We were talking about the cultural inertia and provincialism which become deeply felt after one settles into Italy, and he thought the decline had set in with the Risorgimento—which is curious not because there is any lack of skepticism today in Italy about the vaunted traditions of the Risorgimento, but because of the example that immediately came to his mind. One was left to infer that the cultural elite had surrendered its prerogatives. Why, in his first years in Italy one could still pick up from Roman push-carts first editions of English eighteenth-century novels which had come straight from the shelves of the old nobility. He finds Italians now lacking in individuality. Curious to see how he touches on all these things quite outside the realm of historical development; he goes straight to fundamental themes of *style*. The long romance with Italy is probably over—obviously "Italy" the aesthetic concept, Italy as he first knew it and as he has retained it at his villa with such devotion and finesse, has had to bear the burden of a certain jarring or contradiction under the pressure of recent events. There must be odd infringements on so exquisite a connoisseur's existence that make one reflect on how hard it is to possess fully everything we buy in this world.

We talked about his old friend Santayana, who is living not far away as a guest of the Nuns of the Blue Sisters—they no longer see each other. Curious to think of these two old intellectual grandees finishing out their lives in Italy, the one a Spaniard and the other a Lithuanian Jew, but both formed by their early life in Boston and at Harvard. They were together at the Boston Latin School, at Harvard, and in Germany thereafter—Santayana always one year ahead, as he is one year older. He greatly admires Santayana, and it was only when talking about him that he seemed younger and less *distingué* than anyone else you ever heard of—but they are estranged, and to judge from the oily and characteristically malicious tone Santayana takes to him in his memoirs, the friendship ended on his side rather than on Berenson's. In Santayana's eyes, Berenson was simply a pushing Jew; he has never liked Jews who do not know their place; despite the magnificent presence, the *soigné* air, the echoes of Pater and Matthew Arnold, the great fortune built up by Berenson as a consultant to millionaire collectors, the villa, and the "Jewish aristocracy" of Lithuania, one is compelled, after sixty years, to recall Berenson as a young immigrant given his start by Mrs. Jack Gardner. But how he looks up to Santayana, and how he rejects the faintest criticism of that great man, who is always the idol of nonphilosophic minds who are never quite sure what he is getting at! Berenson himself hadn't read the Santayana memoirs; his secretary told him not to, he would be too distressed. And very pleasantly and understandably, he didn't care about men like Whitehead—pure thinkers who thought about thinking. Yet I was not to offer the slightest possible irreverence on the subject of Santayana—my faint complaint being his addiction to pseudo-classic Wisdom. In some way Santayana's life has always been a touchstone for his own—the manner conceals an extraordinary humility, it seems. And meanwhile there is Santayana in his convent cell and Berenson in his villa: not "expatriates," not "Americans," simply unbound to any particular country. Both with that strange formative early life in New England, and with no place to go back to, the last New England heroes of the James saga, yet quietly and firmly superior to all national limitations—truly citizens of the world, and discoursing of essential things, above all contemporary battles, in an English that comes straight down to us from the Boston of seventy years ago.

Florence, June 16—Café scene in the Piazza della Repubblica, which everyone absentmindedly still calls the Piazza Vittorio Emanuele. In the moonlight hundreds of people sitting at those long lines of tables, row on row, between the hedges of rubber plants that mark off one café from another; an audience waiting to make its own play. Wonderful to watch the long appraising stares, like an expert judging horseflesh, with which these open-air troglodytes look each newcomer up and down. No one misses a thing. They may look bored and weary to death, with scales over their half-closed eyes, sipping indifferently at their miniscule cup of *espresso* as if there were all the time in the world and they had been sitting here, with that same cup of coffee, spoon, and water carafe, since the Etruscans. But in the air the preparatory vapors of a seduction; these are buds that open only at night. As soon as a new one walks into the lighted den, making the grand tour up and around the long line of tables, faint waves radiate from brains chattering with thought and speculation. Ah, some more of the *Americani.* The waiter in his soiled and patched evening clothes grins and bows; the three whores glumly sitting together go through the girls with unforgiving eyes like one of those electric signal boxes in a prison corridor that ring an alarm bell if there is any metal on your person. The cigarette vendors come screeching around like a flock of gulls maddened by the smell of food off the ship's bow—old, young, sick, every age and every human condition, each of them with his little suitcase held out before him like a tray. *Sigarette? . . . Nazionali . . . Americane!* Every five minutes a beggar appears at the table—usually old women with black shawls and the look of the eternal mother of sorrows, leading little barefoot girls whose faces are so gray and bent with suffering, whose arms hang so miserably at their sides as if they had been scratching old sores, that you find yourself either responding to the situation or rewarding the impersonation. Under the table more barefoot kids in discarded GI pants and American Air Force jackets, hunting cigarette ends and storing them carefully in little tin pails; it will all go to make "new" American cigarettes. In the history of Europe this age should go down as that of the Pax Americana, or the second-hand butt.

The beggars cover the café in waves; they make sure never to come up together or at too close intervals, and while one makes his rounds the others stand at the hedge, like actors waiting to go on. Notice how the Italians give, every time. They may look indifferent and after the tenth approach exasperated beyond words, but after shrugging their shoulders or trying the frontal attack method (*Signora! Have mercy! Do you think I'm the Bank of Italy?*) they come up with the usual. The crucial test comes when someone at a table tries to look away. Hopeless. The beggar simply keeps turning with him and stares him down.

In the brilliantly humming summer night all these café dwellers, each moored in his cultural swamp, gently pushing at the world outside like a fly caught in a dish of honey. The faces lack that paunchy, pasty look of the normally overfed at home: here you can actually see the bony structure brought into the world at birth. The general level of good looks is amazing: face after face with that focused sensuality that is always the personal ticket of young actors and actresses. Most of them emptily looking out to sea, or engaged in a little deal. The air is damp with sex, but you can hear sums being recited at table after table; the whole piazza is one great bourse for the black market. *Centotrenta lire . . . centosessanta . . . tremila quaranta.* A fierce-looking boy in his late teens rides up on a bicycle and unerringly goes straight to the American faces and clothes. Will you buy American cigarettes—real *American* cigarettes, not counterfeit? Wanna change your money, mista! Heh, mista? Will you for God's sake *sell* him something? You think he hasn't got the money? Takes out a great wad of sweaty lire. "Listen!" he says disgustedly, about to ride off—"I'll buy anything you got! ANYTHING!" Funny in that place to hear the long wailing singsong of the cigarette vendors, which as the evening drags on becomes simply: "America!"

Rome, Sept. 3—Almost impossible to find a book of Silone's in the shops, but everyone goes at him constantly—as if he were not simply a legend brought from overseas who writes "bad Italian," but a convenience to everyone's sense of superiority. It is very tiring to hear him knocked down with the same contemptuous phrases by every literary creature one meets. Even

C., who does those little articles and cartoons for the Socialist press, and may fairly be described as an amiable hack of not overpowering gifts, loves to discourse on the "outside world's" absurd overestimation of Silone—it puts him right in style, and gives him the only point of contact he has with opinion outside Italy. "You people cannot imagine how crudely he writes," and screwing up his shoulders with that well-worn Mediterranean gesture which denotes some intractable human error or folly, takes up the argument after everyone at the table had given it up as hopeless: "Silone! Always Silone! You people have never heard of anyone else!"

He writes, it seems, badly; he is a "political," not really a man of letters—a deputy, an active Socialist, editor of his own political weekly, etc.; he does not shine in conversation, but is in fact a depressed and depressing character; his reputation is out of all proportion to the real situation in Italian writing. The main point, obviously, is that Italian intellectuals are not disposed to honor a novelist who has been pushed at them as a symbol of the "real," the anti-Fascist, Italy. Curious situation: on the one hand there is a certain defensiveness about compliance with a regime which only the boldest cared to defy head-on, and which, as they say, "was after all, not so bad as Hitler. You have no idea how easygoing it was. With us, even authoritarian government is always a little bit of a joke." I have noticed that even Gaetano Salvemini's return has aroused mixed feelings—"he criticizes too much." On the other hand, whatever moral debt some Italians may have incurred for Fascism, none of them is likely to feel any great repentance now, considering the misery into which so many have been plunged after being bombed, pillaged, and cheated up and down the peninsula. They are understandably furious with those Anglo-Americans who were Mussolini's really *sincere* admirers, and then worked their precious moral superiority both ways—denouncing them first for Fascism and then laughing at them for its ineffectuality. The modern Italians are, anyway, oversensitive on every question of prestige, and are now even more so, with so much of the country's economy pinned to the black market. They are annoyed with those who approach them on set political lines—who go around like L., that proverbial American liberal, saying in effect: "Your country is beautiful and I have the greatest admiration for your leading writers, Mr. Dante and Mr. Silone. But are *you* quite free of sin?"

Mrs. C. told me that *Fontamara* was a terrible book and that the first she had seen of it was an Italian edition sent over especially by Silone's English publisher—not easy for them to take that! And he is not a "literary" writer, a deep matter in a country where style works on writers like a narcotic. ("My greatest pleasure," said A., who is very intelligent, "is spending a morning polishing my paragraphs.") So Silone is considered a gross writer, and with so much of his time taken up with inter-Socialist politics, a curiosity. Yet harsh and peculiarly personal as so many of these attacks are—essential to Italian self-esteem—there *is* a curious muddleheadedness to Silone which I can see more clearly here than I could at home. He has gone through an intense religious evolution without getting out of the shell of party Marxism, and up to recently kept up with Nenni and the anti-Communist opposition in the Socialist movement out of some vague idea of reconciling them. But essentially, as P. says, he is disliked because he personifies the one type the Italians cannot take—the moral dissenter. "He simply will not reduce everything to the canonical Italian level of the 'family affair.' " Similarly one can see that the personal character of his Socialism represents more and more a longing to get back to the immediate human relatedness with peasants and artisans he enjoyed in his early days in the Abruzzi. What I have always loved in Silone is his feeling for the bottom people—a fact that would be equally admired in Italy if he did not let the intellectuals feel that he is making dour ethical judgments on *them*. But the peasant types whom Carlo Levi described in *Christ Stopped at Eboli* with such easy detachment, creatures of living mythology and native farce, are to Silone just those "who do not betray." He may be muddled and intolerably gloomy, but he is striking out for unfashionable values. In Catholic Italy it is very queer to take Christianity that seriously.

Sept. 5—Rome keeps eluding me, as Florence never did, or even Assisi—the one almost too perfectly pure in style, the other simply mysterious, lost to our age like a buried city. I knew in Assisi that I must remain outside it, that I could not reach across the wall of old sacredness, and was content to be amazed and to go away. But Rome makes everything initially so easy and yet ends by being the greatest enigma of all.

And this is not because the past has made a camouflage city over the "real" one, an historic patina barring the depths to the city's inner life. I had expected it to be so, but what is astonishing here is the realization that all these streets and streets of gray, Baroque church fronts, old stones, arches, inscriptions, temples, palaces are casually interwoven with the greater modern city and are entirely lacking the "picturesque." The city is not *grand*. Except for that hideous birthday cake, the Vittorio Emanuele monument, and the great sweeping roads which Mussolini erected to the Colosseum, there is nothing imperious about Rome as there is about Washington or the Paris laid out by Baron Haussmann. The greater part of it has a softly informal quality, as if the stone had rotted over the dark cramped streets like vegetation, and the over-ripe gourds of Baroque churches had begun to melt at the edges, emitting a thin juice of blood and dirt. The city always seems small without ever being compact. It was not until I came to the Pincio along the park, and looked down on the city, with its domes, obelisks, and spires upflashing in the sun like an heraldic coat of arms, that I realized how enormous are those churches which, when you pass their doors, seem to obtrude, each over its little front of street, like an old chatelaine barring the way.

It is perhaps just this long inner weathering, softening, crampening that makes the city immediately so *easy,* as if it had been used up and used up, generation after generation, and now had no pretense with anyone. Yet it is in this very blandness and intimacy with which Rome takes you in, this lack of outward "surface," that ambiguity begins. Here the remains of the successive generations have been piled up and piled up with such indifference that they finally melt into equivalent phases of the same weariness with time. People say: "How amazing that the various periods blend so well." How amazing, rather, that the city should still be able to absorb them all and keep us equidistant in time from each. The obelisk in the Piazza del Popolo is as "Roman" now as the great stone goddess dumped into a corner of the courtyard of the Palazzo Venezia; the statue of Marcus Aurelius in the Campidoglio, the Palazzo Farnese, the temple of the vestal virgins along the Tiber, that great heap of Latin Rome set up like a goldfish bowl in the middle of the Piazza Argentina, those Baroque churches on the Corso, behind those sooty fronts of European gray which always look as if they had been trod over by millions of feet in the long procession of Christendom, churches where the gilt and coiled pillars writhe and mount in irreversible dreams of splendor, in a style that summons back the death agony of empires—all, seen week after week, take on an impossible unity of experience. Returning late last night along the Via del Babbuino, I noticed in the corridor of a small house a wall decorated with shards off some Roman wall, and had this strange picture in my mind of Rome today wearing its own past as slyly as a savage decked out in the glass beads and metal crucifixes donated by missionaries.

Nov. 8—E. T., whom I used to see in that 23rd Street cafeteria scribbling away at his anti-Fascist novels, and who was almost the type of the Italian anarchist, with his unworldliness, his ungovernable *brio,* his fifteen or seventeen years of prison under Mussolini, and his fierce dislike of Communist totalitarians (he even spent some weeks on Riker's Island for beating one up), has since his deportation suddenly blossomed out as the C.P.'s anti-American expert. I have been reading in *L'Unità* an article by him which announces the following facts to the Italian proletariat: (1) Truman is a gangster; (2) this is so because he got his political start from the Pendergast gang in Kansas City; (3) there used to be a Capone gang in Chicago, and Chicago is very near Kansas City; (4) there is also a Tammany gang in New York, which is connected with political gangs in Washington and Chicago; (5) Q.E.D., America is dominated by gangsters.

Nov. 15—Our "landlord," Prince L., has gone off for a few days and there is a meek little retired sea captain in his studio who is elaborately deferent to us on all occasions. Came over to my window this morning and asked me to have a coffee with him, to discuss the writer's problems. He is doing a fantasy on the Third World War, the point of which is that America will assuredly lose it. Not a Communist but an old-fashioned liberal—"my only politics is Italy." But he has soaked up the C.P. line with such thoroughness that I can spare myself much study by listening to him. All strikes are forbidden in America; Lewis was put in jail for starting one; Negroes are lynched weekly in New York and Chicago; the ruling class is itching to use the atom bomb on Russia, and will drop some on Italy if the workers seize power. Russia? He shrugs: a far-off country, run by Oriental despots; it does not interest him; he is *not* a Communist. But America has all the wealth and all the ships and all the bombs and is mad to rule the world. "You may be amiable, but you have everythin and we have nothing."

Dec. 1—Dinner with Silone and Carlo Levi in a sweltering mo at the pizzeria *Il Re degli Amici*—accordion players, Neapolita blues singers, a grotesque one-man band loaded front and bac with instruments and beating time to the upward and dow ward surge of a rusty black derby squeezed over his eyes, wande ing beggars and nuns collecting alms. Sociability unlimited, th café of all good Roman artists, Socialists, and Actionists—th beautiful Italian bedlam and intellectual merriment, people cal ing and flirting from table to table: all one great family part Always at such moments, as when walking the streets at noo and feeling the relatedness of people to each other, the fami motif binding Italians together seems stronger than the pe sonality of each one. I keep thinking of a dance on the villag green.

Even Silone looked almost gay tonight, though taking adva tage of Levi's valiant efforts to speak English, which he pr tends not to understand at all, he put his face in a great mass o fish, meat, and greens, and remained dolorously alone with hi own thoughts. Levi in his most resplendent mood and most car free costume, with a crazy fur cap given him by a Florentin carriage driver and a long checked overcoat straight out o Harold Teen. Falstaff in a zoot suit, grinning from ear to ea the most pagan of all the Jews. He looks like a Roman senato out on the street, and glad of it. Everything interests him, ever strand in Italian politics, art, and gossip runs through his hand as he talks. As he sits there, papa at the head of the table, sighin one minute for the New York girls, the other relating stories o Florence under the occupation, imperturbably self-centered as child but bringing up light and gaiety on all possible subject by his delight in his appetites and his own mind, one thinks o

Bacon's discovery that *the plant, man, grows more vigorous in Italy*. Paints in the morning, writes in the afternoon, rounds out his day with a cartoon for *Italia socialista,* and then makes his grand entrance here, an old stogy in his mouth, amiable as a Congressman back home on Main Street—the pinnacle of Italian self-enjoyment. Tells me with enormous relish that he did a cartoon satirizing Nenni lost in the Communist jungle, and that Nenni, misunderstanding, called up to congratulate him. Reports that the people he described in *Christ Stopped at Eboli,* which recounts his confinement for three years under Fascism, have taken to wearing markers on their clothes reading: "I am a character in Carlo Levi's *Christ Stopped at Eboli.*" What will you have? It is a marvelous people, the Italians! And he sits there, roaring his head off, making eyes at every pretty girl who passes. The years have hardly worn at him; he shares in everything and belongs to no one—it has all gone into a *bouillabaisse* of experience—the times in and out of prison, the period of exile in Lucania when, as a political prisoner with no other way of reaching the people but his early training as a physician, he discovered for the Italians themselves the most impoverished and beaten section of the peasantry; and now postwar Rome, out of which he protrudes with undiminished force, and every aspect of whose life he makes seem as local to his own as if he were the neighborhood scribe, writing letters for all the peasants in the village.

Curious to watch Silone and Levi together—both men of the same generation, both formed entirely outside the shell of Fascism and characteristically better known in other countries than in their own, fundamental types of the writer "engaged" to action, yet so different in mind and temperament that the extremes of the Italian character have been called on to produce them—the one awkwardly self-conscious, soured with political and literary disappointments ("He has been told so often he is a bad novelist," M. says, "he is ready to believe it"), but a man who defends sadly the most creative urgings of our age; the other riding the cres of the wave, hearty and ineffably self-assured, relying on hi Italianism for every experience. In the "outside world" people are beginning to compare them, to find in them tokens of the "new" Italy; here the formula simply doesn't operate—the Silone one knows is not to be found in a crazy-quilt evening, but in his work, with its scruples, its awkward tenderness, and its humor— and the work is no longer separable here from Italy; it is one more chapter in the inner history of the Italian masses.

And afterward, toiling home through the cold, stopping for an *espresso,* admiring the nymphs in the Piazza del Popolo, a bag of chestnuts from the old woman on the corner warming herself at the fire, while in the faint light of the lamps in the park, just beyond Michelangelo's gates, that Roman god and emperor whose name I have never learned still stands with his arm half-raised, beautiful and indifferent.

Eighteen

THE WRITER'S FRIEND

Editor to Author, the letters of Maxwell Perkins, edited by John Hall Wheelock, was, on its appearance some time ago, politely and noncommittally reviewed, in deference to Perkins' great reputation as chief editor of Scribner's for twenty years. I wonder why everyone has been so careful, at least in print, not to mention the fact that the letters themselves are distinguished mainly by their humility. For it is just their awkward affection for his writers, their painful efforts to put into words his veneration of the writer's craft, that impress upon anyone who did not know him the human services Perkins obviously rendered Scribner authors, and that light up the personal situation he made for himself—that of the editor who does not write himself but lives by giving himself away to those who do.

No, the letters are certainly not brilliant. They show, as one would expect, his love of good writing and his stubborn defense of the writers he most admired—Wolfe especially, Hemingway, Fitzgerald—and was the first to publish in America. But they also reveal a mind that seems amazingly schoolmasterish when you consider the literary company he liked to keep; Perkins' approach to general ideas was conventional, and he tended to overwork his favorite notion that "intelligence," alas, has never triumphed over "emotion" as the deciding factor in history. "The most obvious example of this, perhaps," he once wrote to Dixon Wecter, suggesting that the latter might want to do a book on the subject, "is the instance of Erasmus and Luther. Luther was a man of great intellect, too, but he was a man of violence and impetuosity. Erasmus tried to keep him from breaking up Christendom, believing that the Church could be reformed gradually, without destruction. I am putting this in a very simplified way, of course, but Erasmus did represent the man of cool intelligence, and Luther the impetuous and intense one. This goes all through history." And if you should compare these stiffly dictated letters with those long, handwritten, and unctuously clever missives that used to be turned out every other day for their cronies by such old-school Scribner editors as Richard Watson Gilder and William Crary Brownell, Perkins' seem intellectually threadbare, and even a peculiarly depressing example of what the pressures of a modern publishing office and the habit of dictating to a secretary against the din of taxi horns on Fifth Avenue can do to the language of a man who loves good English style. Here is Perkins mollifying an indignant reader who had written in to protest against the publication of *The Great Gatsby:*

> The author was prompted to write this book by surveying the tragic situation of many people because of the utter confusion of ideals into which they have fallen, with the result that they cannot distinguish the good from the bad. . . . He wished to present such a society to the American public so they would realize what a grotesque situation existed. . . . The author intended the story to be repugnant. . . . He wanted to show that this was a horrible, grotesque, and tragic fact of life today. He could not possibly present these people effectively if he refused to face their abhorrent characteristics. . . . If the author had not presented these abhorrent characteristics, he would not have drawn a true picture of these people.

Yet the significant point of this letter is that Perkins was trying to win for an important new American writer the understanding and sympathy of an older reader who was used to more genteel publications from the House of Scribner. There are many letters like it. The Gilders and Brownells wrote better, but you cannot picture them fighting for writers the way Perkins did, or working so intensely over manuscripts night after night as he did over Thomas Wolfe's, or spelling out with such excruciating patience, to all the Jews, Catholics, and aggrieved patriots who complained that some book or other should not have been published, Perkins' simple and beautiful belief that every possible freedom should be given writers who are worth publishing at all. In fact, if you consider what Gilder and Brownell did with some of the really important American books that in their time came into the Scribner office, you find Gilder boasting that he had bowdlerized *Huckleberry Finn* in the pages of *Scribner's Magazine,* and Brownell turning down, as "premature," Van Wyck Brooks' *America's Coming-of-Age*. Perkins thought of himself as an editor, not a literary pontiff; he was interested not in literary schools but in finding and developing good American novelists. (Professionally, at least, he seems, of course, to have cared only for fiction, and, though he reread *War and Peace* regularly with ecstatic admiration and was always telling his writers to study it, really for fiction by Americans.) Whatever his own literary frustrations had been, or the limitations of taste that glare up at you from this book, he had the modesty and the wisdom to find his own creativeness in helping along individual American writers, no matter how much he may have disagreed with them or been annoyed by them. And it was always the individual writer he was concerned with—bringing out his hidden resources, giving him useful criticism, and, above all, encouraging him.

It would seem from Perkins' letters that what a good book editor does mostly for a writer is to be his friend. People who write books in America generally need encouragement, and they need it in great doses. It takes time to do a book creditably; there is usually more money in stories and articles; the pressures that work against a man's giving the requisite attention to a book are many and intense—nor are they always the writer's financial need, his other job, if he has one, or his family life. There is something about our culture that can make even the writer himself begrudge the time and patience and faith that are needed for a book. Perkins understood all that; he knew how to be the writer's friend, the friend in the office, the nearest and yet the most official contact a writer has these days with his publisher—which is not quite the same thing as being the writer's confidant, nurse, broker, easy touch, and lay analyst, though I am sure Perkins had to be these things, too. The writer's friend is the man who acts on the belief, as Perkins once expressed it to Thomas Wolfe, that "There could be nothing so important as a book can be." It is not necessary for him to write brilliant letters. It is preferable that he not spend his time thinking up best-selling projects into which writers may fit. It may not even be wise for him to offer technical advice—Perkins' is not always impressive—so long as he can put his finger on the weak spots. All that is required of him is that he understand and encourage and stubbornly keep in view, so that even the writer at his lowest won't forget it, that part of the writer that is his anima, the secret of his vocation, the reason for which he writes. It is the kind of understanding that is more important to a real writer than praise; that keeps him going despite the predominance of those who, as Perkins said, "just follow the trade of writing and who always know just where they are going and go there like business men"; and that, so far as the writer himself is concerned, is most usefully expressed in concrete human relationships, for it is founded on the friend's continuing personal attention, on his ability to respond freshly to unexpected developments, and even on his love.

What I had never fully taken in until I read these letters is the effect that the most famous of these friendships—the one with Thomas Wolfe—had on Perkins himself. Everyone knows that Wolfe owed Perkins a great deal, and Wolfe certainly expressed himself generously on the subject—so much so that he finally became alarmed that people would think he could not function without Perkins and, largely as a gesture of defiant independence, switched over to another publisher. But one has to read these letters to realize that the adoring and boundless tributes Wolfe paid to Perkins were, in the latter's own way, entirely reciprocated:

> The plain truth is that working on your writings, however it has turned out for good or bad, has been the greatest pleasure, for all its pain, and the most interesting episode of my editorial life.
>
> No one I ever knew has said more of the things that I believed than you.
>
> I never knew a soul with whom I felt I was in such fundamentally complete agreement as you.
>
> You are the writer I have most greatly admired.
>
> Your work has been the foremost interest in my life.

In reading these letters you have to make allowance, of course, for the fact that Wolfe was usually depressed or in a rage and constantly needed Perkins' assurances in order to keep working. Nevertheless, there is a vein of deeply personal feeling in them that is utterly unexpected and quite touching. It makes one wonder just what it was that had been inhibited so long in that prim and shy Vermonter who pessimistically based all his hopes on "the man of cool intelligence," like Erasmus, that responded so gratefully to Wolfe's bombast.

Some of the most affectionate and admiring letters to Wolfe were written when Wolfe was at his worst. Wolfe naturally resented Perkins' help on his manuscripts, even when he demanded it. He hysterically accused Perkins of trying to censor his Left Wing opinions, when he had them. He complained—only Wolfe would have thought of this—that Perkins found his sufferings "amusing." Perkins must have been considerably puzzled by the portrait of himself as Foxhall Edwards in Wolfe's last novel, *You Can't Go Home Again*—a portrait that, to anyone who puts together Perkins' personality from these letters, is additional proof that after *Look Homeward, Angel* Wolfe was always too busy reporting on himself as America's Greatest Novelist ever to describe with acuteness or love the people who were closest to him. Yet Wolfe probably was the great event of Perkins' life. And it was obviously Perkins, with his comparative indifference to European writing and the kind of national provincialism that has always led Americans, out of a fear that their whole story has not been told in literature, to look for the Great American Novel, the Leading American Novelist, the Final Truth About America in Fiction—it was obviously Perkins who helped to sustain Wolfe in the myth that he was the Voice of America, that myth now so dear to teen-agers and to cultivated German émigrés who in childhood based their ideas of American literature on the size of the country. Since I agree with F. Scott Fitzgerald that Wolfe lacked something to say, I find it hard to understand how a man who relished Hemingway and Fitzgerald, to say nothing of *War and Peace,* could have rated Wolfe so high. But it is not his comparative critical judgment that identifies an editor like Perkins; it is his devotion to the individual writer. And that devotion Perkins gave Wolfe in full—with a humility that entirely brings home the satisfactions of the friend who must always live in the shadow of another's writing.

Nineteen

E. E. CUMMINGS AND HIS FATHERS

The Charles Eliot Norton Professorship at Harvard is awarded each year to a distinguished modern writer, composer, or critic of the fine arts. For the academic year 1952-53, the Norton Professor was E. E. Cummings, Harvard '15, who told his delighted audience that "I haven't the remotest intention of posing as a lecturer," and then proceeded, in his highly personal style, to summarize his life and opinions and to campaign for love, beauty, and individuality by reading from his own works and from no one else more contemporary than Dante, Chaucer, Shakespeare, Donne, Wordsworth, and Swinburne. His talks have now been published under the inevitable title of *i: six nonlectures.*

Although Cummings considers himself a dangerous crank and the last individualist of our collectivist and totalitarian century, he is probably regarded by most people who read him—and certainly by those who don't—as a funnyman, a great card, a deliberate showman. This is the reputation of many leading poets now, for although they naturally complain of the age, on a platform they tend to become the very incarnation of literature, the only literary performers around who recall such famous actors as Dickens and Mark Twain. But Dickens and Mark Twain pretended to play characters from their own works, to audiences that doted on these books. Today a poet like Cummings simply plays himself, in the role that is always, provokingly and unerringly, that of the "poet"—the last of the clowns, the one fool left with innocence or brass enough to stand up before a crowd, bare his heart, and sass the age. Many a literary audience in this country, composed of people as liberal as anyone else, has roared with laughter when Cummings has denounced trade unions as slavery or has said things about the New Deal that, if found on the editorial page of a newspaper, would reduce this audience to despair. It is not always the poetry that comes through; it is the poet himself—in the marvelous, the ineradicable difference from other people that gets him to be a poet at all. The result is that his opinions are regarded not even as quaint but as the portable furniture that is part of his public performance. There must be thousands of people in this country who can never look at Cummings' name in lower-case type without seeing in him what their grandfathers saw in Mark Twain or Mr. Dooley.

Cummings has certainly assisted in making this reputation. He has done this by creating a style whose trademark is by now as instantly recognizable as an automobile's—by giving to its very appearance on the page the instant feel of spontaneity, of lyric bitterness against the mob age; by constantly unhorsing all words sacred to our conformism and replacing them with private words; by the living contrasts within a language that is full of abstractions but that is always coming apart at the seams, slangy and mock-important. A lifelong addict of the circus, vaudeville, and burlesque, Cummings loves to puncture words so that he can fling their stale rhetoric like straw all over the floor of his circus tent, to take a pompous stance that collapses under him, to come out with an ad-lib that seems positively to stagger him. But the very point of all this is that it occurs within a vocabulary that is essentially abstract and romantic, and that the performance is by a man who remains always aloof, whose invocation of love, spring, roses, balloons, and the free human heart stems from a permanent mistrust of any audience.

This duality of the traditionalist and the clown, of the self-consciously arrogant individualist and the slapstick artist, makes up Cummings' world, and it is this that gives special interest to the autobiographical sections of a book that otherwise, though as delightful as anything he has ever written, tends to lapse into defensive quotations from his own writings and opinions. For in coming to Harvard he came back to his own—to the town he was born in, to the university whose intellectual inheritance he so particularly represents, to the memory of his father, a Boston minister and onetime Harvard instructor, whose influence is so dominant in his best work. The remarkably exalted memories Cummings gives us of his Cambridge boyhood—his loving, characteristically idyllic picture of the big house in Cambridge; of the trees; of the great English poems his mother copied into a little book and read to him; of William James, who introduced his parents to each other; of Josiah Royce, who introduced him to the beauties of the English sonnet—all this, which is no less a fairy tale, as Cummings tells it, for being true, is the background of his familiar opposition between the idyllic past and the New York world in which he has to live. Cummings is not merely a traditionalist in the mold of so many American poets, a mold that recalls those other American inventors and originals, such as Ford and Edison and Lindbergh, who are forever trying to reclaim the past their own feats have changed; he is the personification of the old transcendentalist passion for abstract ideals. In his knowingness with words, in his passion for Greek and Latin, he takes one back to Emerson and Thoreau, who were perpetually pulling words apart to illustrate their lost spiritual meaning. Underneath the slapstick and the typographical squiggles, Cummings likes to play with words so that he can show the ideals they once referred to—and this always with the same admonitory, didactic intent and much of Thoreau's shrewd emphasis on his own singularity.

It is these old traits that give such delightfulness, and occasionally something of his hoped-for disagreeableness, to Cummings' "egocentricity," which he pretends in these lectures to apologize for yet which is actually, of course, not a subjective or narcissistic quality at all but the very heart of his Protestant and fiercely individualistic tradition. And certainly that tradition has in no recent literature received such tributes as Cummings pays here to his father, who was killed when a railroad train ran into his car. One of Cummings' best poems is called "my father moved through dooms of love," in which the dead man's probity, lovingness, and joyfulness are so achingly contrasted with the lives of most men that by the time the poem swells to its triumphant conclusion he has taken on virtually the attributes of Christ. In this book, Cummings quotes an old letter of his, which reported (and it is interesting to note the rush of these details) that his father

was a New Hampshire man, 6 foot 2, a crack shot & a famous fly-fisherman & a firstrate sailor (his sloop was named the Actress) & a woodsman who could find his way through forests primeval without a compass & a canoeist who'd still-paddle you up to a deer without ruffling the surface of a pond & an ornithologist & taxidermist & (when he gave up hunting) an expert photographer (the best I've ever seen) & an actor who played Julius Caesar in Sanders Theater & a painter (both in oils & watercolours) & a better carpenter than any professional & an architect who designed his own houses before building them & (when he liked) a plumber who just for the fun of it installed all his own waterworks & (while at Harvard) a teacher with small use for professors—by whom . . . we were literally surrounded (but not defeated)—& later . . . a preacher who announced, during the last war, that the Gott Mit Uns boys were in error since the only thing which mattered was for man to be on God's side (& one beautiful Sunday in Spring remarked from the pulpit that he couldn't understand why anyone had come to hear him on such a day) & horribly shocked his pewholders by crying "the Kingdom of Heaven is no spiritual roofgarden: it's inside you" & my father had the first telephone in Cambridge . . . & my father's voice was so magnificent that he was called on to impersonate God speaking from Beacon Hill (he was heard all over the common) & my father gave me Plato's metaphor of the cave with my mother's milk.

In the new American scriptures, fathers don't count. But Cummings' cult of his father is, precisely because it will strike many Americans as wholly unreal, the clue to all that makes Cummings so elusive and uncharacteristic a figure today. For just as the occasional frivolousness of his poetry is irritating because it is *not* gay, because it is snobbish and querulous and self-consciously forlorn in its distance from the great urban mob he dislikes, so the nobility and elevation of his poetry—which has become steadily more solid, more experimental and moving—is unreal to many people because of the positive way in which he flings the *true* tradition in our faces with an air that betrays his confidence that he will not be understood.

Cummings' wit always starts from the same tone in which Thoreau said that "I should not talk so much about myself if there were anybody else whom I knew as well." It is both a conscious insulation of his "eccentricity" and an exploitation of his role. But Emerson and Thoreau, even in the rosy haze of transcendentalism, were resolute thinkers, provokers of disorder, revolutionaries who were always working on the minds of their contemporaries; Cummings' recourse is not to the present, to the opportunities of the age, but to the past. And that past has now become so ideal, and the mildly bawdy satires he used to write against the Cambridge ladies of yesteryear have yielded to such an ecstasy of provincial self-approval, that we find him in these lectures openly pitying his audience because it did not have the good sense to be born in his father's house, and quoting never from his contemporaries but only from the familiar masterpieces of English poetry his mother read to him. He has always made a point of defying the Philistines, but at Harvard he stood up against our terrible century armed only with his memories and the Golden Treasury.

Cummings' poetry has ripened amazingly of recent years, but it has not grown. And charming and touching as he is in this little autobiography, he remains incurably sentimental. This sentimentality, I hasten to add, is not in his values, in his dislike of collectivism, in his rousing sense of human freedom; it is in his failure to clothe the abstractions of his fathers with the flesh of actuality, with love for the living. The greatness of the New England transcendentalists was their ability to reclaim, from the commonsensical despairs of a dying religion, faith in the visionary powers of the mind. More and more, in Cummings' recent books, one sees how this belief in imagination, this ability to see life from within, has enabled him to develop, out of the provocative mannerisms of his early work, a verse that is like lyric shorthand—extraordinarily elastic, light, fresh, and resonant of feeling. At a time when a good deal of "advanced" poetry has begun to wear under its convention of anxiety, Cummings' verse has seemed particularly felt, astringent, and musical. But it is precisely because Cummings is a poet one always encounters with excitement and delight, precisely because it is his gift to make the world seem more joyful, that one reads a book like this with disappointment at hearing so many familiar jokes told over again, while the poet escapes into a fairyland of his fathers and points with a shudder to all who are not, equally with him, his father's son.

Twenty

ON MELVILLE AS SCRIPTURE

Of all the recent studies of Melville I have seen, Richard Chase's *Herman Melville: A Critical Study,* seems to me the most brilliant; and since it must be taken very seriously, the most frustrating. For while it is most clearly, and passionately, concerned with the moral significance of Melville's symbolism, and is surely the most affirmative statement ever made of Melville's distinction as a thinker, its conception of his art is static and even provincial. It is a devoted, combative book, with a richly felt sense of Melville's urgency; anyone who cares for Melville will recognize that it has started up from deep inside his thought. There are some very moving insights, and a power of hauntingly exact definition, that could have come only from great devotedness. But I do not really take in Mr. Chase's subsidiary aim, which is to present Melville as a supreme example, or moral imagination, for the "New Liberalism." And its critical method, especially on the works after *Moby-Dick,* seems to me astonishingly immature, and is so full of the most reckless guesses and assumptions, that I wonder if he has not simply turned in Melville the artist and the man, about whom we know so little, for the Messiah of the "New Liberalism"—a movement that seems to exist mostly in the minds of Mr. Chase and of Arthur Schlesinger, Jr., but to judge by the difference between the moral quality of this book and that of *The Vital Center,* can hardly be the same movement.

Mr. Chase's approach to literature is very modishly framed in myth and folklore; his book is built on personifications. Some are named after characters, like Ishmael and The Confidence Man; some after obvious prototypes, like The True Prometheus and The Handsome Sailor; some from symbolic incidence, like The Christ, The Maimed Man in the Glen, The False Prometheus. But they are all generic quantities with a meaning above Melville's works, and are applied freely to recurrent phases of his mind, and of American personality, folklore and politics as well. Moreover, the book is addressed to a personified reader, The Chastened American Liberal Who Has Turned His Back on Stalinism and Progressivism—The New Liberal—and is an onslaught on The False Liberal, and less severely but firmly, on still another, The Ordealist Critic, or The Preacher of Alienation. So that in a very real sense the book is a morality play, in which The True Prometheus, The False Prometheus, The Confidence Man, The Ordealist Critic and The New Liberal vie with each other, in this period of intense political introspection, for the Soul of America the Alienated at the Mid-Century.

They are very large, these personifications; some are original, and all are provoking; they surely exist, to speak here only of the Melvillean ones, as those archetypal images of the self's divisions which are very real to anyone who has read through Melville. But they are applied with such finality to the American scene, move so autonomously across Melville's works, and are obviously so much more stimulating to Mr. Chase's mind than the concrete artistic experiences from which they have been taken, that Melville as man and practicing artist gets lost from sight, for he is always too diffusely and superhumanly in sight. Of all Mr. Chase's personifications, he is the mightiest—a kind of brooding Promethean intelligence, Our Tattooed Titan on Whose Skin May Be Deciphered the General Myths and the Local Folklore—the peak of the American ordeal, and its moral victory. He is now the Young American Wanderer, now the Maimed Man in the Glen, now Ishmael of course, but always Prometheus the Humanist—a figure often in suffering, but heroic; sometimes imperfect, but cumulatively glorious. He is a personification, in fact, in whom it is difficult to see the young roustabout, for here he is all the young men out in the world; or the harried husband and father who cried out in *Moby-Dick* for "Time, Strength, Cash and Patience," for here he turns up as the Successful Family Man; or the solitary who in those magnificent letters of the period (far better literature than several items on which Mr. Chase has trained his symbol-extracting machinery) proudly asked for Hawthorne's friendship, for to Mr. Chase's mind Melville's loneliness is somehow diminished if we show him immersed in native materials; but who does emerge, sometimes very movingly, as our Wisest Man of Sorrows, our Prometheus, our greatest Light-Bearer.

Now this Prometheus is a very appealing figure to us (our fathers did not know his greatness, but we have seen his face); and Mr. Chase's many happy insights, his beautiful essay on the moral drama in *Moby-Dick,* are the richest instance I know of Melville's power to call out of Americans in this generation a kind of intense personal relatedness not felt now, in such numbers, for any other American writer—a claim on his uniqueness, I would add, that points up these "inner estrangements" in the American situation Mr. Chase is so afraid will keep us from having a "high culture." But this figure is expected also to consecrate The New Liberalism, and for purposes of our national self-criticism, to use the phrase with which Mr. Chase rounds out his hymn to *The Confidence Man,* "ought to be scripture." And since I do not identify the New Liberalism so complacently as Mr. Chase does, and indeed, find it hard to think of Melville as a Liberal, or as "scripture," for to me he is a very great, unstable, fiery daemonic artist, more akin to Blake and Rimbaud than to academic humanism, I can only say that I find much of Mr. Chase's exegesis irrelevant to Melville's marvelous force and energy, to his Ahab-like creative will, and to that style in which one hears the torrential rhythms of the creation.

If there is one thing I am sure about in "The New Liberalism," it is its infatuation with abstractions, its wish to believe names equal to things. This comes, I think, from its extreme self-consciousness as an educational élite, from its exasperated sense of urgency and protest against shallow views of human nature, from the academic tendency to see the artist as a corpus of knowledge rather than as a distinctly individual experience, and from some old alienation that still cuts deeper than its grateful affection for the American advantage in the struggle against totalitarianism. Thus we find Mr. Chase raging rather incoherently at the end against the old liberalism as the lover of all our estrangements, from "the divorce of parts" to "the hiatus between the sexes, the abyss that separates generations, the enmity between the terrified ego and the unconscious, between action and motive, between reason and myth, between father and son." Is The New Liberal to heal all this? Mr. Chase is trying to prove too much. Passionate as he is about Melville's thought, his point of view lacks emotional authenticity, for Bulkington in *Moby-Dick*—"wonderfully concise. . . . Man fully formed, fully human, fully wise,"—means more to him than does Ahab; *The Confidence Man* becomes Melville's "second-best" book, and unable to say openly that *Clarel* is a stuffed and badly written poem, Mr. Chase tells us that if it were "mercilessly compressed, it would sound a great deal like T. S. Eliot's *Waste Land*"—a judgment that seems to me meaningless, for the poetic styles of the two works are antithetical, and works are not rendered alike by being reduced to common size.

Insofar as it exists in action, The New Liberalism is the intellectual wing of the party now in power, and to judge from Mr. Schlesinger's *The Vital Center,* sees nothing wrong with that master Confidence Man, F.D.R., admires Theodore Roosevelt, and scorns "utopians and wailers" who protest the abuses of power. But generally, its approach to life is through literature, for The New Liberal has usually not made his mind up about religion, knows little philosophy or science, and (almost always) is loftily superior to politics. Yet he does not present literature itself as an experience; he reduces the artist to his myths or ideologies or structural stratagems—that is, he rewrites the artist in his own favorite personification as Tiresias the Universal Savant, or the almighty critic, who is a little contemptuous of King Oedipus the artist for carrying on so, or what Mr. Chase at one point irritably calls Melville's "clumsy emotions." And if need be, he sacrifices the truth of his own experience, the experience with which he directly receives the artist's work, to the charms of a moral lesson or Personification. This is Mr. Chase, when he tells us that "*Clarel* is not a supremely contrived poem, but there is a certain order and felicity in the symbols." Or that "reading and rereading *Pierre,* we find that its meanings proliferate and its texture becomes rich." As this is put ("*and* its texture becomes rich"), one might infer that the texture of a work grows in proportion to the "meanings" we disengage from it. But obviously "meanings" in a work of art, or any other human experience, can be of different value. And even if they "proliferate" in the critic's mind, it is still his first responsibility to show whether, and how, they are actively felt in the developmental structure and stylistic vision of the book, and how deeply they are realized in the imagination of the writer and the reader. Art is hardly the whole of reality, but it is a form of love, or perfected communication, in which everything depends on what is given and received between one person and another. "Texture" is not a gross total of "meanings"; it is the intermediate sphere between the final aim of the writer (which may be unknown to himself) and our readiness to apprehend and to share in a consciousness different from our own; it is the place in space our experience of art immediately occupies. Bulkington may be "Man fully formed, fully human, fully wise," but he is "wonderfully concise" only if one presumes that Melville calculated every stroke in advance, which is evidently untrue, and if one sees the book *only* as a morality, which belies the fact that the False Prometheus (Ahab) gets all the great lines, and the True Prometheus (Bulkington) gets praised (a shade hysterically).

But then, Mr. Chase never permits much to an artist's spontaneity, or fancy, or caprice; even when he quotes from the beginning of *Billy Budd* Melville's rhapsody over the beauty of a Negro sailor who wore a Scotch Highland bonnet with a tartan band, he does so to connect us back to *Pierre*—"the emblem of Lucy Tartan enlightens the forehead of the Handsome Sailor as he emerges from the depths of Night into the consciousness of Day. . . . He moves as ponderously, but with as much strength and beauty . . . as revolutionary America itself, setting forth on the path of civilization." Is Melville never to be allowed a memory or a detail or a figure of speech that answers simply to his own exuberance? Does Mr. Chase think it Melville's distinction that he had as many symbols at his fingertips as James Joyce? He tells us, for example, that "a minor theme of *Pierre* is the theme of the keys. As in Joyce's *Ulysses,* the keys are those of St. Peter, whose name Melville's hero bears. The key symbolizes the secret of Pierre's paternity. In his earlier portrait, Pierre's father wears a seal and a key on his watch chain. . . ." Or: "etymologically, we perceive, Pierre Glendinning and Glendinning Stanly are the same name, since 'Stanly' comes from a Germanic word for 'stone' and 'Pierre' comes from a Greek word meaning the same." Or: "Mrs. Glendinning in her role as History has reached her state of perfection (false though it is) by giving birth to Pierre (America) and making him her one true lover. . . . She is 'not far from her grand climacteric,' which, as a piece of symbolism, means that she is about to achieve the perfection of Society."

I mistrust Mr. Chase's understanding of how an artist operates; he is much too fond of showing that Melville was almost as wise as Arnold Toynbee. Yet when the works are not identified with their symbols, Melville is chided for a "deficiency of symbolization," or for being "too little the continuously professional writer." Quoting Melville's very winning and characteristic exclamation in *Moby-Dick,* "I try all things; I achieve what I can," Mr. Chase assures us that "his plight as an epic writer was less desperate than his words might imply," though Melville was not necessarily thinking here of the epic form. He *did* try all things, often in a single work, and that is half his charm as an "unprofessional" author, as it helps to explain why he failed as a professional one. Much as he needed a public in order to make a living, he needed even more to spill over in every direction, to fit his new learning to his old wanderings, to act as reporter, prophet, wise man, and general mystic factotum to his "raw" countrymen—a very characteristic mark of the American writer from Whitman to Ezra Pound. But though he did become over-conscious of his symbols in proportion as he began to write purely for himself—a point Mr. Chase can never state explicitly because it is of the very argument of his book that Melville's interest in symbols was uniform —I still do not think that Melville ever sat down to write *about* symbols, which is the impression this book leaves. To Mr. Chase, Captain Vere in *Billy Budd* is Man, because *vir* is Latin for man; when Billy accidentally spills the soup in Claggart's path, Claggart feels insulted because "Billy has symbolically exposed himself to Claggart as the Host, the vessel from which issues 'virtue.' . . . The spilled soup has also exposed Claggart's guilt as an eater of the Host and, furthermore, Claggart's fear of his own unconscious desire to be like Billy; for the psychological content of Claggart's desire to share Billy's innocence is his desire to be the passive host." Did Melville sense all this? If I doubt it, it is not least because Mr. Chase never looks for an explanation in the human events nearest him. He has told us above, for example, that Pierre bears the name of St. Peter, who is in *Ulysses,* but not that a cousin of Melville's bore the name of Pierre. In any event, Mr. Chase does not say what Melville himself thought; but since his subject is a Personification of modern wisdom, it may be presumed that he thought of everything. A *writer,* however, particularly so spontaneous and airily half-learned a writer as Melville, is usually in a more limited state of intellectual grace, for art is so difficult that he must take the larger part of his "content" for granted. If Melville had been half as keen on symbols as Mr. Chase is, he would not have moved an inch, and he would certainly have lost the rich personal coloring that comes from the juncture of unconscious symbols and the conscious word, to say nothing of that effect of fertility, from word to word, which is so peculiarly his own—even in so intellectualized a work as *Billy Budd.*

To Mr. Chase, *The Confidence Man* is the grand justification of his conception of Melville. Now this book is very plainly the product of a first-rate imagination; it has been unfairly neglected; and it may very well be almost as political as Mr. Chase says. He has read it far more patiently and lovingly than anyone else I know, and he has disentangled from its summary and difficult pages a whole tableau of native folklore. But it is significant that his argument is based on the politics of the book, which he interprets very piously, and on the incidence of folklore types and themes, without proving to us that the book was fully realized by Melville.

The presence of folklore elements does not of itself establish a book's value—witness so much of the antiquarian junk in the attic of American literature, and so, so much of Mark Twain. Mr. Chase has very understandably been influenced by Constance Rourke, whose delicate style is the happiest of any American cultural historian, and from whose harmonious spirit he would seem to have absorbed much of the economical force and pungency of his own writing here. But Constance Rourke worked as a reviver, to show the continuity in the American pattern; she was a historian of materials, who did not pass judgment on them, except as she showed the different inspirations. In his own enthusiasm on the subject of folklore, Mr. Chase gets so rapt proving Melville was an *echt Amerikaner* who worked "in the American grain," and that his alienation has been overstressed by the Ordealists, that he never asks himself *what* values are awakened in the artist by an interest in folklore, or of the different ways in which it can be applied. The raftmen's speech in *Life On the Mississippi-Huckleberry Finn* is one of the prime examples of "folklore" in American literature, but it is still bosh, Mark Twain's particular after-dinner performance; the first meeting of Huck and Tom in *Tom Sawyer* is incomparable, it truly incarnates a *national* literature, for it represents an upwelling, from local figures of speech, of all that is most charming, fresh and free in the nostalgia for the frontier and its legendary youth.

The critic who reduces a work to its elements of folklore or myth has the advantage over the social critic that he is always inside the story; but he may have even less to say *about* it. In fact, it is the specialists in this field who are now farthest from the true spirit of criticism, for they make the fewest discriminations between good work and bad. The great weakness of the myth approach in criticism is that it freezes man to the universal, for by showing man everywhere to be the same, it reduces history to an illustration. The great weakness of the folklore approach is that it shows man only as a type or costume of his local culture. In the one, history becomes a figure of speech; in the other, man himself. Yet both these approaches are used by Mr. Chase throughout his book, for he conceives of Melville's works as an illustration of the specifically American pattern on the universal pattern of myth. Or as he puts it about *Moby-Dick,* "What he had to do was adduce the body of supporting mythology, clothe the skeleton with flesh and the habiliments of style." No wonder that he finds so many examples to his purpose in *The Confidence Man,* and can interpret it *ad libitum!* But *The Confidence Man* marks the full eruption of Melville's wrath against the American belief—liberal, conservative, and radical—that reality is always calculable, that things are never as desperate as they seem, that the world is a moral constant in the mind of History or God. It is a book which perhaps only European intellectuals who have passed through the concentration camps can fully understand, for the heart of it is anguish, an almost unbearable sense of betrayal before the inadequacy of the civil human gift to explain what men do feel when—in Bartleby's words—they know where they are. It is an attack on the spirit of consolation, for consolation justifies the most extreme violations against the living. It is an attack on the spirit of "moderation," on "the picked and prudent sentiments," as the Missourian calls them in his great attack on the Confidence Man. It is not a "compassionate" book; it is an embittered, tense, splintery book; it moves with the rapidities of anger. And it is not simply an attack on the naiveté of the old American liberalism, on the strut-and-brag of American commercialism, on the innocence of transcendentalism; it is a great cry against the deception appearance practices upon reality.

This is not a Melville Mr. Chase easily tolerates. Melville said of Matthew Arnold that he had "the prudential worldly element wherewithal [he] has conciliated the conventionalists," but this Mr. Chase finds "actively offensive," and notes that "Herman Melville might have done better and been happier if he had not shied quite so readily from the ways of the world. . . ." Necessarily, Mr. Chase applies *The Confidence Man* against Henry Wallace and the fellow-travelers; but never on the "sweet voice" which crooned at the beginning of the Roosevelt era that our crisis was only economic, not spiritual; and at the end, had the atom bomb tested on eighty thousand human beings at Hiroshima. I do not find *The Confidence Man* so great a work as Mr. Chase does, for I find it too full of the "organic disorder," too blinding an excess of rage; it moves so quickly that it ends, literally, by putting out the light of the world. But if The New Liberalism wants to make scripture out of it, it will have to look below its "folklore" to Melville's unappeasable fury against the human situation.

Still, these are criticisms one raises only because Mr. Chase insists on bringing us Melville as scripture. For if it is lessons for a new liberal humanism we seek from literature, there are several writers rather more harmonious and dependable in this regard; and if it is "scripture," we shall have to make up our minds what our religion is, and what it is we do believe. The great advantage of myth to the liberal mind is that it presents so many gods, one need not believe in any one. It is the agnostic's theology. Melville is not an agnostic: he said that man's life was haunted by divinity, but that God could no longer cope with the human claim upon Him. Melville was not a liberal: he believed that reality was not susceptible to a political interpretation. Melville is not a reconciler: he did not try to weld appearances together; he pierces through. His love for the world was very uncertain; and in fact, love is hardly his strong point. But he is one of the few men in America who ever sounded, to the depths, the transcendental ache at the heart of being; and he has that peculiar gift—not necessarily the most valuable in literature, but distinctly his—which is concerned with the "soul" of man, not with his "heart"; with his attitude toward the creation, not with his relationship to other men. It is what Ezra Pound, in another connection, tried to convey when he spoke of "the raw cut out of concrete reality, combined with the tremendous energy, the contact with the natural force." Melville had that contact; and while it is not necessarily better than Liberalism, than scripture, than a "high culture," at least let us not sacrifice a unique experience to the abstracts of a moral lesson or ideology.

Twenty-one

THE GIFT

In 1942, Simone Weil, a French scholar working with the Free French in London, was asked to submit a memorandum outlining her ideas on what could be done to bring about a regeneration of France. This project could not have been taken very seriously by her superiors; as a matter of fact, it was assigned largely to give her something to do and to divert her from her insistent wish to be allowed to parachute into France. Such a project must have seemed to the eminently practical men in charge of such things only a little more odd than Simone Weil herself, who was a frail, awkward, and bookish young lycée teacher with a peculiar need to share the most arduous and painful experiences of her generation; she had already injured her health working in the Renault factory and as an agricultural laborer and by fighting with the Spanish Republican Army during the Civil War. She was also Jewish and looked it, which would instantly have condemned her if she had been caught by the Germans.

Early in 1943, Simone Weil completed her assignment—*L'Enracinement* (published in this country as *The Need for Roots*), an extremely keen but passionately visionary work whose subtitle noted that it was a "Prelude to a Declaration of Duties Toward Mankind." This was not a book most Frenchmen would have read very sympathetically during the Occupation. The author wrote with a piercing simplicity, but she stood apart from all contemporary ideologies, she proposed a severe new code of moral obligations for the French, she counseled her countrymen in exile "first of all to choose everything that is purely and genuinely good, without the slightest consideration for expediency," and she showed how, since the time of Richelieu, the state had become "a cold concern which cannot inspire love, but itself kills, suppresses everything that might be loved; so one is forced to love it, because there is nothing else." By 1940, even that forced love was gone, and the effect of this on French morale was the starting point of her investigation. She was intensely concerned with the smallest details of working-class life, and remarked that "the sense of justice is . . . strong among workmen, even if they are materialists, owing to the fact that they are always under the impression they are being deprived of it." She praised the monarchical principle, at least in its earliest medieval form, because it symbolized man's obedience to God. But she belonged to no political camp, and, though she regarded herself as a Christian, wrote that "Christianity is, in effect, apart from a few isolated centers of inspiration, something socially in accordance with the interests of those who exploit the people." At the heart of her book lay a profound conviction that modern man is rootless because he has lost contact with the divinity of the world itself. This loss she blamed on the Jewish-Christian conception of God as a person, since as men came to doubt the existence of a purely personal Providence, they lost their faith altogether and looked on the world as a mechanism indifferent to their hopes and desires and one that science alone had the power to interpret.

This intransigent document would probably have received no particular attention—it was not published even in France until 1949—but for an unexpected development. A few months after finishing it, Simone Weil, then thirty-four, died in a nursing home, mainly because she had refused, though tubercular and completely exhausted, to eat more than the French under the Occupation were getting on their official ration. When the war ended and her notebooks began to be published—the first extracts were made by two Catholic friends, the Reverend J. M. Perrin and the writer Gustave Thibon, with whom she had often discussed her attraction to the Church—a great many people in France and elsewhere found themselves deeply if often reluctantly impressed by the revelation of her extraordinary qualities, by her relentless preoccupation with every area of suffering in our time, and by the intensely individual religious experiences through which she had passed toward the end of her life. By now, Simone Weil has become a legend and her writings are regarded as a classic document of our period; eight volumes have been published since her death, including a volume of her notebooks, in unedited form, and her diaries and letters on factory life.

T. S. Eliot's cautiously admiring introduction to *The Need for Roots,* the second of Simone Weil's works to appear in English (the first, *Waiting for God,* with a far more vital introduction by Leslie A. Fiedler, came out last fall), tries to place the book by putting it "in that category of prolegomena to politics which politicians seldom read, and which most of them would be unlikely to understand or to know how to apply." He adds, not very optimistically, that it is one of those "books the effect of which, we can only hope, will become apparent in the attitude of mind of another generation." Eliot is careful to distinguish the traditionalist side of her thinking and her saintliness from her "immoderate affirmations" and "excess of temperament," and acknowledges that he has written "with some emphasis upon her errors and exaggerations . . . in the belief that many readers, coming for the first time upon some assertion likely to arouse intellectual incredulity or emotional antagonism, might be deterred from improving their acquaintance with a great soul and a brilliant mind. Simone Weil needs patience from her readers, as she doubtless needed patience from the friends who most admired and appreciated her."

It is understandable that Eliot should approach Simone Weil with all the reserve of a bishop who has just come on John the Baptist crying in the wilderness; it is, in fact, a tribute to her agonizing genuineness and to the noticeable recent widening of his literary tastes that Eliot should have been impressed by her at all. For she was certainly, as he says, violent in her "affections and antipathies," and, especially in *The Need for Roots,* made extremely sweeping pronouncements about civilizations of the past, in a way that must irritate and shock even those who know far less than Eliot does of them. She hated everything about the Romans, idolized the Greeks, insisted that the most profound religious discoveries had been made by the Stoics, praised without qualification everything she found in the Egyptian and Sanskrit scriptures, and felt a positive horror of Judaism, in which she never had the slightest instruction, which she rejected as entirely alien to her education and deepest convictions, but about which she wrote, like many another Jewish prophet, with an unearthly insistence on human perfection. Still, all the "patience" in the world will never make Simone Weil seem any less "difficult, violent, and complex" than she was, and Eliot's introduction does not set forth clearly what she has to give people of our generation. Though he recognizes that "we must simply expose ourselves to the personality of a woman of genius, of a kind of genius akin to that of the saints," he is so naturally sympathetic to the traditionalist side of her thinking, while annoyed by her extremism, that he assumes we can learn from some of her ideas and forgive the rest. But she was not the sort of "brilliant mind" who can comfortably add to our philosophy, nor was she exactly one of those "great souls," like Gandhi and Albert Schweitzer, who by their ethical example can inspire millions. She was a fanatically dedicated participant in the most critical experiences of our time, who tried to live them directly in contact with the supernatural. Her real interest for us lies less in what she said than in the direction of her work, in the particular vision she tried to reach by the whole manner of her life. What she sought more than anything else was a loving attentiveness to all the living world that would lift man above the natural loneliness of existence.

This urge was her essential quality, her gift—not merely intellectual or ethical but remarkably open to all human experience at its most extreme, neglected, and uprooted. It was this that kept her outside the Catholic Church, on the ground, as she explained in *Waiting for God,* that "so many things are outside it, so many things that I love and do not want to give up, so many things that God loves, otherwise they would not be in existence"; that led to her distress at the Catholic formula of excommunication and compelled her, though a Jew who had fled for her life from Hitler, to protest indignantly against the belief that God could have "chosen" any people for any purpose whatever; that still gave her a sense of outrage at the Romans' contempt for their slaves, which, she thought, had carried over into the brutalities inflicted on workingmen, heretics, prisoners, and the colored races; that drove her to the factories, to Spain during the Civil War, and at the very end, when she was not permitted to join her own people under the Occupation, to starve herself in one last desperate expression of solidarity with them.

Everything that is fundamental in her life and thought radiates this closeness to pain, her need to know directly the rending misery of the universe, to imitate the Passion of Christ. "Those who are unhappy," she wrote in *Waiting for God,* "have no need for anything in this world but people capable of giving them their attention. . . . The love of our neighbor in all its fullness simply means being able to say to him, 'What are you going through?' " "Attention" she called "the contrary" of contempt. By it, she meant "a recognition that the sufferer exists, not only as a unit in a collection, or a specimen from the social category labelled 'unfortunate,' but as a man, exactly like us, who was one day stamped with a special mark by affliction. For this reason it is enough, but it is indispensable, to know how to look at him in a certain way." "Attention" was one of her major themes, and some of the most profound pages in *Waiting for God* are devoted to it. "We do not obtain the most precious gifts by going in search of them but by waiting for them. How can we go toward God? Even if we were to walk for hundreds of years, we should do no more than go round and round the world. Even in an airplane we cannot do anything else. We are incapable of progressing vertically. We cannot take a step toward the heavens." We can only wait, with an attentiveness that has no particular object to gain, that is the "highest form of prayer," that exposes us to the full affliction of being alive, but through which we can gain the integral significance of the universe in which we are placed.

When a French apprentice who is new on a job complains that the work hurts him, the older men usually say that "the trade is entering his body." This saying, which Simone Weil picked up in the Renault factory, had a special pathos for her. It expressed her belief that there is a particular closeness we can reach with the world, that the truth is always something to be lived. In *The Need for Roots,* commenting on the impersonal and detached "love of truth" on which science prides itself, she wrote that "truth is not an object of love. It is not an object at all. What one loves is something which exists, which one thinks on. . . . A truth is always the truth with reference to something. Truth is the radiant manifestation of reality. . . . To desire truth is to desire contact with a piece of reality." This "direct contact" was the one aim of her life, and her ability to find it in the darkest, most unexpected places is her special gift to a generation for whom, more than for any other, the living world has become a machine unresponsive to the human heart.

Twenty-two

THE AMERICAN EQUATION

Sixty years ago, a young Wisconsin historian, Frederick Jackson Turner, wrote a paper, "The Significance of the Frontier in American History," that has appealed to more Americans than has any other explanation of our national development. The leading historians of the time were still generally Easterners, and liked to interpret American history as the glorious culmination of a single tradition of Anglo-Saxon democracy. Turner had not merely a Midwesterner's positive feeling that what is characteristically American comes out of the West but an unusual interest, for that period, in regional history. To him "frontier" and the very term "West" itself expressed one long and inexorable push beyond the first settlements in Virginia and Massachusetts. The repeated return to primitive conditions on a continually receding frontier line, Turner insisted, had stamped on Americans their individualism, their inventiveness, their characteristic impatience with theory, their rejection of many European forms and traditions. The frontier, drawing to its unprecedented abundance of free land those who were dissatisfied farther East, had been a safety valve on discontent in America; there had always been more than enough land to start all over again. However, Turner introduced his famous frontier thesis by quoting a government report that there was no longer, in the sense of an unsettled area, any frontier line in the United States. And this, as he said, "marks the closing of a great historic movement. Up to our own day American history has been in a large degree the history of the colonization of the Great West. The existence of an area of free land, its continuous recession, and the advance of American settlement westward, explain American development."

These claims have, at best, long seemed too general to be useful, but probably no one in the last fifty years has written a line on the history of the West without in one way or another leaning on Turner. For obviously his theory is at least well founded; it brings to our minds the westward momentum of all American history, from Columbus to our presence in Japan; it expresses Western pride in the historic fact that, from the earliest vision of the continental integrity of the United States down to Colonel Robert McCormick's suspicion of everything the wrong side of the Appalachians, our idea of American nationality has been recharged—and, alas, all too often satisfied—by occupying the West. But the essential reason for Turner's influence is that he gave us the equation between environment and destiny that makes it so easy for Americans to write their history. That the American people should take over its present area in a little more than two hundred years; that all this once immeasurable free land should have the decided effect of making this people more restless, more practical, more inventive, more self-assertive than their European forebears or relatives—all this, however inspiring it seemed to an Emerson, a de Tocqueville, a Parkman, was nevertheless mixed in with some stern questions on the quality of democracy, the nature of the individual, and whether men in America are always as free as they are equal.

But "to explain American development" by the frontier is to let circumstances do our thinking for us and to see men only in terms of the geographical conditions to which they adapt themselves. When this is done, everything that men originally initiated through the ideas in their heads, along with everything troublesome, subtle, and complex, because infinitely human, yields to the solid and patriotic drama of great masses forever pushing on to a new landscape and completing a nation. This American equation was formulated when the stupendous concentration of industrial power around the Great Lakes was leading Turner's generation to wonder whether the West could retain the "early ideals" of the pioneers. Even American scholars were beginning to think like engineers, impatient of general ideas and seeing every "field" as a set of concrete problems to be solved. But despite this increasingly businesslike atmosphere, the frontier theory recalled the early freshness and wonder of the West. The equation thus satisfied some prime needs; it made possible the writing of history that would at once be sensible and nostalgic.

In *The Great Frontier,* Walter Prescott Webb has applied Turner's thesis to what he considers the world frontier between 1500 and 1900 (the Americas, South Africa, Australia, New Zealand); he interprets virtually all twentieth-century history as the inevitable contraction of human opportunities that has followed the closing of the last frontiers. Professor Webb grew up in West Texas at a time when a man could still just barely touch "the hem of the garment of the Great Frontier"; he is a distinguished historian of American frontier life and has written authoritative books on the Great Plains and on the Texas Rangers; he has conducted for years at the University of Texas a famous seminar in frontier history, many of whose findings are used in this book. His book is bold, honest, and, even if only half true, profoundly discouraging. For what Professor Webb is saying is that the whole tradition of modern liberal democracy as America and Western Europe have known it, and with it all of Western culture since the Renaissance, arose only because we could afford it. The great frontier offered so much land, and sent back to the mother countries so much wealth, that an abnormal boom period—"the wealth was gently falling all around"—set off the individualistic democracy and expansive freedom that would now seem to be in retreat, if not for the one almighty reason Professor Webb gives for all twentieth-century unhappiness.

Professor Webb once enjoyed the unforgettable taste of nineteenth-century freedom. It is this deep experience—and, one suspects, his helplessness before what has turned Texas into possibly the most complacently plutocratic society of our time—that gives his book such simple force. He proves over and over that something grand and fundamental in the old, easy life of the West—it once seemed "as big as God"—is visibly and heartbreakingly vanishing from America. And because he knows what the frontier really was, he says a good many biting things that have long needed to be said about the current exploitation of the word, which has become the glibbest metaphor in the American language. But what *The Great Frontier* does best is to show how much the expansion of European culture after the Renaissance owes to the exploitation of a New World; Elizabeth was able to pay off England's foreign debt with her share of the booty Sir Francis Drake brought back from a single voyage. One has only to compare English writing today with what it was thirty years ago to see how the loss of an empire can affect even those who dislike imperialism.

However, *The Great Frontier* is the kind of history that writes itself. Once you get hold of a "principle of unity in human affairs"—and Professor Webb is sure the frontier was as important as the Renaissance, the Reformation, and the Industrial Revolution—it looks like "something around which events formed themselves." Such history can be very stimulating, but it does not convince us very long. It never shows us what is most intimately present in all experience—the human mind itself specifically in action. As soon as Professor Webb tries to describe how individual human beings were changed by the frontier, he becomes synthetic; according to his theory, each individual behaves just like all other individuals responding to the same pull. This looks fine on a graph; it does not really tell us what happened to any one of those lucky individuals who supposedly flourished en masse between 1500 and 1900. Professor Webb defends the looseness of his book by saying that he means—in the spirit of his seminar—to open this important inquiry, not to close it. But you do not even open an inquiry of such magnitude by coming up with any and all ideas in the free-for-all of the great American bull session; you try to indicate the possible depth of the question, which is where the truth is. Otherwise, history becomes a description of mechanical forces, and is not only gross but, in detail after detail, simply untrue. Here is Professor Webb drawing some implications from his thesis that our picture of the world is now "nearly completed":

> The imagination cannot play any more with the mystery and uncertainty of a half-known world, for there is no such thing. The map is finished, the roads are surveyed, and all the roads to that kind of adventure are plainly marked and tended. . . . All this does not mean that with the passing of the frontier the human imagination will not still operate, that literature will not continue to be produced. It does mean that the imagination must make its way henceforth amidst a different set of conditions, that it must operate *among* men and not beyond them, that it must deal with what is well known rather than with what is only vaguely known.

Language like this does not inspire belief; Professor Webb assumes that imagination is always *given* subjects from the outside, like an orderly animal called to its food. But what is mysterious and unknown will always continue to be available because of the limited but continuous activity of intelligence itself. The equation between the frontier and everything "unknown" is not merely doubtful history when stretched out over four centuries of human effort; it violates our natural sense of how unpredictable and persistent the human genius is.

A similar psychology lies behind Bernard DeVoto's *The Course of Empire.* This book completes the assertive and extremely ambitious history of the American West that Mr. DeVoto began with *The Year of Decision: 1846.* That book, which described the climactic events that finally gave the United States its continental area, was followed by *Across the Wide Missouri,* a particularly vivid study of a region that Mr. DeVoto knows well and loves with an exultancy in its wild past that redeems his work from its pretentiousness of tone. *The Course of Empire* completes this trilogy by recounting the long and tortured struggle to find a direct route across the United States—from the first Spanish explorers blindly moving out of Mexico down to the great moment in November, 1805, when Lewis and Clark reached the Pacific by way of the Columbia River, and so at last found the passage to India for which Columbus had set out more than three hundred years before.

The kind of history Mr. DeVoto likes to write has never been satisfactorily defined. Although a staggering amount of research has gone into his trilogy, and, as he makes clear in peppery footnotes and caustic asides, he has aimed at an absolute precision of factual detail that even dry-as-dust scholars cannot always be relied on to give us, his is hardly the sort of pure history we consult just for the facts. Mr. DeVoto is a belligerent partisan of the West who, for reasons that are obscure, is always sure that the westward movement has not been properly celebrated; his work is as full of loose opinions as a columnist's, and he is unfailingly sarcastic about "literary men" who did not grow up in the West but nevertheless have ideas about it. Yet though he is himself certainly a "literary man," and writes in a sweeping, colored style, neither is his work the sort of history that was once written by our greatest historians directly for the general public. In fact—this would seem to be the clue to his historical labors—Mr. DeVoto thinks of his books as a strict demonstration humanized by a peppy style. His theme is always the determination of human actions by geography. He grew up in Utah when it was still within rumor of the frontier, he knows the West perfectly—he has covered all the main routes himself and has read all the books—and his purpose is to show that the need to integrate a continent dictated the course of American history, that "the American Empire was born before the United States." A vital passage in this book admits that there are "intangibles" in history which, although they "deposit no documents in the archives," nevertheless "affect societies." But he gives as an example of this the fact that "in the late phases of the westering" there was "an acceleration which is the only way time decisively affects the equations. . . . The American teleology is geographical."

This pseudoscientific lingo holds Mr. DeVoto's style together like a chain; it is fundamental to his thinking. It expresses the kind of certainty that so often gets him to sneer at human fancy, human fantasy, human myth, human illusion, and to set up against these regrettable lapses *real* knowledge, hard knowledge—which usually turns out to be only a more precise geography. The tone of all this is quieter in *The Course of Empire* than in the preceding volumes of the trilogy, probably because he had such an immense story, extending over three centuries, to pack into this last volume that he could not spare space for more of those withering comments on human illusions. But it is important to note how often he speaks of "the power of wish" or the "syllogism of dream" or the "geography of fable." By these, Mr. DeVoto means the countless errors and fantasies and mirages, even the deliberate lying, through which so many explorers shortened

American geography in order to get themselves a little nearer to the Pacific. Of one explorer, Mr. DeVoto tells us that he proclaimed rivers which existed "by reasoning and in response to need." Of another, that he was a great man "but a literary man. . . . Poetry or a formula for best-sellers came upon him and he created a big lake of salt water in the interior West." Silly, silly men, not to have been as clear-eyed as we are. Although Mr. DeVoto knows better than most how very remarkable many of these explorers were, and how much they managed, bit by bit, to create our superior knowledge—this is a theme of his book—he invariably contrives to patronize them. With his sensible, down-to-earth, ever-alert awareness of human frailty, he interestingly leaves out the definite article before words like "wish" and "dream," as if these expressed not the wishes and dreams of individual men but some unpleasant weakness of human nature.

All this makes Mr. DeVoto's book curious reading. Although he has a great story to tell, writes with furious energy and obvious skill, and is always reminding us of the significance of this geographical epic for the American people, he constantly gets lost in details. The reader often has the strange feeling that he may not always know what is going on but that Mr. DeVoto is writing with tremendous passion and knowledge. Just as Professor Webb makes you feel in his book that individuals are only the playthings of space, so Mr. DeVoto, though he is an old hand at the set character sketch and is a novelist in his own right, never makes any of his Spaniards, Frenchmen, Canadians, and Americans very clear, since they are only events in the great, impersonal nebulae streaming into his pages from the "energies" of American expansion westward.

What has the frontier left us? In Mr. DeVoto's eyes it is the drama of the overwhelming force that geography has exerted on the American mind. But can it be geopolitics alone, which is neither original nor noble, that has led Mr. DeVoto through so many passionate and patient years of research? Is it for this that he loves to retrace every route followed by the explorers and scouts? Geopolitics excited the Nazis, and "manifest destiny," of a kind, is behind the Russians' boast that they have a still open frontier in Siberia and in the Arctic. But can these be enough for us? Is there anything in this drama of space that brings back the wonder and the beauty of that discovery of America which, as de Tocqueville said, was a providential event in the history of the world? Of course Mr. DeVoto does not think that frontiers are ever anything more than a new opportunity for man, and of course he has based his immense labors on our having a democracy to carry westward, not labor camps. Yet he writes as if this expansion merely swept along human faith, human ideas, the human mind. It was the other way around. That is why Mr. DeVoto has gone steadily backward in the chronology of his work, leaving us finally in the world of marvels and legends and visions in which America was conceived. That is why Mr. DeVoto has given so much of himself to the story of what is gone.

Twenty-three

THE LETTERS OF SHERWOOD ANDERSON

Sherwood Anderson, as no one needs to be told who has ever read a page of his, was a very lonely man. He was throughout his actually brief literary career also a very uncertain man, who could never be quite sure that he had made good in that unpredictable literary world for which he had abandoned a business career at forty. And he was at the same time a man who just had to keep writing—writing was a profession, a way of life, a condition of his survival. He needed to write all the time, and what he wrote most of, we know now, were letters. He often wrote dozens of letters before settling down to his daily task; he sometimes spent a whole day writing letters, though he did not always mail them—they gave him contact with others, they released and stimulated him to write stories and novels, and above all they kept him in motion, at the very act of writing.

So there are a lot of letters by Sherwood Anderson—five thousand in the Newberry Library in Chicago. Out of these Howard Mumford Jones and Walter B. Rideout have selected four hundred, which cover exactly the twenty-five years of Anderson's literary career, from 1916 to his death in 1941, and have been chosen, the editors tell us, to represent Anderson's attitudes toward writing and his relations with other writers. The job could not have been an easy one, for Anderson's handwriting was atrocious, his spelling was unbelievable, and he repeated himself as naturally as breathing. But since the letters have been chosen with special reference to Anderson's literary career, the book becomes, quite apart from our interest in Anderson himself, a cardinal document in the history of that great generation which, whatever its private bitternesses and personal failures, put American literature finally on the map.

Nevertheless, too many of these letters say the same things in the same words. It is the unknown, the germinal, the not-yet messianic and artistic Anderson, who would be news to us. Just as it is hilarious and revealing to read the excruciatingly "practical" letters Dreiser wrote as editor of fashion magazines early in the century; just as we relish in Whitman's slovenly and unselfconscious letters what even Henry James enjoyed as their "affectionate, illiterate colloquy," so it would be at least a change to see another Anderson than the one who in this book seems always to be writing letters about his eternal dream of becoming a writer.

The fact is—it will hardly astonish anyone who knows his mind—that Anderson on the subject of writing is moving rather than interesting. There are wonderful moments in this correspondence, for Sherwood Anderson was an extraordinarily open, charming and generous person. But he did write too many of these letters just to keep himself writing; he wrote even when he had little to say—or, what is the same thing for anyone writing letters—he often wrote to people as if he were writing novels at them rather than because he had something to say *to* them that could be said only in a letter. What one misses in this correspondence is the poise, the close directness, even the gossipiness, of the great letter writers—whose letters are great because they are in the world, and are not trying to remake it, and themselves, out of their loneliness. Anderson's letters are almost too serious to be good, and they are so full of his being a writer that it is sometimes hard to tell whether we are reading a page from his novels or an apologia for them. The writing is so generally benign that we sit up with pleasure when he suddenly lashes out at some literary stuffed shirt who has been snooty to him at a writers' conference. The spontaneity is altogether too desperate, and therefore not quite natural, as befits a man whose real fault is that he fooled himself into the belief that, "Every thought going through my head is something to say." For Anderson, writing was not just a means of personal expression, but a search for salvation; it was the way he saved his own life, every day he wrote, in the hope that he was also helping to save his country.

But this is a very American fault: writing for itself alone, writing as something really gratuitous, inwardly free and wise, is the rarest thing in our literature. Reading these letters, with their heartbreaking recital of all those projects begun but laid aside, of books he finished but were not good enough to publish—and all the while writing had to give him a living, satisfy his conscience, and release him from himself—one wonders if the tragedy of Anderson was really, as is so often said, that he began so late. What would have happened if he had not walked out of that factory? What if he had been content to remain a writer in his spare time, content, like so many modest English writers, to fulfill a small, touching vision of life in a series of miniatures—which is what his books come down to anyway—instead of breaking up his life and hitching his talent to every new cause and doctrine in sight that might keep him flowing, that would help him to produce a new book each year?

An absurd thought, for of course it is just the immersed, sweating, visionary side of Anderson—the Anderson who needed to reach what he called "the sacred city"—that makes him one of ours. In England a man with so little formal education and always so self-consciously plebeian would never have begun to write at all. So we must take him as he was, with all his high hopes, his suffering, his naive artfulness, his fidelity to the vision. And here the letters have their own story to tell; here is where they become genuine, as a portrait of the artist in America. The early letters to Waldo Frank, Paul Rosenfeld, Van Wyck Brooks show him humbly deferential to his mentors and "betters"—those critics who were the first to support him, but whose own faults he shrewdly saw and shyly pointed out to them even while he looked up to them with such fearful respect—after all, they had all been to college! What is charming here is Anderson's interior firmness, as in those letters to Van Wyck Brooks where, with his strongly Midwestern allegiance to Mark Twain, he pointed out the lack of fundamental appreciation in *The Ordeal of Mark Twain,* and despite the antipathy to Henry James we would expect, shows Brooks where the latter failed to do justice to genius in *The Pilgrimage of Henry James.* These early letters, with their authentic Whitmanesque cry of "Brother," their eagerness and high hopes for a whole generation fighting its way out of the nineteenth century, are a moving reminder of the fraternalism among writers that died with our entry into the First World War.

It is when we get into the 'twenties, when *Winesburg* so quickly became a classic and Anderson enjoyed the one unqualified success he ever really knew, that we begin to catch those first notes of entreaty, of panic, of needing to attach himself to some cause or doctrine, that was the symbol of Anderson's trouble. For successful as he was and generally admired, he was simply not growing as an artist must. How many cities he tried to escape to! The very names on the letters are a silent record of Anderson's desperate flights around the country, of his search for the "primitive" in New Orleans or Mexico or wherever, of his broken marriages, of his hopes to find in some out-of-the-way hotel either comradeship with "simple" people or just peace enough to get on with his novels. These letters already prepare one for that visible breakdown of his talent in the 'thirties which led him to attach himself to tenant farmers in the South and to labor struggles as he had once attached himself to "the man and woman thing." "Anyway," he writes in one terrible and revealing sentence, "I am going to try that now." Of course Anderson felt a real identification with workers and farmers, and it was certainly more real than anything the "proletarian" novelists ever knew. But how much it tells us about his fundamental ingenuousness and downright ignorance to find him eventually, after his quick disillusionment with the Communists, crying out that he wishes "Karl Marx had never lived." By the late 'thirties he seems to have been often desperate, glad to get commissions from magazines he formerly despised, and—though the most generous of friends—inevitably saddened by the extent to which his erstwhile protégés, Faulkner and Hemingway, had outdistanced him.

Yet even in this last, painful period we catch, amid the yearning and repetitiousness, more than one reminder of the essential, the unforgettable, the beautiful Anderson. How like him to say, still: "Always the imagined world is more important than what we call reality"; to protest that "the young painters . . . of our day are a bit too much inclined to take other humans merely as symbols. There is a lot of 'big thinking' going on"; to note, long before it became as marked as it is now, that under the onslaught of dictatorship there has been set up even in this country "a kind of wall between all individuals." No, he was himself not a "big thinker," and no doubt he would have been happier and more genuinely Sherwood Anderson if he had quietly turned his back on all the "big thinkers" he always thought he needed to write to; which is one reason why his letters are so muddy. But how well he understood that "Man's real life is lived out there in the imaginative world, and that is where we sell him out"; how real he was, in what he really was. He never let go of that trembling vision of love which is all we ever offer to the great mystery around us.

Twenty-four

THE WRITER AND THE MADMAN

Although there were certainly no two other nineteenth-century writers so incongruous as Ruskin and Maupassant in their personal conduct, their literary ideals, and even the causes of the malady that brought them both down, Peter Quennell's *John Ruskin: The Portrait of a Prophet* and Francis Steegmuller's *Maupassant: A Lion in the Path* ask to be brought together. Both these biographers are more concerned with the personalities of their subjects than with the hidden places in their writings. Both lean on new documentary evidence to provide another instance of the sexual eccentricities of the great. Both are dealing with a large body of work which—whether as little read today as Ruskin's, or as snobbishly underrated in England and America as Maupassant's—calls for serious reappraisal, if only because of its enduring hold on our culture. Both Mr. Quennell and Mr. Steegmuller are practiced and professional hands at the kind of literary biography that is responsible in its scholarship (Mr. Steegmuller's is even full of first-hand discoveries) but not academic. And, finally, it is noteworthy that each of these books recounts the disintegration of a great talent; that in each the disaster is explained by the psychology in which our age is so rich, but not enough with the kind of critical insight and patient study of the creative imagination that sees the writer in the man, that believes the writer is the greater part of the man. Neither of these biographers shows that when a great writer grows "mad," it may be *also* because he is no longer able to address himself to the problem, set for him by the nature of genius, of how to close the gap between art and life.

Mr. Quennell's book is of no particular value. While it is, as one would expect, very elegantly written, it has no intellectual urgency whatever, and is not likely to arouse any new interest in Ruskin's work. Its *raison d'être,* one might almost say its excuse, is the series of letters, published two years ago in England and America by Admiral Sir William James, the grandson of Effie Gray and Sir John Millais, which reveal that her first marriage, to Ruskin, was, by his wish, never consummated, and that Ruskin and his doting parents—who eagerly reclaimed their much-spoiled only child even before the annulment—defamed Effie Gray, her parents, and Millais to conceal his own "unnatural conduct."

These letters, exchanged between the principals in the affair, are a Victorian document of extraordinary interest. They present us again with that well-known bedroom tragedy, The Home Life of a Great Victorian (no longer so uproarious as it would have been to a Lytton Strachey). They prove what one has so often been tempted to guess from the sterile magnificence in Ruskin's style—that he could love only at a distance, comfortably free from all adult risks and encounters. They show that the prophet who so tirelessly sermonized his age on Beauty and Good Works perhaps enjoyed torturing his wife during the marriage, and that he put off on her the blame for its failure, though he gratefully consented to the annulment. And when added to what we have already known of Ruskin's only other serious love affair—his frustrated idealization of a little girl—they round out the pathos of his breakdown, with its compulsive profanities and obscenities.

But while Mr. Quennell has woven this evidence into a graceful correction of Ruskin's official biographers and more sentimental admirers, I cannot see that he had any more pressing reason for writing this book. He seems bored by Ruskin, which is understandable, but not in a man who has undertaken a fresh study of him; refers more than once to the burden of those thirty-nine volumes in the collected edition; ignores entirely the formation of the prodigious style; and in general, while he dutifully notes the various aspects of Ruskin's thought, shows no great interest in any one. Writing from Socialist Britain about a man whose sensitivity to injustice, whatever its emotional origins, has meant so much to the British working class, Mr. Quennell announces at the start that he will not go deeply into Ruskin's "efforts and influence as a social reformer" (what a detestable textbook phrase for this mighty subject). And in a period of notable interest in British art—a period, too, that has obviously brought to an end the nineteenth-century saga of private art collectors and wealthy connoisseurs like Ruskin—Mr. Quennell manages also to restrain himself from studying closely Ruskin's "opinions as an art critic." Of course, Ruskin is "a vast subject"; Victorians usually are. But the frigidity of Mr. Quennell's writing shows how indifferent he is even to the man. Ruskin, he writes in a passage on his long unhappiness, was "not one of those lovers whose minds remain relatively independent of the storms that overtake the heart. . . . Besides a heart ravaged, we see a mind beleaguered. It is a spectacle that the biographer, who has a regard for his subject, approaches with some diffidence. Yet, if the subject is to be explored as its merits require . . ." No wonder that at the end Ruskin, inexpressibly monotonous in his pathos, even less provocative a mind than we might have thought him before, simply trots back into the dusty Victorian tomb of his collected edition—a giant, Mr. Quennell affirms, but in effect only a great bore, for here he is a writer more deprived of his art than his neurosis ever deprived him of love.

I will not say that Mr. Quennell is concerned with Ruskin's malady to the exclusion of Ruskin the writer, but he certainly does not make us see a connection between the two. "Madness"—to use an old-fashioned term still not entirely inappropriate to a Hamlet, a Swift, a Blake, so long as we distinguish between what the world once called their folly and what we know to have been their rage—is a subject about which we know more, technically, than the Victorians. But it still requires more than the facile documentation of an unhappy childhood to explain the violations a great imagination can commit against itself. Nowadays one needs to quote Pascal a little differently: the imagination has motives that a vicarious psychoanalysis knows nothing of. In relation to a mind like Ruskin's, our psychology is too pragmatic to be true. Of course, we will see in Ruskin's deliriums the penalty for his abnormal upbringing, his lifelong repression, his unconscious homosexuality. Faced with the ecstatic inflations of the style that so impressed his age and now seems so remote, we draw the obvious conclusion that he mounted on the wings of his prose to compensate for enduring humiliations and loneliness. There can be no doubt that Ruskin did "compensate," that he compensated feverishly, and more and more unintelligibly, for the fantasies and nympholeptic visions of his life. But Ruskin's style is itself a vision, of the kind every great writer is dominated by in his secret enchantment with a life different from that lived by all other men. It is a vision inseparable from Ruskin's passion for language, which makes Mr. Quennell so uneasy; from his "strange fervor," from the very rapture of the word. Ruskin's lifelong ordeal is not least the story of the great impressionistic and imaginative critic who tries to render up the burden on his senses of the whole individual experience of art. He was the schoolmaster of the senses to a society in which he had no place. He tried to preserve in language, in the face of approaching horrors he clearly foresaw, the evanescent Europe that he loved. May it not be that his "egoism" (on which Mr. Quennell sounds as severe as he would have liked Ruskin to be) explains his loneliness far less than the final unavailability of language to a man possessed by language? May it not be that Ruskin's prime daemon, his style, gives us a better clue to his wistful inhumanity than his contradictory feelings about women? I raise these questions to remind myself that the pathetic subject of this book was first a *writer;* Mr. Quennell's book will give no one reason to reread him.

Mr. Steegmuller's book, on the contrary, is stimulating. It has the great virtue of opening up the whole question of Maupassant's relation to contemporary literature. In some of its writing and many of its critical observations, it is pretty slapdash, but as everyone knows who has read that valuable and charming book, *Flaubert and Madame Bovary,* Mr. Steegmuller has an enthusiastic command of the necessary materials, and he is particularly good at assembling a story from documents he has brilliantly, and indeed very entertainingly, translated. If he does not really face up to the moral inertia in Maupassant's work, one must nevertheless thank him for reaffirming the power of an extraordinary talent. It is time that Maupassant came back to life in English, against the intellectual drama of nineteenth-century realism; he has not often been translated or interpreted at his full value.

Still, Maupassant is not an inspiring figure, especially when seen in the company of his great teacher, Flaubert; this book is never so good as when Flaubert is in it, erupting from his letters in all his passion, probity, and indignation against Maupassant's sensuality and literary careerism. The wonderful scolding letter of Flaubert, beginning on page 87, which mounts into "Too many whores! . . . From five in the evening until ten in the morning all your time can be consecrated to the muse, who is still the best bitch of all. . . . A little more pride, by God!," is one of the great documents of the writer's faith; I wish Mr. Steegmuller had pointed up more sharply Maupassant's failure to live up to it. The superiority of master to pupil is a point he takes for granted, but if it had been more openly analyzed, it would have given his book a consistency of thought it lacks and would have saved him from such banal exclamations at Maupassant's achievement as "an undoubted masterpiece," "a marvel of storytelling," "the magic of his art." Flaubert's hatred of mere "realism" is more than ever an example for writers seriously concerned with the advance of fiction; Maupassant's spiritual mediocrity long ago warned that realism had become something of a racket. His talent was prodigious, his outward manner is still endlessly imitated, but he is a block to many contemporary writers. To Mr. Steegmuller, this is simply because Maupassant brought the short story to a harsh perfection that frustrates contemporary short-story writers and makes him still "a lion in the path"—Henry James's homage to his sensual and technical power. Chekhov, whom Mr. Steegmuller so lightly couples with Maupassant as the other great master of the "objective" story, probably wrote fewer good stories than Maupassant, and many of his newspaper sketches are even more trivial than the latter's and without their brilliant edge and satiric bite. But Chekhov is a bridge to the art of James Joyce and Virginia Woolf; his work incarnates that reverence for the individual consciousness that lies at the heart of twentieth-century writing. Maupassant's hard professionalism, his rather complacent irony, have become the stereotype of the kind of short story which, whether the ending is tricky or not—Mr. Steegmuller rightly protests that this side of Maupassant has been exaggerated—is essentially sociological, for it serves to make the reader feel that he has a grasp of a social situation and need know nothing more of the individuals in it.

Maupassant died in an insane asylum of paresis, at forty-three.

Long after he was fatally infected (which he did not suspect), he was still obsessed with sexual conquest. The story of his cynical dandyism, of his constant need to humiliate, in the husbands of his mistresses, the image of the father whom he hated, is a pattern Mr. Steegmuller connects with the early separation of his parents and his abnormal attachment to his mother. As his biographer shows, Maupassant's bitterness against his father is a major theme in his work and explains his unwearying delight in the subject of cuckoldry. But Mr. Steegmuller does not note that Maupassant's conception of the sexual relation is very typical of the "muckerism" that Flaubert called modern life. Though Maupassant's eventual insanity is a clinical fact directly attributable to the spirochete in his brain, his hardness was itself a disease not unfamiliar in our "realistic" culture, and explains Maupassant's easy success with us. The cold prurience, the everlastingly cynical "situation," his passion for showing up people, for liking to make his readers, as he said, "feel bad," his despair of any enduring trust between the sexes—these still make Maupassant the epitome of the writer who, a little sadly but not unprofitably, exploits in sex the brutishness and unfeelingness he denounces in society. The *Spirochaeta pallida* was the final and effective agent that cut Maupassant off from life. But he had separated himself long before by the quality of his thought. As the recent example of Ezra Pound reminds us again, the madness of a great writer is always a tragedy of thought. It is only out of all his thought, out of the deepest places in his thought, that his true biography can be written.

Twenty-five

DREISER

Robert H. Elias' *Theodore Dreiser: Apostle of Nature,* despite its portentous subtitle, is not an interpretation but an almost unnaturally objective biography, by a young scholar who has devoted himself for years to amassing the necessary facts with a kind of professional zeal not usually spent on anyone so out of style as Dreiser. It is about as detailed and reliable a life of Dreiser as we are likely to get for some time. But since it appears at the time when his reputation is at its lowest, I wonder why Mr. Elias did not explain what has drawn him to Dreiser over such a long period, and so at least define his own pleasure in the novels for a generation that began to read them long after Dreiser's method, like the "brilliant" hotel lobbies, horsecars, and women's clothes on which he lavished so much detail, had gone out of fashion. Mr. Elias is so concerned with Dreiser's "ideas"—the least original side of a writer more notable for his tragic grip on life than for the coherence of his thinking—that from his account it is hard to see why one should read the novels at all.

Mr. Elias' explanation for his work is that Dreiser is a "challenging" figure, but what he means by this is that his development was so erratic and his thinking so self-contradictory that they demand investigation of the kind of man who moved from an absolute belief in determinism to a succession of radical causes, vho—one might go on further—could identify himself only with he extremes of power and of suffering, and, after years of being he Communists' chief literary prize and decoy in this country, inally made of his long-pondered novel *The Bulwark* a dull re-igious chromo, then found a rare moment of happiness impul-ively taking communion in a Hollywood church. Dreiser 'challenging"? On the contrary: the "scientific" materialism of ıis early work is no longer a serious issue in twentieth-century hought, his novels are too often read as documents on a vanished ocial period, and the famous awkwardness of his art would ıave been sufficient to repel a literary generation haunted by the liscipline of Eliot and Hemingway if it had not already turned ıgainst naturalistic fiction long before his career was over. The ruth is that Dreiser has become the property of literary scholars ınd historians, for whom he rounds out an era, and that he seems o mean very little to most writers today. What craft would a ıovelist starting out today learn from him? Even those embattled ıaturalists like James T. Farrell who are always invoking Dreiser's example in support of their own work seem to defend ıim because they are working in a time hostile to naturalism, and ıot because they derive from him in any creative way.

And certainly Mr. Elias' biography is not going to stir up any resh interest in the novels. With its full, inexplicably dry, un-paring account of Dreiser's miseries and intellectual confusions, t can inspire only pity for the man, or, at most, wonder that any-ne so deprived, limited, and injured, so rooted in popular rejudices and idolatries, could have created those still unforget-able explorations of our early-twentieth-century life in America —books that, with all their clumsiness, uncertainty of style, and lespondent air, as of a man struggling with materials too large or him, nevertheless have such emotional truth. Mr. Elias' is a valuable record, and he has found some rare documents for it— or example, an amusing letter from Dreiser, as editor of the

Delineator in 1909, to Charles G. Ross, in which we see the very man whose first novel, *Sister Carrie,* had been withheld from circulation by its publisher because of its courageous realism writing that "We like sentiment, we like humor, we like realism, but it must be tinged with sufficient idealism to make it all of a truly uplifting character. Our field in this respect is limited by the same limitations which govern the well-regulated home. . . . I am personally opposed . . . to stories which . . . are disgusting in their realism and fidelity to life." But, like those liberals who take up Dreiser out of a sense of intellectual duty, Mr. Elias does not even touch on that which is still so moving in a Hurstwood, a Sister Carrie, a Jennie Gerhardt, a Clyde Griffiths. By stressing Dreiser's "philosophy" rather than his sensibility and the inner world of his novels, by avoiding the crucial question of his creative sympathies and identifications, his novelist's gift for searching an individual life to its depths, Mr. Elias has managed to bypass Dreiser's art as effectively as those liberals who think they honor him by praising a social consciousness that was not always in the liberal tradition, to say the least.

All these literary and political doctrines in whose name people still uphold Dreiser have as little to do with his imagination, his stolid but authentic personal gift, as those weaknesses of style for which critics used to dismiss him when showing how badly he wrote. He did write "badly" when he adopted a fancy style for his high-toned characters, who were unreal to him, but while his style was certainly dull, it was exactly the instrument he needed for building up those vast coral reefs of observed facts. Dreiser's approach to fiction was always archaic, and seems especially so now, when the "well-made" novel has become indispensable—just when we are no longer quite sure what the novel is about. The novelist today writes as if he could depend on his intelligence alone. Dreiser was a reporter who, when he turned to the novel, always recorded in the most "lifelike" manner. For him, ction was still a branch of history. He seized upon certain large onceptions floating about in his period and hoped that by an ccumulation of small realistic details, social documents, and ediorial reveries on the behavior of his characters a testimony to the ature of life in his time would appear; like Whitman, he was urprised by his own gift. He was dominated by the social myths nd dreams of a generation enraptured with materialism, and he ould conceive of the novel only as a backhanded tribute to the uthority of power. Yet, even as he showed his characters derauded by a purely acquisitive society, he preserved in them a ertain wonder, a forgotten, provincial detachment from the rutalities around them, that gives them the quality of conemplatives in a world they no longer hope to master. They have hat brooding attachment to strange new forces in life that we ind in old sagas—a quality that I have always felt to be at the enter of Dreiser's work but that is hard to define, for they are ot resistant enough to be tragic and yet they are not merely sad; hey are like figures in a dream that they are astonished to be weaving around themselves. It is this that always moves me in the novels when I go back to them: the processional of relatives and newspaper friends and dusty old eccentrics in *Twelve Men;* the wonderful night scene in which Sister Carrie measures herself against the immensity of Chicago, and in which we see a generation just off the farms and out of the small towns confronting the modern city for the first time; the scene in which Carrie comes on Hurstwood sitting in the dark; Jennie Gerhardt's growing solitude, even after the birth of her child; and, beyond the mechanical documentation in *The Financier* and *An American Tragedy,* the power drives of Frank Cowperwood and Clyde Griffiths.

Dreiser's greatest characters are all the more real because they are unconscious of their classic burdens; they have the sort of worn, deeply engraved dignity that is given to those who

know only that they are doomed to face in one directio
and never another. Yet Sister Carrie, Hurstwood, Jenni
Gerhardt, and Clyde Griffiths are not, like the characters c
Dos Passos, simply nasty and truncated examples of a socia
tendency. They are individual human beings, and they neve
seem less than human because they are engaged in a hopeles
struggle; rather, they gain an enormous kind of realized lif
by their very inability to shirk the terms of their commitment. O
course their world is drab, lacking in nuance, merely *fated*. I
comes back to us now in harsh images of absolute success an
failure, of a parochial life so bereft of everything but savag
competition below and meaningless mystery above, so limited t
a cycle of titans and their victims, that it is only the novelist'
ignorance that there is anything else, his helpless confinement t
the American success story for every idea, that gives his work it
awful and crushing power. Close as it is to us in time, it is diffi
cult for us to feel its immediacy, for the business leader of whon
Dreiser was in awe is no longer the hero of our society; we won
der that so much could once have been made of social documen
tation when it is now done by coolly impersonal research expert
without any moral complexity, when the failures we know ar
hardly limited to abandoned mistresses, thieving hotel managers
bankrupt financiers, and widowed farmers. Dreiser's work is on
in which business success, adultery, and "the survival of th
fittest" are the prime elements, like the fire and water and air tha
the earliest Greek philosophers thought moved the world. It is a
once rudimentary social history and cosmology, the first literatur
of some early society. But I never feel in it—as I do in the work
of cleverer naturalists, like Frank Norris and Dos Passos—con
tempt for the author's characters and even some intellectual satis
faction that so many unpleasant types have come to a bad end
The degeneration of Hurstwood in *Sister Carrie*—one of th
most impressive technical performances in the modern novel—

frightening precisely because we are made to feel that a human eing like ourselves is falling out of life directly in front of our yes, and that nothing can be done about it, for his failure is ecessary to Carrie's success; the general indifference to his fate s the very color and tone of the story. Dreiser saw that indiference as the law of the universe, and he kept thinking that he ould explain it by science and philosophy, fields for which he vas not well equipped. Nevertheless, he was always amazed by t. In his best work, that amazement rushes back at us with a ound primitive, innocent, and grand, like man's first discovery f the nature of his existence.

Twenty-six

THE WRITER AND THE UNIVERSITY

Once, American writers all seemed to be clergymen—just as a time would come when they would all seem to be former clergymen. Then, often as not, they were politicians, and later, printers. The printers like Mark Twain became journalists before they became "authors," and almost, it would seem, in order to become authors. In fact, by the end of the nineteenth century, the tendency of American writers to begin in journalism, and even to stay in it as part of their creative life as writers, was so well established that this persisted into the 1920's, when reporters like Lardner and Hemingway carried on the tradition of Hearn, Crane, Dreiser, Mencken. The city room was still a legendary place for American writers, and just as every recruit in Napoleon's army carried a marshal's baton in his knapsack, so a reporter hid in the drawers of his desk, amid the crumpled pieces of carbon paper and the whisky bottle that was his excuse to posterity for not finishing it, a chapter of the great American novel.

Nowadays, however, a great many writers tend to be in the universities—and I mean *writers,* those for whom writing is a personal necessity and who, whatever else they may do, see the world with a writer's mind. The university today includes not merely critics, who would seem to belong there, but poets, novelists, and dramatists of one kind or another who can be ound up and down the country being the Norton professor at Harvard, the Christian Gauss lecturer at Princeton, the Neilson professor at Smith, the poet-in-residence at the University of Cincinnati, the visiting critic at the University of Indiana. Even the writers who stay out of academic enterprises at home turn up in Europe under the auspices of the Rockefeller Foundation, the Ford Foundation, the Fulbright program, the Salzburg Seminar in American Civilization, the visiting professorship in American culture at Florence or Cologne. Many writers are professors in full harness, like Wallace Stegner, Lionel Trilling, Mark Van Doren, Yvor Winters, Peter Viereck. There can be very few new American poets who are not wrapped in what has been called the "academic cocoon." E. E. Cummings will never be a professor, T. S. Eliot always gets back to publishing, and Wallace Stevens at seventy-six is still in the insurance business at Hartford; William Carlos Williams is a baby doctor in New Jersey and, despite a lifetime of visiting in colleges and universities, Robert Frost has never—at least not since his youth—really been in regular service. But among the good younger poets, Theodore Roethke teaches, and Randall Jarrell, and Richard Wilbur; Karl Shapiro gave up a post at Johns Hopkins to become editor of *Poetry,* which can hardly be called an unacademic post; Robert Lowell teaches a good deal, if not regularly; but it is rare to find a poet of this generation, as, say, Elizabeth Bishop, who will not teach at all. As for the critics!—the critics, including some who forgot to go to college at all, are not merely professors, they tend even to become heads of departments, chiefs of divisions, directors of educational surveys and programs both at home and abroad.

What we are seeing just now is more than the university's friendly hospitality to writers; it is an attempt to play the active role of patron—to support the creation of literature, to take writers into the academic community, and thus to show that it regards them as assimilable, harmonious—and necessary. Dr J. Robert Oppenheimer, closing the celebration of Columbia' two-hundredth anniversary with a survey of "Prospects in th Arts and Sciences," noted, as part of the transformation of th American scene in these last years, that now the artist "needs t be a part of the community, and the community can only, wit loss and peril, be without him. Thus it is with a sense of interes and hope that we see a growing recognition that the creativ artist is a proper charge on the university, and the university proper home for him; that a composer or a poet or a playwrigh or painter needs the toleration, the understanding, the rather loca and parochial patronage that a university can give; and that thi will protect him to some extent from the tyranny of man's com munication and professional promotion. . . . For here there is a honest chance that what the artist has of insight and of beaut will take root in the community and some human bonds ca mark his relations with his patrons. . . ."

All this represents a very great change. When I was in colleg in the 'thirties, it was still well understood that scholars were on class and writers quite another. They did not belong to the sam order of mind, they seemed quite antithetical in purpose an temperament, and at the very least, they needed different place to work in. There is no need to recall all the satire, scorn, and downright bitterness which has been showered by writers on the academic class—and has been reciprocated. You can no more imagine Hemingway or Fitzgerald in a university than you picture one of the new critics out of it. In those days it was understood that scholarship was itself a trust, gravely presided over by men and women who were custodians of the best that had been thought and learned. Knowledge was seen historically; it consisted of a tradition, *the* tradition. It was not always possible to say where this tradition began, but so far as literature was concerned, it ended at the cemetery. In 1938, a classmate of mine wanted to do his doctor's thesis on Dreiser, but was told flatly that he would not get permission until Dreiser was dead. This, with its obtuse hostility to a writer whose best work was behind him, nevertheless represented a principle that some of us were bound to respect, precisely because it was not ours. It defined the opposition between tradition and the new generation; it showed us the authority we had to fight. The scholar, on his side, knew what he knew, he knew what his subject was, and it was *not* to be confused with every confounded and ill-considered literary enthusiasm that came along. Enough time had to elapse for his subject to take its shape, for the evidence to appear. D. H. Lawrence (1885-1930) and James Joyce (1880-   ) were questionable and problematical additions to the canonical history of English literature. Just as a professor was, in those days, someone who *looked* the professor, so was he someone who watched over knowledge, who preserved it—and so often, alas, thought that he owned it. The scholar saw himself in relation to the tradition of which he was an officer, and whether he sat on a board interrogating a candidate at a doctor's oral, or wrote a paper "establishing" the influence of a major poet on a lesser poet, he knew that he was custodian of the custodians, and so trained those who were to carry on the same work after him. Indeed, the very picture that scholars had in those days of certain institutions of democracy proceeding in a straight line from the Anglo-Saxons in the German forests to their descendants on the American frontier, or of English literature evolving somewhat awkwardly but steadily from Beowulf to Thomas Hardy, expressed perfectly, as an image of history generally tends to, the scholar's conception of his subject and of his own approach to it. All scientists were adding to our knowledge, all scholars were working with the precise impersonality and cautious certitudes of science, and the tradition was so real that it possessed moral authority in itself.

It followed from this that the literary scholar's attitude toward the contemporary writer was, at best, one of understandable scepticism. For how can you evaluate soundly, how can you judge truly, how can you even *know*—when the writer is still living, when the arc has not been closed by death, when the pattern may be interrupted or even changed by a masterpiece or a failure? It is easy, now, to laugh at the caution with which departments of English used to look at contemporary American literature, and in our day, when the young are brought up on it and are made to analyze stories by Hemingway and poems by Cummings, to remember with derision the time when Paul Elmer More called a novel by Dos Passos "an explosion in a cesspool," and when it was well understood, in many a cozy professorial conclave, that *The Waste Land* and *Ulysses* were deliberate hoaxes on the public. But the scholar honestly thought that there was a tradition to look after, and if he tended to be too cautious in adding to it, even the writer himself might well respect the other for knowing his subject so well and for trying to preserve it.

It was only when this idea of a tradition broke down that writers could become part of the university. It is all very well for writers to say why *they* need the university—to complain of how difficult it is for them to earn a living, or how deadly the modern streamlined newspaper has become. They may lament that while Hemingway learned many elements of his style on the *Kansas City Star,* a paper famous for its literary reporters, newspapers now are simply too much alike, and have become much too few, in fact, to support the diversity and vaguely bohemian literary atmosphere that once made newspaper work so stimulating to literary hopefuls. But obviously the writer cannot enter the university unless the university will have him there. It is exactly the point at which the tradition broke down among the professors themselves, when *they* became "modern" and "creative," ashamed above all of seeming dull—it was exactly at this point that the writer was welcomed in a university whose proper study came to seem not the past, in its closed historic shape, but the constant interflow of "life," of contemporary experience, of every and any phenomenon that could be weighed, measured and described.

"Aren't we writers, too?" a distinguished scholar said to me, more puzzled than reproachful, when I made this point at the faculty club. "Do you think that I'm academic?" the most academic man of my acquaintance asked me, exactly in the tone of voice with which an invalid might ask a doctor if the case were hopeless. He lives among professors of literature who are always referring to contemporary literature, or lecturing on contemporary literature, or analyzing it with the I.B.M. machine of modern criticism, or anthologizing contemporary literature—and he feels out of touch. The old order has not, of course, passed entirely: pedants will be pedants, but nowadays no longer have to be scholars. The real scholars, on the other hand, are no longer sure where they fit into the scheme of things. For it is the authority of culture itself that is going today, and in the world of values, there are no longer any parents for the young to rebel against. Parents and children, professors and students, all are young together and want incoherently to remain "young" as long as possible. Scholarship persists as an art; the scholar himself is no longer looked up to as a judge.

Our very conception of time has changed. The past is no longer all that came before us, all that asks to be *learned*—it is something which comes to us as fashions to imitate, and which past it is to be, current literature now dictates. Time past is only that which serves time present, so that people study Donne only because of Eliot and know Homer only through Joyce. The university which in 1938 would not permit a doctor's thesis on Dreiser recently sponsored one on something called "Post-Depression Drama"—which interested me, not least, because if in the old days scholarship studied only the literature it could connect with history, nowadays it brings up analysis even where there isn't any literature. The visiting poet, or the critic-in-residence, lives in a world where sociologists work only in teams and are imitating psychologists; where it is clear not merely that scholars are interested in everything they can use for a subject, but where they will even allow themselves to be photographed in the act of making history. The old picture of the scholar as a cloistered eccentric must be replaced by the hard-breathing young social psychologist, textbook maker, anthologist, and therapist to the lonely crowd who, ever since the days of the brain truster, has turned the American scholar into a slightly synthetic personality—always "liberal" and a regular fellow, as much the product of mass culture as his students, usually a journalist and mostly a rewrite man.

It is in this new atmosphere that the writer has come into the university—an atmosphere in which values are in confusion and in which many fields run into each other; in which the constant search is for a philosophy, ideas, a perspective, any slant by which to leaven the great mass of facts which American scholarship piles up every year. Many scholars now give the appearance of living intellectually from hand to mouth, and it is this that explains the unbelievable influence of the critics who, in a culture that has forgotten religion and has never known philosophy, act as "idea men." We live in a culture so materially rich, so powerful, so well able to support experiment and so eager to develop itself, that the writer is urged, almost in desperation, to contribute to the discussion and is sometimes looked on as a miracle if he comes up with an idea. The creative writer serves all sorts of purposes in our new culture. He is something of a dancing teacher to the children of the new rich; only, instead of teaching them the art of the dance, he can show them how to analyze down to the bone what others have written. This prosperous, aspiring, *parvenu* side of American life explains a great deal about the writer's presence in the university. There is money around, and some of the money can be used to hire well-known writers, whose names lend prestige to the university and whose antics will supply the faculty club with gossip all winter. The writer becomes an attraction, able to bring in not only the summer session crowd and the extension division crowd, but to make the university officials advance the claim that they are taking learning straight to the people; the writer is either a stimulant or an irritant, and in any case, a challenge. Above all, he serves directly in those fields, like creative writing and literary criticism of the more practical sort, which seem to have become the domain of visiting writers. And what the university does for the writer is equally obvious. It gives him, what writing can never do, a measure of security; and what is of extreme importance to anyone who knows what a lonely trade writing can be, an intellectual community of a kind which simply does not exist elsewhere; it does give him a sense of belonging, and encourages his writing in many graceful and grateful ways, just as it obviously limits it in others.

Still, the relationship of the writer to the university is basically an unreal one, and while the university needs writers and (some) writers need the university, it would be well to realize the fundamental differences between them and not to minimize them. The scholar thinks of his field, still, as a body of knowledge to which facts are added and in which clarifications are constantly being made. But to the writer reality is something to be *transformed*—and not by the patient discussion and analysis of impersonal items, but by a creative act. The virtues of scholarship at its best—patience and humility and disinterestedness—are not necessarily the writer's virtues, except that he needs the patience to realize his hunch, the humility to allow his work to have its way with him, and enough steadiness to bring his work to a successful conclusion. It is an illusion that people interested in the same subject necessarily share the same attitude toward it; in truth, it is the essentially personal attitude that we have, the innermost point of view that we bring to anything from our very souls, and not the subject itself, that brings minds together.

Above all, the writer does not work with anyone; he is not a collaborator, he is not co-operative, and it can be to his very peril as a writer if he sacrifices the excruciating precision of his vision and his unrelenting impatience of mediocrity in order to please, to accommodate himself, to fit in. Academic life, though it may exercise no control over his writing, only over his teaching, can in all sorts of small ways exert pressure and influence on his writing. We live in a culture where the highest aim is not to live in the spirit, but to be comfortable; not to give offense or to take it, but to get along, to be happy. But no one in his senses would choose writing in order to become happy. The writer, the artist, is a man plagued by homesickness, and in furious resistance to the most commonplace treacheries, and forever in love with Him who is not the God of this world. "I put a piece of paper and a pencil under my pillow," said Thoreau, "and when I could not sleep I wrote in the dark." Academic life thrives on co-operative specialization, on a body of scholars who not only answer to each other but who all need each other. It thrives on promotions, honors, acceptance—and on publication at any price. In the same spirit of utter good will it offers the writer promotions, too, and recognition and acceptance. But these do not help the writer in his lonely work. They may be actually harmful, for they can distract and deceive and soften him up.

But these differences and distinctions apart, it is obvious that the writer will remain part of the university and that more and more universities are likely to want writers. The writers will welcome this. Quite apart from the fact that it *is* becoming increasingly difficult for a serious writer to live by his writing the money in publishing these days is in secondary media, like television and those soft-cover books which, in the great majority, still feature the more sensational and "popular" kind of writing. Newspapers are more than ever just now, by reason of their timidity and standardization, poor training grounds for the free creative spirit, and a Mr. Dooley, a Broun, a Thurber, have yielded to a world of Timestyle, of the syndicated review, and—this is where it really hurts—to the columnist who is more likely to be Westbrook Pegler than Walter Lippmann.

Basically, the writer is in the university because of what has happened to America in the last few years—the new thoughtfulness of wealth, the amazing break-up of the conservative tradition, the open competition of the university with other intellectual agencies. The university has become one of the real movers and shakers of American life, as witness Congressman Reece's indignant charge that the Rockefeller Foundation and the Encyclopaedia of Social Sciences had virtually brought socialism to America. The presence of so many writers in the university is really a chapter in the still undescribed revolution of America since the war. But what needs finally to be said, on the writer's part, is that he is in the university because he wants to be there. It enables him to play a role—as moralist, as philosopher, as literary guide and teacher to his tribe—which American writers have always loved to play, which the country has wanted them to play, and which, in a culture so devoted to self-improvement as ours, the university best enables them to play. What all this has done to American writing is another story; but who knows whether to blame our new writers on the academy or to admit that so many of them flock to the university because that is the natural center of their interests just now? However one may lament what has happened to our writing ever since it entered the university, there should be no doubt that from the writer's own point of view, his choice is made in the deepest freedom. It is all his own doing, all his own career, his talent, his fate—and always his task to bear. That, in fact, is what it means to be a writer, and it is because of this intense act of will, of choice, of freedom, that only the writer can say what being in the university means to him, and what he gets out of it.

Twenty-seven

DOSTOEVSKY AND THE AGE OF ANXIETY

In this season of deep human winter, when so much facile humanism lies frozen on the stalk of our science and our ethics, it is good—but no doubt a little uncomfortable—to face again that devout Russian iconoclast whose legendary illness has always served to give men intellectual health. Dostoevsky would have bridled at that last phrase, of course; he thought he came to bring men not ideas but religious security. Like so many Slavophiles (but somehow more than most, as his need of an absolute faith was greater), he dreamed of a time when "Russian virtue" and the "religious Russian heart" would fecundate the West, set it free of its materialism and its shallow ideals of progress. In his own mind his books, when he was not rushing them through to pay his creditors and his landlord, would be bridges to a new apocalypse—that moment to be made possible only by the spiritual genius of Byzantine Russia, the sacred authority of the Romanoffs, and books like his, when patriotism, authority and religion would turn contemporary "anarchists" into the humble and happy creatures of the new revelation.

It is not faith that Dostoevsky has ever brought us; the day when his message could be taken even by the Russians, on his terms, has long since passed. His gift has been icy and merciless clarity; an awareness of man, as man, in his social loneliness, his emotional cheating, his fertile and agile hostility, his limited power to love—always, Dostoevsky's subject is the war in man. It was those he considered his enemies, the Russian socialists, who brought the West a new faith. Think of the different ways in which men read *Das Kapital* and *The Brothers Karamazov,* and how much keener anticipation of totalitarianism and modern secular religions is to be found in Ivan Karamazov's tale of The Grand Inquisitor than in the hopeful literature of socialism! By one of those ironies which lay implicit in the national struggle between the Westerners and the Slavophiles in old Russia, the Westerners took power in one decade and found they could anchor it in another only by attaching their scientific materialism to nationalist and authoritarian ideas—to a political program at bottom very much like Dostoevsky's own. The most incisive and the most pragmatic of the Russian Westerners lies before the Kremlin as an eternal human icon. Dostoevsky, the tormented God-seeker, the harried journalist seeking to be a seer, hovers at the side of our complacencies as the prime questioner and satiric destroyer; really a very unpleasant man, as all his friends and family knew and as Tolstoy suspected without meeting him; but terribly hard to get rid of. For the light he sheds on human motives—brokenly, mischievously, always with his programmatic mind on "the defeat of anarchism"—is one nothing can ever break, so long as we take it up in ourselves.

Here is a pretty historical irony. The only strain of it that descends to us unchanged from the agony of Czarist Russia is the universalism of its best minds. Just as the revolutionary seeds planted in the Russian October have sprouted into all the real political conflicts of our time, so Dostoevsky's notes on nineteenth-century Russian futility, sloth and yearning for a new faith emerge as the real parables of modern character and of that "neurotic personality of our time" whose deeper ambiguities you won't find in Karen Horney. In this "age of anxiety," as Auden puts it, this age when man can no longer tell in his atomic insecurity how much his inner conflicts, human-duplicated, contribute to the social disorder and how much they are made by it; this age when the sense of guilt is so ripe and universal that it is the freshest device of innocence; when in fact it would take a whole new moral vocabulary to deliver men of their nominal aches and fears—and only then would the real creative struggle of man to know his meaning in the universe begin—in such an age Dostoevsky's heroes, stumbling blindly along the old Russian street, appear before us as pillars of honesty, heroes of truth.

Unlike us, they are perplexed by everything except the deepest issues of their perplexity; they *know,* in a world in which activity is impossible. We are all a little Russian these days—some by *force majeure,* some by disgust with our own culture, some out of sheer material infatuation with the force of that heartland that has pushed its way west and east. But we are even more Russian in our growing approximation to that absolute spiritual crisis which Dostoevsky's heroes accept as the ground of their lives. And it is a crisis, however measured by political disorder, that is not to be defined in political terms alone any more than the Raskolnikovs, Stavrogins, and Ivan Karamazovs measured their opposition to the reality of their day in political terms alone. It lies in the effort of man to assert his full reality—that is, to discover it—in the face of deterministic psychologies, material consolation, and his own gift for converting potential good into immediate evil.

If Dostoevsky speaks so directly to us today it is because the problems of which his characters are composed are not national or historical, and because these men spare themselves and us nothing in their effort to seek out the real meaning of their suffering. They begin with the realization that their suffering is culturally and spiritually real, not merely clinical and personal. Dostoevsky himself was so obviously dismayed by his own inability to escape some final truth that he was forever trying to resolve it into an authoritarian, pseudo-religious faith. But authoritarianism is easy, and the pseudo-religions are easier still. The faith by which Dostoevsky redeems his characters, from the vantage-point of which alone he dares to paint them in all their ambiguity and their striving, does not really count. Just as the Bible-reading Raskolnikov in the last part of *Crime and Punishment* adds nothing to the real story of the novel except in his shrewd dream of the world being devoured by microbes, so the ends of Dostoevsky's characters, when they are salvational ends, mean nothing to us after we have learned their means—and life to them is only the means by which they read it and occasionally escape it. The real thing in Dostoevsky is always the enveloping human moment of hostility, self-deception, cardinal vanity and forced realization: the living present of man's need to squirm out of the fact that he exists, and that all his learning and all his busy-ness are not sufficient to clear up his problem.

Tolstoy comes to us with cold pity, and asks us to be noble, to deny a little here and save a little of ourselves there; to see how deeply we damage ourselves by pleasure or conquest so that we shall be forced to be good. Chekhov, as Gorky wrote in his beautiful tribute, is forever looking at us—with real pity—asking: "Oh, my friends, why do you live like this?" But Dostoevsky's question is daemonic. He knows that men live as they do because they think as they do, and that their thoughts cannot be replaced by other thoughts until they have reached the bottom of their own. He asks: "Do you know who you are?" That is why he cannot give us faith, and why it is just as well; his job is not to console or heal us. The little rooms in which his characters are forever assaulting each other with real questions are in us and nowhere else; they are our world. Dostoevsky is occupied with the irreversible reality of the universal isolation.

Twenty-eight

FAULKNER IN HIS FURY

TO HANNAH ARENDT AND HEINRICH BLÜCHER

Speaking at Stockholm last December, Mr. Faulkner said, in part: "Our tragedy today is a general and universal physical fear so long sustained by now that we can even bear it. There are no longer problems of the spirit. There is only the question: When will I be blown up? Because of this, the young man or woman writing today has forgotten the problems of the human heart in conflict with itself which alone can make good writing, because only that is worth writing about, worth the agony and the sweat . . .

"He must learn them again. He must teach himself that the basest of all things is to be afraid; and teaching himself that, forget it forever, leaving no room in his workshop for anything but the old verities and truths of the heart, the old universal truths lacking which any story is ephemeral and doomed—love and honor and pity and pride and compassion and sacrifice . . .

"Until he relearns these things, he will write as though he stood among and watched the end of man. I decline to accept the end of man. It is easy enough to say that man is immortal simply because he will endure: that when the last ding-dong of doom has clanged and faded from the last worthless rock hanging tideless in the last red and dying evening, that even then there will still be one more sound: that of his puny inexhaustible voice, still talking. I refuse to accept this. I believe that man will not merely endure: he will prevail. He is immortal, not because he alone among creatures has an inexhaustible voice but because he has a soul, a spirit capable of compassion and sacrifice and endurance. The poet's, the writer's, duty is to write about these things."

We in America do not often hear such talk from our novelists—and perhaps we expect it least from a realistic novelist whose work is still identified with the sadistically meticulous account of Southern "decadence" we so often get from the fashionable new novelists. Even Faulkner's larger reputation in Europe, at least in the form in which it comes back to us, shows that if that hydra-headed monster, the twentieth-century American novelist—he whose name is simply Faulkner-Hemingway-Caldwell-Steinbeck—is still thought of as the last word in brutality and savage materialism, it is predominantly Faulkner who so personifies him to the outside world.

But the thrill of pleasure I felt on reading Faulkner's Nobel Prize speech was based not only on my gratitude that such words should be spoken today at all—and how badly our frightened intellectuals need to hear them—but also on a sense of recognition. *What* Faulkner said at Stockholm is in its explicit adjunction unusual for him and even untypical. I would not have said that it is to lift our hearts that he writes. But that voice, that unashamedly eloquent voice in all its true terseness, reminding us by the very rush and edge of his sentences that all human affairs are settled first within the heart, returning back and back to those large words like love and honor and pity and pride by which, after all, we do try to live; pointing to the fear-racked man of our age in his secret daily aloneness—it is precisely that voice, passionate and steady, that seems to hold his novels together in their fierceness, line by line. Even the most perfunctory reading of a page should intimate to us the nature of the mind we are dealing with, warn us that he is different in kind rather than in degree from our other novelists today.

Yet many people seem able to read Faulkner through, even to analyze his work on its secondary levels with the greatest shrewdness, without finding any very constructive purpose to his style. For what is the usual objection to that style? Why, that it is *needlessly* involved, that it is perversely thick with parentheses, even with parentheses within parentheses; that it is a pity a man who can tell a story so well should get so heated in the telling and be so long-winded. I have just read an article in the latest number of *Partisan Review* that states his art is wholly uneven, hopelessly lost between two styles—"one is simple and full of references to nature; there is nothing to equal it in American writing today . . . In his other style, which dominates his writing, Faulkner constructs his legend of the South. It is here that all his famous traits are found: the rhetoric, the difficult, involved sentences, gratuitous and exaggerated, the tangle of meanings and motive." "So little is left of the touching simplicity and openness," this article goes on, "it is hard to believe that the same man writes in both styles." Your thoroughly sensible critic finds Faulkner a talented man who unfortunately tends to get lost in floods of excess sensibility; your humanist liberal, that he rants; I have recently heard a Marxist criticism that he is simply a floridly uncontrolled reactionary brooding over the decline of his class. Even someone who understands him so well as Malcolm Cowley thinks that the defects of his style can be attributed to the traditional isolation of the American writer. "His novels," Cowley says in the introduction to his brilliantly arranged Portable Faulkner, "are the books of a man who broods about literature but doesn't often discuss it with his friends; there is no ease about them, no feeling that they come from a background of taste refined by argument and of opinions held in common . . . Like Hawthorne, Faulkner is a solitary worker by choice, and he has done great things with double the pains to himself that they might have cost if they had been produced in more genial circumstances . . . All of them are full of overblown words that he would have used with more discretion, or not at all, if he had followed Hemingway's example and served an apprenticeship to an older writer."

Now these objections—and I have contributed to them myself—spring in part from a certain false professionalism in our attitude toward style. One might call it the Hemingway influence. Hemingway's own early style, and his—a whole generation's—particular craving for simplicity and naturalness, are something else again. The Hemingway influence has now become an article of commerce. The dregs of that influence can be seen not merely in the shallow and smug language of a slick news-weekly like *Time,* but even more in the method of production that puts the magazine together on the belief that anything can be rewritten, and apparently by anyone. I have often detected in the language of editors and critics the unconscious belief that all writers have the same needs, and that all write to the same audience. They favor that "clear," because convenient, style through which one can see immediately to the bottom of any subject—and indeed, to judge from Hemingway's recent work, the bottom is very quickly reached. I call it a falsely professional attitude—Richard Chase complains in a recent book on Melville that even he was too little the continuously professional writer!—because it stems from that morbid overconsciousness of the audience that afflicts even the most serious writers in this country. We have become so intent on getting the audience to understand quickly, rather than on encouraging the writer to have his full say, that we brutally dispose of the individual differences between writers.

Now Faulkner, as is well known, is less conscious of his audience than most novelists today. He has even written in a letter to Cowley: "I think I have written a lot and sent it off to print before I actually realized strangers might read it." Many objections to his style, I am convinced, stem from our disbelief that a writer in America *can* write without thinking of the "strangers" who might read him; that he will not sacrifice an iota of his realization to "communication" at any price. But the primary reason for our objections to Faulkner's style is our refusal to believe that what he writes about is entirely real even to him. Most of his critics show a genuine indifference to his point of view.

By point of view I mean not a writer's social opinions, which he may and usually does share with many people, especially if he is a Southerner; not those psychological interpretations by which we now so easily interpret and think we entirely reveal someone's character; not even his moral philosophy, whether on its most realistic or exalted level. I mean the angle of vision from which one recurringly sees the universe—that native disposition of mind which plants in us very early those particular words, those haunted stresses and inflections, those mysteriously echolaic repetitions, to which we most instinctively return—and which at our best we accept with joy, and sometimes even understand.

It is his point of view, his personal conviction of the shape life has, that presents any writer with that resurgent theme from which he chooses the subject of his art and even many of its devices. For a real artist never simply borrows a technique even when he may seem to, but uses it as if no one had used it before him. It is by his point of view, surely, that we *know* Dostoevsky, who is more than the sum of his reactionary social opinions; Proust, who is more, even, than *his* sensibility; Melville, who is more than his pessimistic abasement before the magnitude of the divine. It is a writer's point of view that gives us our immediate experience of his mind in all its rich particularity. It is *in* his point of view, though not necessarily for his point of view, that we read him.

But it is amazing how many people disregard what is most

immediately present to their minds when they read a page of Faulkner. It is very hard for me to believe that the often tumultuous and deeply spiritual experience we have in reading something like "The Bear" adds only to another "parable of the Deep South," or the fact that he is really—the holy simplicity of literary historians!—a "romantic." (The word today apparently signifies that one romantic is just like another.) I do not think Faulkner would have been any different if he had gone to school to Ezra Pound, had learned to trim his style, to be more sparing of those "overblown" words. I think he needs those words. Hemingway may not; Faulkner does. I would suggest that he means something by them essential to his stubbornly individual vision of the world. I would guess they have been in his mind a very long time, that it was almost to see them live a life separate from his own that he began to write, that it is to rediscover their meanings through and through the whole range of his adult life that he continues to write.

For what are those words to which Faulkner constantly returns? Cowley cites *"immemorial, imponderable, immutable."* But the more active words, actually, are *astonishment, outrage, furious, intractable, implacable, inflexible, impervious, amazed, outlast, endure, repudiate, rage, sourceless*—and less and less in the recent works, but always present, for they awoke the image of the soaring arch and of the ecstasy in retracing its height that are both so essential to his mind—*upsoar, avatar, apotheosis.* And significantly, most of these words are applied to individuals of every type and in every class—not only to his intellectuals or visionaries, like Quentin Compson, Horace Benbow, the Reverend Gail Hightower, or his tiresomely sage spokesman, Gavin Stevens; but to a Snopes as well as a Major DeSpain; to the farmers in the field and sitting Saturday afternoons in their "clean well patched overalls" around Varner's store; to the old hunter Ike McCaslin; to a criminal like Popeye; to some children and most boys; to the hunted Negro in "Red Leaves" trying to escape being buried alive with his dead Indian master; to the Negro slaves and to their silently wise descendants still doing the dirty work in the kitchens after the war is over. They are used with particular force about the unscrupulous Jason Compson in *The Sound and the Fury* and the hunted and murdering Joe Christmas in *Light in August;* they are applied to houses, hills, roads, dogs, the dark and mighty figure of the bear in Faulkner's great story of that name; about doors, and at least once, by implication, about God.

These words are not merely interjections, or—as they might often seem—assertions trailing off the loose ends of his narrative. They are the very ground bass, to borrow a figure from music, above which he sets his narrative theme; in and out of which his story is composed. They are the atmosphere in which Faulkner's characters move—even God Himself in the middle section of "The Bear," that God so struck with the outrage and the horror of man's blind exploitation of the land that He was prepared to repudiate him altogether until John Brown, who was fully a man, and so astonished even Him, stayed His hand. All of them, Negro or white, Southern or Northern, old settlers or new exploiters, feel this outrage, this astonishment, this fury. It is the living state—not merely of ourselves caught for a moment above the motion of life, but of everything within our ken and which we color with the violence of our state—astonished and furious and outraged, outraged freshly over again every day and every hour, yet still trying to be impervious, to believe ourselves implacable, and by claiming our own intactness, showing that we seek to endure. And it is a state that is known to his characters and about each other not in moments of contemplation only, for that would arrest the momentum, but—like the constant echo of the ground bass that we hear in Bach—as that particular knowledge to which they must all return.

Now it is with this word *return* that I can perhaps at last get at what is so distinctive in Faulkner's vision—the fact that, more often than not, his characters view things without surprise. It is not the happening that makes a story of Faulkner's move; it is the confirmation. Everything seems to have been known beforehand. The event itself seems to be assimilated first in brooding expectancy; then to occur as a confirmation; then requickens the familiar outrage and astonishment that it should happen at all. So that when the event does occur as expected, and the usual baleful grim glance is thrown over it, it seems to have been not so much lived as relived. Thus one feels—particularly about his most thoroughly realized characters, like Jason Compson and Joe Christmas—that their suffering and their thinking incorporate the very momentum of life. It is as if *their lives were thinking for them.* All through the greater part of *Light in August* one seems to see Joe Christmas running, constantly running ahead on the public highway, yet with his face turned to us, amazed that everything he has expected so long *should* finally be happening to him—even as he runs. All through the great monologue of Jason Compson in *The Sound and the Fury* one sees him rushing about the streets, or hunting his niece from his automobile, yet investing each terrible moment with this greater frightfulness—the fact that his whole life is present in his ordeal, and that he should have expected life to come to a crisis just so, for he has really spent his life thinking it over.

I believe it is this expectancy, this forehand knowledge they bear about with them through each moment of their lives, that gives Faulkner's people that peculiar tension of watching and listening under which he sometimes seems to stagger from page to page of his novels like a man lifting a heavy plaster cast. Surely there is no other living novelist who has lavished so much attention on the human face in its inflexible watchful concentration, who has pinned down so much of the simultaneous impact of human events upon the eye. Each character seems to bear the whole weight of his actual and potential knowledge on his face —yet to doubt that knowledge, not out of any genuine disbelief, but out of astonishment and outrage that he must bear it. And along with it, that fiery screen of background detail, of historical causality as it pertains to his own life and the tradition-racked consciousness of the South, that enters into his mind like those background details of a dream that we take in without always knowing that we do.

In short, Faulkner burdens his characters with the integral human state; he will not let them off. This is the undergrowth of every day—sometimes unbearable in its keenness and recoil—which Joe Christmas must trample through even as he runs. This is that inflamed sense of one's whole life entirely present before one that is the real agony of Jason Compson all that terrible day, "April 6, 1928,"—and that makes him, though infinitely repellent, so giant a paradigm of man clutching at the air of this world as, assailed by every conceivable pain and anxiety, he searches for the niece who has stolen the money he had originally stolen from *her*. In *Intruder in the Dust* Faulkner calls it "that naked agony of inesthetisable nerve-ends which for lack of a better word men call being alive." In "Beyond," that beautiful little story of the responsibilities we still bear dreaming of our death, the Judge describes it as that "certain integral consistency which, whether it be right or wrong, a man must cherish because it alone will ever permit him to die."

It is this "consistency" as the very foundation of awareness, which rejoices in awareness as its most joyful and healthy end, that I see in Faulkner's conception of human integrity. It is this consistency that gives him his inner freedom as a storyteller, and as a stylist, that fierceness and openness of tone beside which so many voices today sound peevish.

Now obviously this integrity is not what we usually mean by

the word today—that which Stuart Chase once so significantly described as a "luxury." As one hears the word nowadays, integrity seems to represent something we should like to have, that we know—if only for our health's sake!—that we need to have, but, nevertheless, is always the paradise lost in the conflicting allegiances of our middle-class existence. And in fact, by our imperative, but still in one sense unworthy, calculations whether we dare to say this thing, to write this article, to defy that boss; by our wearing and wistful questioning of the "integrity" of our simplest relationships, the most casual things we do, we have come to feel that the tidal waves of prosperous unhappiness constantly sweeping over modern American life may represent chiefly a bad conscience. Faulkner starts beyond this point; I do not suppose he has ever written a line simply to please a magazine editor or to impress his audience. At one time, as I have noted, he didn't even know he had one. If he has a bad conscience, it is the bad conscience of the sensitive Southerner who bears in his heart the whole history of the culture he loves, and that culture Faulkner has examined over and over with paramount good faith and that necessary love for one's own people, simply because one is *of* them, without which our judgments of other people are arbitrary and usually destructive. For him integrity represents not that hoped-for state of "integration" which enables us to "function," but that which alone enables us to grasp our existence.

Ironically enough, those critics who insist on reading Faulkner exclusively as an historian of the South, "another Balzac," find it easier to think of him as a profound social thinker than to face up to his philosophical emphasis. Yet if you study carefully something so fundamental to his thought as the long dialogue on slavery and the land which composes the middle section of "The Bear," you find that the obscurities of his work stem not from any particular profundity or complexity of ideas, but from the fact that his mind is so astonishingly energetic, his sensibility so vividly aroused by all the issues present to his mind, that he is always leaping from one to the other in excited discovery. Faulkner writes like a man thinking aloud. And quite often, indeed, like a man who has suddenly fallen into a hypnotic trance of thinking about any issue that may present itself to him in the midst of a story. Nor, despite the quiet boldness of his thinking about the South and slavery, is he particularly free—how could he be?—of the tangle of motives, self-defensive rights and wrongs, that we usually detect in Southerners reviewing the history of slavery. For every positive acceptance of its great wrong and guilt—and no other Southern novelist has gripped the subject so frankly—he will go out of his way to plead the despotic kindness of the old slaveholders. There is a particularly amusing example of this in the middle section of "The Bear," where the extraordinary crescendo of argument leading up to the imminent revelation of God's curse upon the land suddenly falls away into a crooning lullaby of the kindness the women showed the slaves when they were ill—and then is capped by the admission that these same services were performed for cattle, but not by those lower-class people, ancestors of the Snopeses, no doubt, who had to hire their horses from a livery stable! Faulkner is a Southerner; and very much a man of his class. But let us not forget that for him the guilt of slavery is tempered by the realization that the exploiter, too, is a man; that no more than the slave can he be dismissed from the other end of the relationship. Yet it is not entirely fair to him, it conventionalizes him, to assume that he sees all these things simply under the general and individual rubric of human guilt. Faulkner does not give the impression that so many Southern poets and critics do—that their highest aim as *writers* is to become good Christians again. He seems more intent on understanding the human situation than on being saved.

But to return to his specific quality as an artist. It is what I have already noted as his momentum. Faulkner's imagination seems to be characterized by a velocity of memory that one finds only in writers of genius—by the ability to sustain details in so long and dynamic a single period that they finally compose a single order of progression. A characteristic example of this can be found early in *Intruder in the Dust.* It is worth quoting here not because this novel, or even the passage itself, is among his best—indeed, I would say that since *The Sound and the Fury* and *Light in August,* written about the same age that Melville was when he wrote *Moby-Dick,* Faulkner has done nothing so good, and lately seems suspiciously as mellow as Melville became at too early an age—but because it shows to what extent Faulkner's momentum will assert itself in a novel interpreted by our best critics as a Southerner's conventional case against President Truman's Civil Rights Bill.

It is the scene in which the boy Charles Mallison is taken, after he has fallen through the ice while hunting, to the house of the Negro Lucas Beauchamp. He knows, of course, that the man is a descendant of the old planter Carothers McCaslin, and like everyone else in town is constantly irritated by the Negro's pride, his air always "intractable and composed," his refusal of the customary servility. And now, as he trails sheepishly behind, he is more than ever aware of this elderly Negro who with calm dignity insists on taking him into his house and who humiliatingly reminds him that, like his own grandfather, "the man striding ahead was simply incapable of conceiving himself by a child contradicted and defied."

So he didn't even check when they passed the gate, he didn't even look at it and they were in no well-used tended lane leading to tenant or servant quarters and marked by walking feet but a savage gash half gully and half road mounting a hill with an air solitary independent and intractable too and then he saw the house, the cabin and remembered the rest of the story, the legend: how Edmonds' father had deeded to his Negro first cousin and his heirs in perpetuity the house and the ten acres of land it sat in—an oblong of earth set forever in the middle of the two-thousand-acre plantation like a postage stamp in the center of an envelope—the paintless wooden house, the paintless picket fence whose paintless latchless gate the man kneed open still without stopping or once looking back and, he following and Aleck Sander and Edmonds' boy following him, strode on into the yard. It would have been grassless even in summer; he could imagine it, completely bare, no weed no sprig of anything, the dust each morning swept by some of Lucas' women-folks with a broom made of willow switches bound together, into an intricate series of whorls and overlapping loops which as the day advanced would be gradually and slowly defaced by the droppings and the cryptic three-toed prints of chickens like (remembering it now at sixteen) a terrain in miniature out of the age of the great lizards, the four of them walking in what was less than walk because its surface was dirt too yet more than path, the footpacked strip running plumbline straight between two borders of tin cans and empty bottles and shards of china and earthenware set into the ground, up to the paintless steps and the paintless gallery along whose edge sat more cans but larger—empty gallon buckets which had once contained molasses or perhaps paint and wornout water or milk pails and one five-gallon can for kerosene with its top cut off and half of what had once been somebody's (Edmonds' without doubt) kitchen hot water tank sliced longways like a banana—out of which flowers had grown last summer and from which the dead stalks and the dried and brittle tendrils still leaned and drooped, and beyond this the house itself, gray and weathered and not so much paintless as independent of and intractable to paint so that the house was not only the one possible continuation of the stern untended road but was its crown too as the carven ailanthus leaves are the Greek column's capital.

Nor did the man pause yet, up the steps and across the gallery and opened the door and entered and he and then Edmonds' boy and Aleck Sander followed: a hall dim even almost dark after the bright outdoors and already he could smell that smell which he had accepted without question all his life as being the smell always of the places where people with any trace of Negro blood live as he had that all people named Mallison are Methodists, then a bedroom: a bare worn quite clean paintless rugless floor, in one corner and spread with a bright patchwork quilt a vast shadowy tester bed which had probably come out of old Carothers McCaslin's house, and a battered cheap Grand Rapids dresser and then for the moment no more or at least little more; only later would he notice—or remember that he had seen—the cluttered mantel on which sat a kerosene lamp handpainted with flowers and a vase filled with spills of twisted newspaper and above the mantel the colored lithograph of a three-year old calendar in which Pocahontas in the quilled fringed buckskins of a Sioux or Chippewa chief stood against a balustrade of Italian marble above a garden of formal cypresses and shadowy in the corner opposite the bed a chromo portrait of two people framed heavily in gold-painted wood on a gold-painted easel. But he hadn't seen that at all yet because that was behind him and all he now saw was the fire—the clay-daubed fieldstone chimney in which a half-burned backlog glowed and smoldered in the gray ashes and beside it in a rocking chair something which he thought was a child until he saw the face, and then he did pause long enough to look at her because he was about to remember something else his uncle had told him about or at least in regard to Lucas Beauchamp, and looking at her he realized for the first time how old the man actually was, must be—a tiny old almost doll-sized woman much darker than the man, in a shawl and an apron, her head bound in an immaculate white cloth on top of which sat a painted straw hat bearing some kind of ornament.

I shall not dwell here on the remarkable inwoven textures of this passage, or—what for technical reasons is perhaps most interesting to any writer of prose—on the peculiarly impelled rightness of those words which by their ecstatic repetition hold and propel the phrases so that Faulkner can release the whole scene already present to his mind. But I should like to define the necessity behind the passage. For what I see and hear in the soar and thud of these details is an effort to convey—not merely *to* the consciousness of a single mind but *along* the whole circuit of time and thought through which we move—that which *is* our life in all its presentness. We suddenly feel in some momentary shock to our physical being that we are being played on by history, by the forces of our own character, by that tangle of rights and wrongs, of present injustice and perhaps ultimate injustice, too, that asserts itself in every human situation. And it is only such an awareness, such a willingness to live the situation with everything we are, that mollifies the ache of being alive. For this is who we are—"this living entity at this point at this day."

Faulkner's insistence on embracing all actuality in the moment is more than a novelist's innovation or technique. It goes far beyond the stream-of-consciousness method, with its emphasis on the underground level of man's knowing—a method that always shows man as half-asleep, and just becoming aware how much he lies to himself. It is an attempt to realize continuity with all our genesis, our "progenitors"—another of Faulkner's favorite words—with all we have touched, known, loved. *This* is why he needs those long successive parentheses, and parentheses within parentheses. They exemplify the chain of human succession. The greatest horror his characters know is to feel they have been dropped out of this stream of being, to think of themselves as "self-progenitive" or "sourceless." But no matter how many parentheses he may use, he knows how to leave them behind him, to come out flush to the end of a sentence with a fresh, stabbing, often humorously concrete thought. We may live in our tradition, be haunted by it as Southerners are: but we are not our tradition; we are individual and alive.

With Faulkner it would seem as if the theme of the journey which is so elemental in American literature, always present to our minds because of our very history as a people, has here been contracted to display the real journey each human being makes through time—minute by minute of the universe with which we are filled. And so thoroughly is the moment lived and relived that only when it is over can we look back and see how rich our lives are. Here is one main source of Faulkner's humor, which is so often the wild grin he throws over a situation after it has been lived; it is his own amused astonishment at how much a human being can take in, how long a road he travels through in his own mind. And here, too, we approach that ultimate word which means so much to him—endurance. This endurance, or "outlasting," is not the mark simply of his favorite Negroes, like Dilsey in *The Sound and the Fury*. The Negroes are its greatest *social* example. For the Negroes, like the Jews, have the curious bitter advantage—and how often they have wished they could lose it—of having suffered an historic injustice so long that the noblest individuals among them can finally take in the whole of their situation precisely because they know it is the *human* situation, and so in some sense cannot be remedied. What endurance seems to mean to Faulkner is that if one sees one's whole life in time, only then can we realize our secret courage, our will to have endured; and only so relinquish our life to others. Only through integrity can we feel that our existence has fully been done justice to—for we have *lived* it.

One word more. It is often said that Faulkner owes his place in American literature to the fact that he has been fortunate in his background, which is so filled with "tradition and drama"—or perhaps simply to the fact that he has had the remarkable patience, or unusual good sense, to stay with his subject. It is implied that other writers, had they not been so rootless, had they not been open to the usual temptations, might have done as well.

And perhaps it is true that any writer—say Sinclair Lewis or

Thomas Wolfe—might, if only he had stayed in his Minnesota or his North Carolina, have been able to work *his* way through the region he knows best, to write finally not only of what men do, but of what they mean.

But I wonder if there is not another way of putting it. Perhaps it is only the writer who knows that men are not the same everywhere, who believes that each human being is original and has a soul—perhaps it is only such a writer who will stick to his birthplace as if the whole of life were as much there as anywhere.